FROM BOARDROOM TO BUILD

A BLUEPRINT FOR AI GOVERNANCE, RISK, AND TECHNICAL SECURITY

CARLOS CABRERA

FROM BOARDROOM TO BUILD

A Blueprint for AI Governance, Risk, and Technical Security

Carlos Cabrera

(Copyright page — the reverse of the title page)

ISBN 979-8-9967050-1-6 (paperback)

ISBN 979-8-9967050-0-9 (ebook)

Library of Congress Control Number: 2026916035

Published by Cabrera Press

New Jersey, USA

First Edition: June 2026

For permissions, bulk orders, or inquiries:

carlosrcabrera@yahoo.com

*For **Ana García de Cabrera** — for your support and your belief, your counsel and your trust.*

*And for my daughter, **Alanna** — for believing in me, for expecting my best, and for knowing, always, that my family is my priority.*

*And for my parents, Francisco **"Frank"** Cabrera and Jacinta **"Matilde"** Rodríguez de Cabrera, may they both rest in peace — for always wanting the best for me.*

*And for **Augusto Delgado** — for always listening to my ideas, and exploring them with me.*

ACKNOWLEDGMENTS

A book about connecting people was, fittingly, not written alone.

My deepest thanks go to my wife, **Ana**, who gave me the space to think and whose counsel steadied me. And to my daughter, **Alanna**, who has always listened and supported me, and whose belief was a quiet engine behind these pages. Whatever time this book took, it was taken from them, and they gave it gladly.

My thanks also to **Augusto Delgado**, who listened to these ideas as they took shape—often before they made any sense—and explored them with me.

I owe a particular debt to **Horace Robinson**, who guided me at the very beginning of my technology career and set me on the path—the knowledge, the discipline, and the certifications—that made the rest of it possible.

Beyond that early guidance, much of my education came from organizations whose public work became my teacher across nearly three decades—the freely available research, frameworks, and guidance from NIST, OWASP, ISO, ISC2, ISACA, MITRE, AWS, and Microsoft, among others. So much of what I know I learned by reading what these communities shared openly, and this book is, in part, an attempt to give something back.

And, finally, to **Rocco**, our family dog, whose relentless happiness and energy—no matter the situation—pulled me out of more than a few of the day's stresses and tribulations, usually without my noticing it was happening.

Any errors that remain are mine alone.

— *Carlos Cabrera*

INTRODUCTION: HOW TO READ THIS BOOK

From Boardroom to Build: A Blueprint for AI Governance, Risk, and Technical Security

There is a conversation that happens in almost every organization adopting artificial intelligence, and it usually goes badly. In one room, leaders ask what AI means for the business—the opportunity, the risk, the liability, who owns it. In another, engineers build and deploy the systems—the pipelines, the models, the integrations. The two rooms speak different languages, optimize for different things, and too often discover only after something goes wrong that they were never really connected. The board set a policy no one enforced. The team built a control no one mandated. The AI shipped, and the gap between intent and implementation became the place the problems lived.

This book is written to close that gap. Its title is its argument: the work of securing and governing AI runs *from the boardroom to the build* —from the leader's first question about whether to use a technology, all the way down to the engineer's decision about how to configure it—and it only works when those two ends are connected. A strategy that never becomes a control is a wish. A control that no one decided to require is an orphan. The whole point of this book is to make the journey between the boardroom and the build a single, coherent path that both the people who set direction and the people who do the building can walk together.

Who this book is for. That means this book has two readers, deliberately. It is for the executive, the board member, the founder, and the manager who must make decisions about AI without necessarily being able to write the code—and it is equally for the engineer, the security practitioner, the architect, and the technical lead who must turn those decisions into systems that actually hold. Most books pick one of those audiences. This one refuses to, because the entire problem is that those two audiences need to understand each other.

How the book is built to serve both readers. To make a single book work for two audiences, every chapter but one—the closing blueprint in Chapter 17—is split into two lenses. The **Leadership Lens** is written for the decision-maker: it covers what matters, who must own it, what to fund, and what to ask. The **Execution Lens** is written for the implementer: it goes deeper and more technical, into how the thing is actually built, configured, and operated. This structure has a consequence worth using:

- If you are a leader and short on time, you can read the openings and the **Leadership Lenses** straight through, skipping the deep technical sections, and still come away with a complete and coherent book. *Every Leadership Lens ends with "The one question"—a single sharp question to ask your team this week.*
- If you are an implementer, *the* **Execution Lenses** *are where the hands-on guidance lives, each ending with "The one move"—a single concrete action to take this week*—but read the Leadership Lenses too, because they tell you *why* the work matters and what the people funding it are thinking.
- If you are a team of one wearing both hats—the founder who is also the engineer, the lead who is also the strategist—read all of it; it was written for exactly your situation.

How the book is organized. The chapters are grouped into three phases that follow the journey itself.

- **Phase I — The Leadership Fast-Track (Chapters 1–6)** is the boardroom: recognizing that AI is already in your organization, knowing what you have, governing it, treating its risks as enterprise risks, giving it an owner, and learning to calibrate your effort to what's actually at stake. A leader could read this phase alone and be meaningfully more prepared.
- **Phase II — The Execution Core (Chapters 7–14)** is the build: securing the pipeline, the supply chain, and the cloud; monitoring systems in production; attacking them before adversaries do; planning for incidents; protecting data and fairness; and doing all of it at whatever scale your team can sustain.
- **Phase III — Governance & Future Horizons (Chapters 15–17)** is the bridge that connects the two: navigating AI regulation, building ethical guardrails, and looking at where this is all heading—closing with a single blueprint that pulls the whole book together.

A few things to know going in. This book favors *principles over specifics,* deliberately, because AI moves fast and any specific—a product name, a regulatory deadline, a benchmark number—will age faster than the underlying idea. Where specifics appear, they are illustrations of durable principles, and they are flagged as the moving targets they are. The book is also honest about what is *not* solved: several of the hardest problems in AI security have no clean fix yet, and you will find them described as the open problems they are rather than dressed up as settled. That honesty is deliberate, because a security posture built on false confidence is worse than one built on none.

You will also notice a few ideas that recur from chapter to chapter —a way of reading any system's stakes, a continuous loop that never quite closes, a principle about limiting what a compromised system can do, a recurring instruction to start with a single system. These repetitions are the spine of the book. They are what turn seventeen separate topics into one argument.

Where to start. Start with Chapter 1 if you want the full journey.

Start with the Leadership Lenses of Phase I if you are a leader who needs to be useful by the end of the week. But wherever you start, carry the book's central conviction with you: AI can be adopted deliberately and safely, by organizations of any size and any level of resource—not by doing everything at once, but by connecting the room where decisions are made to the room where they are built, and taking the next deliberate step. That is the road. Let's walk it.

TABLE OF CONTENTS

CHAPTER GUIDE

From Boardroom to Build: A Blueprint for AI Governance, Risk, and Technical Security

Phase I — The Leadership Fast-Track

Chapter 1 — The AI Imperative Why AI is already in your organization whether you sanctioned it or not, and why the choice is to govern it or be surprised by it.

Chapter 2 — Know Your Landscape The types of AI an organization actually runs, and why you can't secure what you can't name.

Chapter 3 — The Governance Backbone Building governance as a structure, not a finish line—implement once, satisfy framework, standard, and law together.

Chapter 4 — AI Risk as Enterprise Risk Using the risk machinery you already have, speaking the language of the business, and setting a risk appetite so you can say yes deliberately.

Chapter 5 — The New Hierarchy: Who Owns AI Risk? Because what falls between roles falls to no one.

Chapter 6 — The Industry Playbook The three dials—consequence, data sensitivity, regulatory weight—that calibrate how much rigor any system has earned. (Phase I capstone.)

Phase II — The Execution Core

Chapter 7 — Securing ML & GenAI Systems AI as a pipeline, not a product: securing data, training, the model, and inference—and verifying what you can't trust.

Chapter 8 — The AI Supply Chain The attack surface you didn't build: pretrained models, third-party data, and the dependencies your scanners can't read.

Chapter 9 — Modernizing the SOC Why AI fails at the behavior and output layer where traditional monitoring is blind—and how to watch it.

Chapter 10 — Red-Teaming AI Adversarial testing as an ongoing practice, because the test is never finished.

Chapter 11 — Beyond the Breach: AI-Specific Incident Response Responding to failure at machine speed: capture before you contain, and close the loop.

Chapter 12 — Privacy by Design: Protecting the Data Fuel Why data baked into the model breaks the traditional privacy playbook—and the engineering toolkit for protecting it.

Chapter 13 — Scaling Securely: Leveraging AWS, Azure, and Google AI Services The cloud as a force multiplier in both directions—owning your half of the shared-responsibility line.

Chapter 14 — Lean Security: Enabling Business Velocity Without Sacrificing Protection Doing the right fraction on purpose: prioritize ruthlessly, automate relentlessly, multiply with AI. (Phase II capstone.)

Phase III — Governance & Future Horizons

Chapter 15 — Navigating the Maze: Global AI Regulation and Compliance Don't chase individual laws—build to the principles they converge on, and let your security artifacts be your compliance evidence.

Chapter 16 — The Ethical Guardrails: Bias, Fairness, and Trans-

parency Why fairness is a choice, not a setting—and the discipline of measuring, mitigating, explaining, and monitoring it.

Chapter 17 — The Road Ahead: The agentic horizon, the whole book pulled into a single blueprint, and the one move to carry forward. (Phase III capstone.)

CHAPTER 1
THE AI IMPERATIVE: SECURING VALUE IN AN AI-FIRST WORLD

From Boardroom to Build: A Blueprint for AI Governance, Risk, and Technical Security

OPENING

In the spring of 2023, Samsung's semiconductor division did something that sounds, on paper, entirely reasonable. They let their engineers use ChatGPT.

The logic was sound. These were brilliant people solving hard problems, and a tool that could help them debug code and summarize meetings faster was an obvious productivity win. So the company lifted its internal ban and opened the door.

Within about three weeks, that door let something out. One engineer, stuck on a bug, pasted proprietary semiconductor source code into the chatbot to get help fixing it. Another fed in the transcript of an internal meeting to generate clean notes. A third submitted a test sequence used to identify defective chips. Three separate incidents, all within roughly twenty days, all involving some of the most sensitive intellectual property the company owned—now sitting on servers

Samsung didn't control, potentially absorbed into a model's training data, effectively impossible to claw back.

By May, Samsung had banned generative AI on company devices outright.

Here's what I want you to notice about that story, because it's the reason this book exists: **nobody in it was a villain, and nobody was an idiot.** The engineers weren't being reckless. They were being productive, using the best tool available to do their jobs well. Leadership wasn't being negligent in some obvious, lazy way—they made a reasonable call to enable their teams. And yet the outcome was a serious, irreversible exposure of trade secrets.

That is the central problem of securing AI, and it looks nothing like the security problems we're used to. There was no hacker. No malware. No breached firewall. The "attack" was just talented people using a helpful tool faster than anyone had thought to put guardrails around it.

And Samsung was not special.

What made the headlines was the leak. What should have made the headlines was how ordinary it was. Just weeks earlier, a survey of nearly twelve thousand professionals had found that among those already using AI tools like ChatGPT for work, 68% were doing so without telling their managers.[1] Not maliciously—they simply found a tool that helped and started using it, the way people always adopt whatever makes their day easier. Within months, companies like Amazon, JPMorgan, Goldman Sachs, and eventually Samsung itself moved to restrict or ban these tools[2], not because they had caught their employees doing something wrong, but because they had suddenly realized they had no idea what their employees were doing at all.

This is the phenomenon I call **Shadow AI**—the AI tools, integrations, and workflows operating inside your organization right now that nobody formally approved, nobody is monitoring, and in many cases nobody in leadership even knows exist. If your reaction is "that's not happening here," I'd gently suggest that's exactly what every one of those companies believed the week before they found out otherwise.

So let me ask you the question this whole book is built to answer: **Is your organization's AI actually secure—or are you just hoping it is?**

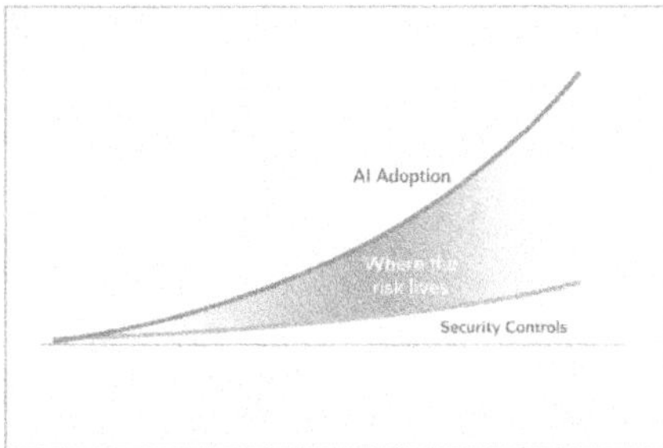

Figure 1.1 — The Adoption-vs-Control Gap A conceptual illustration showing how organizational AI adoption accelerates faster than the implementation of security controls. The widening shaded area between the two curves represents the growing zone of unmanaged risk—the space "where the risk lives."

THE LEADERSHIP LENS

If you read only the Leadership Lens sections of this book, you'll still come away with a complete picture of what AI security demands of you as a decision-maker. This is the track for the people who set direction, allocate budget, and answer to the board. The Execution Lens that follows each brief is for the people who turn that direction into working systems—your architects, engineers, and analysts. You're welcome in both, but you're never required to read past your own.

The Executive Brief — Why this risk is yours to own

Here is the uncomfortable truth the Samsung story points to: your organization has almost certainly already adopted AI faster than it has secured it. That gap—between adoption and control—is the single biggest source of new enterprise risk in the next decade, and closing it is now a leadership responsibility, not a technical afterthought.

What's actually at stake is broader than data. For most of the history of cybersecurity, we protected *information*—records, credentials, transactions. AI changes the target. When a model approves a loan, routes a shipment, or flags a medical scan, the most valuable thing in your organization is no longer a database. It's the *logic making your decisions.* Compromise that, and you haven't just lost data; you've lost the integrity of how your business operates. And the target is still moving:

AI systems are beginning to act, not just answer—executing tasks and touching other systems rather than recommending—and every stake in this chapter rises with that autonomy. We'll meet that horizon fully in Chapter 17. That's why AI risk has to be treated as enterprise risk, owned at the top, and not delegated quietly to whoever runs IT.

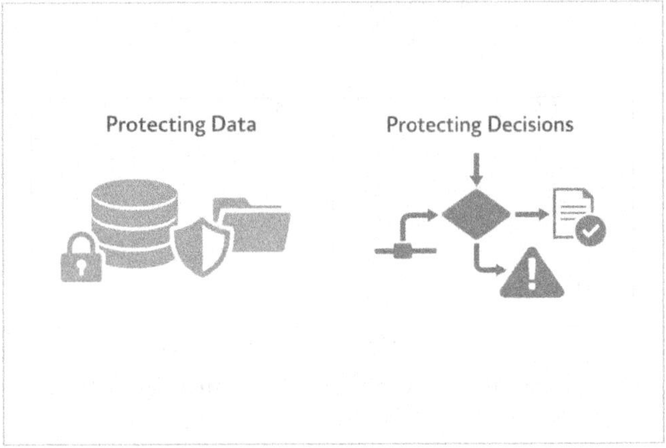

Figure 1.2 — From Protecting Data to Protecting Decisions *A side-by-side conceptual illustration contrasting traditional cybersecurity, which safeguards stored information such as databases and records, with AI-era security, which protects the logic behind automated decisions. The shift highlights that in modern enterprises, the integrity of decisions—not just data—defines true security.*

The investment case is straightforward. The cost of governing AI well—clear ownership, basic guardrails, monitoring, an incident plan—is small and predictable. The cost of governing it badly is large and unpredictable: irreversible IP loss, regulatory penalties, legal liability for what your AI tells customers, and the kind of reputational damage that outlasts any single news cycle. You are not choosing whether to spend on AI security. You're choosing whether to spend a little now, deliberately, or a lot later, in a crisis.

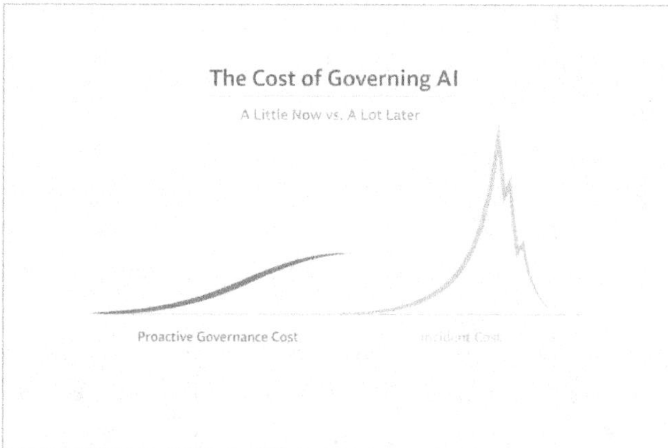

Figure 1.3 — The Cost of Governing AI: A Little Now vs. A Lot Later. A conceptual illustration contrasting the predictable, controlled cost of proactive AI governance with the unpredictable and often much larger cost of reacting to an incident. The smooth curve represents steady investment in governance; the jagged spike represents the cascading impact of IP loss, penalties, liability, and reputational damage when governance is neglected.

The one question to ask your team this week: *"What AI is running in our organization right now that we haven't formally reviewed—and who owns the risk for it?"* A slow or uncertain answer is the finding.

THE EXECUTION LENS

This track is for the people who build and defend the systems—security architects, ML engineers, platform teams, and SOC analysts. Where the Leadership Lens asked "what's at stake and what should we fund," the Execution Lens asks "what do we actually do, and with what." Throughout the book these sections get progressively more hands-on. This first one maps the terrain; the chapters that follow get into the wiring.

Why the Samsung leak was an architecture problem, not a training problem

It's tempting to read the Samsung story and conclude the fix was "tell people not to paste secrets into chatbots." That's a policy, and policies are necessary, but they are not controls. If your only defense against data exfiltration is hoping every employee remembers a rule under deadline pressure, you don't have a security posture—you have a wish.

The implementer's job is to make the safe path the easy path, and to catch the unsafe path when someone takes it anyway. For the class of risk Samsung hit, that breaks down into a few concrete control surfaces:

Visibility first — you can't secure what you can't see. Before any tooling, the practical starting point is discovery: identifying what AI services and integrations are actually being used across the organization, sanctioned or not. This is where AI Security Posture Management (AI-SPM) and egress monitoring come in. AI-SPM tools automatically discover where AI models and keys are hiding in your cloud infrastructure; combined with egress tracking, they surface the "Shadow AI" footprint the Leadership Lens just asked about. A network egress review that flags traffic to known LLM API endpoints is a blunt but effective first pass—and it's the move this chapter ends on.

Data loss prevention, adapted for prompts. Traditional DLP watches email and file transfers. The new surface is the prompt box. Modern DLP and CASB (Cloud Access Security Broker) tooling can be configured to detect sensitive patterns—source code, credentials, regulated data—moving toward generative AI endpoints, and to block or quarantine them before they leave your boundary.

A sanctioned path that's genuinely better. The reason Samsung's engineers used public ChatGPT is that it helped. The durable fix isn't denial; it's providing an enterprise-grade alternative—a private model deployment or an enterprise tier with contractual data-isolation guarantees (no training on your inputs)—so the productive choice and the safe choice are the same choice.

A distinct pattern emerges here, because it recurs throughout this book: the technical response to an AI risk is rarely a single tool. It's visibility, a guardrail, and a better default, layered so that no single human decision is the only thing standing between you and an incident.

The map for the rest of the book. Figure 1.4 previews the technical domains developed in depth during Phase II of this book (Chapters 7 through 14).

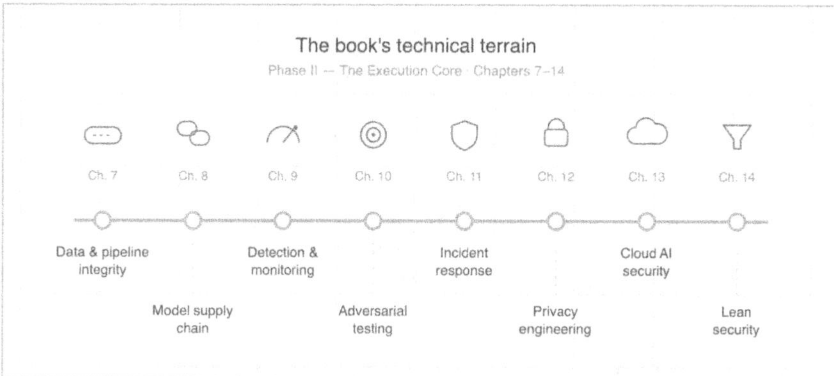

Figure 1.4 — The Book's Technical Terrain. *The eight technical domains of Phase II, mapped as one continuous route: data & pipeline integrity (Ch. 7), model supply chain (Ch. 8), detection & monitoring (Ch. 9), adversarial testing (Ch. 10), incident response (Ch. 11), privacy engineering (Ch. 12), cloud AI security (Ch. 13), and lean security (Ch. 14). Together they form the Execution Lens—the terrain the rest of this book operates in.*

The one move to make this week: run an egress check for traffic to public LLM API endpoints. You're not looking to punish anyone. You're looking to find out how big your Shadow AI footprint actually is. Whatever number comes back is your real baseline, and it's almost always larger than expected.

BRINGING IT TOGETHER

Organizations do what works: they deploy useful tools faster than they govern them. Samsung engineers were not reckless and their leaders were not negligent—everyone acted reasonably, and the result was a data leak. Thousands of employees quietly using AI were no exception. That gap—adoption outpacing control—is this book's problem. Closing it is not a project but a discipline that requires two players sharing one map: Leadership, which sets direction and owns the risk, and Execution, which builds the controls and sustains them.

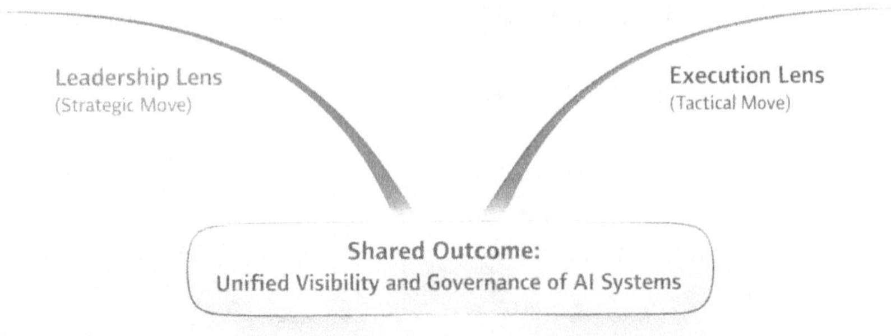

Figure 1.5 — The Two Lenses, One Outcome *A conceptual illustration showing how the Leadership Lens (strategic move) and Execution Lens (tactical move) converge toward a shared outcome:* ***Unified Visibility and Governance of AI Systems****.*

Leaders: commission a baseline inventory—what AI runs here, and who owns its risk. Do not call it a witch-hunt; call it a baseline. Implementers: run an egress check for traffic to public LLM endpoints and report a single number. That metric turns abstract worry into a board-level decision and supplies the evidence to fund the controls this book describes.

Do those two things, and you shift from blind optimism to objective verification.

Coming next — In Chapter 2, before we touch a single framework or control, we answer a question most AI security books skip entirely: *what kind of AI are you actually securing?* The SaaS tool with AI bolted on, the cloud API your developers call, the model your own team fine-tuned—each carries a different risk profile and a different set of defenses. You can't secure what you can't categorize, so that's where we begin.

CHAPTER 1 IN REVIEW

The core idea: Organizations adopt AI faster than they secure it. That gap between adoption and control is the defining enterprise risk of the AI era, and closing it requires leaders and implementers working from the same map.

• • •

For the leader (Leadership Lens):

- AI risk is enterprise risk. It belongs at the top of the organization, owned and funded deliberately—not delegated quietly to IT.
- The target has shifted. AI security protects the *logic behind your decisions*, not just your data. A compromised model corrupts how the business operates, not only what it knows.
- The economics favor acting early. Governing AI well is a small, predictable cost; governing it badly is a large, unpredictable one—IP (Intellectual Property) loss, penalties, liability, and reputational damage.
- Start with visibility. You cannot govern, fund, or defend AI you haven't yet made visible.

For the implementer (Execution Lens):

- Policy is not a control. "Tell people not to do it" is a wish; visibility, guardrails, and a better default are controls.
- The durable response to an AI risk is layered, not singular: see it (AI-SPM, egress monitoring), guard it (DLP/CASB adapted for prompts), and replace it (a sanctioned, safer path that's genuinely better).
- Make the safe path the easy path. People used the risky tool because it helped; the fix is an enterprise alternative that helps just as much without the exposure.
- Your first deliverable is a number: how much Shadow AI is actually in use. That baseline drives everything that follows.

The two actions from this chapter:

- *Strategic Move (leader):* Commission an honest baseline—what AI is running that we haven't reviewed, and who owns its risk?
- *Tactical Move (implementer):* Run an egress check for traffic to public LLM endpoints and report the number.

The throughline to remember: A governance policy with no technical enforcement is a wish. A technical control with no leadership mandate is an orphan. Securing AI is the discipline of making sure neither happens.

CHAPTER 2
KNOW YOUR LANDSCAPE: THE TYPES OF AI A BUSINESS ACTUALLY USES

From Boardroom to Build: A Blueprint for AI Governance, Risk, and Technical Security

OPENING

Here's a question worth sitting with before you read another page: right now, today, how many distinct AI systems are operating inside your organization?

Most leaders, asked this in a meeting, will pause and offer a number. Three. Maybe a dozen if they're being generous—the chatbot tool the company licensed, the coding assistant engineering adopted, the thing marketing uses to draft copy. Whatever number you just thought of, I'd gently suggest it's wrong by an order of magnitude. Not because you're careless, but because most of the AI in your organization never announced itself. It didn't come with a purchase order or a security review. It arrived quietly, folded into tools you already had, and in many cases you didn't choose it at all.

This is why we have to start here, before frameworks, before controls, before a single policy. You cannot secure what you cannot see, and you cannot see what you cannot name. The defining challenge of AI security isn't that the technology is dangerous—it's that it's *diffuse*. It doesn't live in one system you can point to. It's spread across dozens of entry points, each with a different owner, a different risk profile, and a different set of controls available to you.

So this chapter does one thing: it gives you a map. We'll sort the AI in your organization not by what it does, but by **how it got there**—because how AI enters your organization determines almost everything about how you can defend it. The search box you can't configure demands a completely different response than the model your own team trained. By the end, you'll have a way to look at any AI in your environment and immediately know which of five categories it falls into, and therefore where to start.

The five categories sort into three groups, and the logic of the groups matters as much as the categories themselves:

- **The AI You Didn't Choose** — it arrived without a decision. You have the least control and, often, the least awareness.
- **The AI Your People Chose** — employees adopted it to get work done. Control is shared, and so is responsibility.
- **The AI You Built** — you integrated or trained it yourself. You have the most control, which means the risk is now unambiguously yours to own.

Notice the arc: as you move from the first group to the last, you gain control—but you also inherit ownership of the risk. With the AI you didn't choose, the vendor secures the model—but the data your people feed it is nobody's responsibility until you make it yours. The AI you built is entirely yours, model and data alike. Most organizations get this exactly backwards. They pour their security attention into the models they built, which are visible and feel important, while the AI they didn't choose—the larger, more invisible footprint—goes ungoverned. We start with that blind spot.

GROUP 1: THE AI YOU DIDN'T CHOOSE

Category 1 — Ambient AI: The AI You Never Decided to Use

Start with the most invisible category of all, because it's the one almost no security program accounts for.

For roughly twenty years, the search box was a neutral utility. You typed a question, you got back a list of links, and nothing about that transaction felt like it required a second thought. That mental model is now obsolete. The danger is that the box looks exactly the same as it always did. Today, when an employee types a query into Google, Bing, or a tool like Perplexity, that query may be processed by a generative model: interpreted, reasoned over, and in some configurations retained and reviewed. The interface didn't change. What happens behind it did, completely.

This is **Ambient AI** — artificial intelligence that operates inside tools your people already use, that nobody adopted, configured, or approved, and that often can't be turned off. No one signed up for it. No one read its terms. It simply became the default behavior of a tool everyone already had open.

Why this is more dangerous than the obvious cases. In Chapter 1, Samsung's engineers at least made a *decision*—they chose to open ChatGPT and paste code into it. That decision, however unwise, is a thing you can govern: you can train against it, build policy around it, block the tool. Ambient AI offers no such decision point. People type things into a search box that they would never knowingly paste into an AI tool, precisely because the search box has never felt like an AI tool. A query like "how do we structure the layoffs in the [specific division] without triggering [specific regulation]" reveals confidential strategy—and the person typing it isn't thinking of it as feeding sensitive data to a model. They're thinking of it as a search, the same way they've searched for two decades.

The behavioral risk is real and measurable. Recent research found that 77% of employees paste data into generative AI tools, and 82% of that activity flows through unmanaged personal accounts that sit entirely outside enterprise oversight.[1] Ambient AI is where much of that happens invisibly, because it doesn't register in anyone's mind as "using AI."

The control concept that defines this category: consumer versus enterprise posture. This is the single most important thing to understand about Ambient AI, and it's subtle. The *same product, from the same vendor,* can have two completely different data postures depending on which version your employee is using. An enterprise-tenant version may contractually guarantee that your data stays within your organization and is never used to train the vendor's models. The consumer version of that very same product may carry the opposite default—where the vendor's own guidance amounts to "don't enter anything you wouldn't want a human reviewer to read," because human reviewers may see it and it may be used to improve the model.[2] Same logo. Same search box. Opposite consequences for your data. And an employee logged into a personal account on a work laptop is almost always in the consumer bucket—with no idea the distinction exists.

Where this is heading. The risk doesn't stay still. Ambient AI is evolving from systems that *answer* into systems that *act*—surfacing information today, taking actions across your connected tools tomorrow. As that shift happens, the invisible query becomes an invisible *action,* and the control problem grows accordingly. We'll return to this when we discuss agentic AI later in the book; for now, it's enough to know that the least-governed category is also the one expanding fastest in capability.

***Figure 2.1 — The Same Search Box, Two Data Realities** A side-by-side illustration showing identical search interfaces under two distinct data-handling regimes. On the left, the **enterprise tenant** keeps data within its boundary and excludes it from model training. On the right, the **consumer account** may retain, review, or use queries for training. The visual makes the difference between enterprise and consumer AI postures concrete and memorable—identical user experience, radically different data realities.*

Category 2 — Embedded AI: The AI Inside Tools You Already Bought

The second category in "The AI You Didn't Choose" is subtler than the first, because here you *did* make a purchasing decision—you just didn't make it about the AI. You bought a CRM, a productivity suite, a project-management tool, a customer-support platform. Then, sometime later, the vendor added AI features. A summarization button appeared. An assistant slid into the sidebar. The tool you vetted two years ago is now, quietly, an AI tool. And nobody re-vetted it when that changed.

This is **Embedded AI**: generative or predictive capability folded into SaaS products your organization already runs. It's everywhere now, because every vendor is racing to add it, and it creates a discovery problem most security programs haven't caught up to. You can no longer assume your sanctioned, approved applications are AI-free—and surfacing the AI features hidden inside the SaaS your employees already use is now a distinct security task in its own right.[3]

Why it's distinct from Ambient AI. The difference is one word: *contract*. With Ambient AI in a free consumer search box, you have essentially no leverage—you didn't sign anything, so you can't negotiate terms. With Embedded AI, you have a vendor relationship, which means you have actual control levers: enterprise tiers with data-handling guarantees, admin consoles to enable or disable AI features, data processing agreements, and the ability to ask hard questions before renewal. The risk is real, but so is your ability to do something about it—*if* you know the feature exists. That "if" is the whole challenge.

The hidden risk: your data's blast radius widens silently. When a SaaS tool adds AI, the AI often has access to everything that tool already holds—which may be a great deal of sensitive data. An AI assistant inside your CRM can potentially read your entire customer database to answer a question. The concern security researchers raise is that when AI has access to multiple connected systems, the blast radius of any single compromise increases sharply, and the risk compounds through *access and integration* far more than through the model itself.[4] The feature that makes the tool helpful is the same feature that turns a contained system into a connected one.

The control question for this category isn't "should we allow this vendor"—you already did. It's "now that this vendor has AI, what does its AI touch, where does that data go, and have we turned on the enterprise protections that are available to us?"

GROUP 2: THE AI YOUR PEOPLE CHOSE

Category 3 — Conversational AI: The AI Your People Chose

Here we cross from "The AI You Didn't Choose" into the second group: **The AI Your People Chose.** This is the category most people picture when they hear "AI security," and it's the one Chapter 1 opened with. An employee decides, deliberately, to use a standalone AI tool—a chatbot, an AI coding assistant, an image generator—to get their work done. They open it, they type into it, they paste into it.

This is **Conversational AI** used as a discrete tool, and the defining feature of this category is *human intent*. Unlike the first two categories, there was a decision: someone chose to use this. That changes the control surface entirely, because now you have a behavior you can govern—you can train against it, set policy, provide sanctioned alternatives, and monitor for it.

But the Samsung story taught us the catch: the decision is usually well-intentioned and individually reasonable, which is exactly what makes it hard to stop with rules alone. The data confirms this is the dominant leak channel. The same research behind the numbers in Category 1 shows employees averaging roughly fourteen pastes a day into these tools through unmanaged personal accounts—at least three of them carrying sensitive data—making copy-paste the single largest vector for corporate data leaving enterprise control.[5] And critically, the bulk of it flows through unmanaged personal accounts rather than corporate ones—connecting this category straight back to the consumer-versus-enterprise posture problem from Chapter 1.[6]

The shared-control insight here is the heart of the second group: responsibility is genuinely split. The employee chose to use the tool; the organization chose whether to offer a safe alternative, whether to monitor, whether to make the secure path the easy one. Neither side owns this risk alone—which is why the durable fix, as we saw with Samsung, is rarely a ban and usually a *better default*. Seen together, the first three categories add up to one thing: the Shadow AI problem from Chapter 1 wearing three different disguises—AI operating inside your organization that leadership neither approved nor monitors.

GROUP 3: THE AI YOU BUILT

Category 4 — API-Integrated AI: The AI Your Developers Build On

Now we enter the third group: **The AI You Built.** And the moment we cross this line, something fundamental changes—the risk stops being primarily about *behavior* and starts being about *architecture*.

API-Integrated AI is what happens when developers wire a third-party hosted model—OpenAI, Anthropic, Google—into your applications via an API. You did not train the model, but you built the system around it; that system now handles your data and your customers, and its failure modes become yours to architect against. A close cousin is a self-hosted open-weight model running on your infrastructure: the data stays inside your boundary, but you swap provider-trust for supply-chain risk—unvetted weights, unpatched serving stacks, and no vendor securing the other end. For our purposes, treat it as sitting between API-integrated and fully custom models.

Consider what the data flow actually looks like: a request travels from your enterprise application, through your middleware, out to the AI provider's API, and into their cloud infrastructure—and back. Security analysis of these integrations emphasizes that even when the provider's enterprise policy promises not to train on your API data, improper implementation on *your* side—misconfiguration, weak handling of keys and data, gaps in the middleware—remains a primary source of exposure.[7] The provider secures their end; the architecture you build around them is your responsibility.

This category also transforms a risk that has been lurking in every category before it: prompt injection. An AI assistant embedded in your email client or CRM that summarizes inbound content is already reading attacker-controlled text—but there, the defense was the vendor's engineering problem and your configuration problem. Here, for the first time, it is yours to engineer. An attacker who controls any input your application feeds the model—a user's text, a document, a web page—can craft it to override instructions, extract data, or trigger unintended actions in connected systems. Security researchers rank prompt injection as the top AI-specific application threat, and note its root cause is architectural: models are not reliably able to distinguish trusted instructions from untrusted data in their input.[8] This is not a behavior you train employees out of—it's a flaw you engineer defenses against. We'll develop this fully in the execution chapters; for now, it marks the line where AI security becomes a genuine engineering discipline.

Category 5 — Custom & Fine-Tuned AI: The AI You Own

The final category is the one with the most control—and with it, the most undivided responsibility. **Custom & Fine-Tuned AI** is a model your organization trained from scratch or—far more commonly—an existing model you fine-tuned on your own proprietary data to make it expert in your domain.

Here, every protection and every failure is yours. There's no vendor whose enterprise tier you can switch on, no provider securing one end of the connection. You own the training data, the model weights, the deployment, and the entire attack surface—which is the largest of any category. Fine-tuning a model on proprietary data delivers real competitive advantage, but it also bakes your sensitive data *into the model itself,* creating risks that don't exist when you're merely using someone else's model: the data can potentially be extracted from the model, the training process can be poisoned, the weights themselves become crown-jewel intellectual property.

This is the category most security programs instinctively focus on, because it's the most visible and feels the most important—you built it, so you guard it. And it should be guarded carefully. But the AI you built is the easiest to remember to secure. It is rarely where the surprise comes from.

THE LEADERSHIP LENS

You now have the map. The question this lens answers is the one a leader actually has to act on: *given five categories of AI in my organization, where do I focus, who owns what, and how do I spend?*

Invert your instinct. Leaders naturally fixate on the AI they built—the custom model, the visible investment with your name on it—but that is usually the thing you already secure. The real surprise lives at the top of the map: the AI you did not choose and the tools your people quietly adopted. Awareness and control run in opposite directions—the more you must watch, the less you can directly control—so direct your attention up the map, not just down it.

Assign an owner to every category, including the ones that feel ownerless. The bottom of the map has obvious owners—engineering for custom models, development for API integrations—but the top is ambiguous: who owns employees pasting data into a consumer search box, or a SaaS feature switched on last month? If the answer is "no one," that category is ungoverned by default. Name an owner for each of the five categories; ungoverned is an ownership gap, not a technical state.

Spend where the gap is widest, not where the technology is most impressive. Budget flows to the exciting, visible AI, but the highest return on a security dollar is where exposure is unmanaged: discovery tooling to reveal Embedded and Ambient AI, enterprise licensing that flips users to governed defaults, and policies that make the safe path the easy path. A dollar spent making invisible AI visible almost always beats a dollar spent hardening the model you were already watching.

The one question to ask your team this week: *"Can we produce a single list of every category of AI operating in our organization—including the AI we didn't choose and the AI inside tools we already bought—and name who owns the risk for each?"* If your team can't produce that list, you've just learned that your organization is securing AI it can name while remaining exposed to AI it can't. That list is the deliverable. Everything in the rest of this book assumes you have it.

THE EXECUTION LENS

The leader's job was to make sure every category has an owner. Yours is harder: you have to actually *find* the AI in each category—much of which is actively invisible to traditional tooling—and then apply controls that fit how each category behaves. The map isn't just a way to think about AI. It's a discovery checklist and a controls architecture, and the two halves of your job map onto the two halves of the chapter's structure: the categories you didn't choose are primarily a **discovery** problem, and the categories you built are primarily an **engineering** problem.

The top of the map is a visibility problem before it's a control problem. You cannot apply a single control to Ambient or Embedded AI until you can see it, and the uncomfortable reality is that your existing stack is mostly blind to it. File-based DLP watches attachments and uploads; it does not watch text pasted into a search box—which, as we've seen, is now the single largest channel for corporate data leaving enterprise control. So discovery here doesn't come from your traditional tools. It comes from three places: **network egress analysis** (traffic to known LLM and AI-service endpoints), **identity and SSO logs** (which surface AI services authenticated through corporate accounts—and, by their *absence,* hint at the unmanaged personal-account usage that dominates this space), and **the emerging AI-SPM and AI-discovery tooling** purpose-built to inventory AI usage across SaaS and identity systems, including the AI features embedded inside applications you already run. Run those three in combination and the invisible top of your map starts to become visible. That inventory *is* the deliverable the leader asked for.

The control surface differs by category — applying one tool everywhere fails. This is the core technical insight of the chapter: each category exposes a different control surface, so your defenses have to be matched to the tier, not applied uniformly.

For **Ambient AI**, you have no contract and no admin console, so your leverage is at the edges: identity controls that route people into enterprise tenants, browser-level controls that govern what happens in the search bar and AI sidebar itself, and DLP modernized to inspect *prompt and query traffic,* not just files. The strategic fix is to make the enterprise version the path of least resistance, so the consumer version isn't the default anyone reaches for.

For **Embedded AI**, you *do* have a contract—so your primary controls are the ones the vendor already gives you: the admin settings that enable or disable AI features, the enterprise data-handling tier, the data processing agreement. The technical work is twofold: discovering which of your existing SaaS tools have switched on AI, and then auditing what data each AI feature can actually reach—because an AI assistant inside a system inherits that system's access, and the blast radius compounds through that access.[9]

For **Conversational AI**, the controls are the ones we previewed with Samsung in Chapter 1: a sanctioned enterprise alternative, DLP on the prompt channel, and monitoring for unsanctioned-tool usage. The engineering goal is the same "make the safe path the easy path" principle, implemented through tooling rather than policy.

For **API-Integrated AI**, you cross fully into engineering. The controls live in *your* architecture: secure handling of API keys and credentials, hardening of the middleware where data passes to the provider, validation and isolation of untrusted input to defend against prompt injection, and verification that your implementation actually invokes the provider's no-training enterprise terms rather than assuming it does.[10] The provider secures their end; everything between your user and their API is yours to harden.

For **Custom & Fine-Tuned AI**, the control surface is the entire ML lifecycle—training-data integrity, protection of the model weights as crown-jewel IP (intellectual property), defense against data extraction and model poisoning. This is the deepest engineering work in the book, and it's why several later chapters exist. Here in Chapter 2, it's enough to recognize that owning the model means owning every layer beneath it.

Step back from the five categories and the technical logic is one line: as you move down the map, control shifts from *configuration* to *engineering*. At the top, securing AI means configuring identity, browsers, and vendor settings—you're tuning controls someone else built. At the bottom, it means architecting and defending systems yourself.

The one move to make this week: run the three discovery methods together—egress analysis, identity/SSO review, and an AI-discovery scan—and produce a first-pass inventory sorted into the five categories. Don't aim for complete; aim for *started*. The first version will be incomplete and probably alarming, and both of those are fine. An incomplete map you're actively filling in beats the complete-feeling blindness you had before you looked.

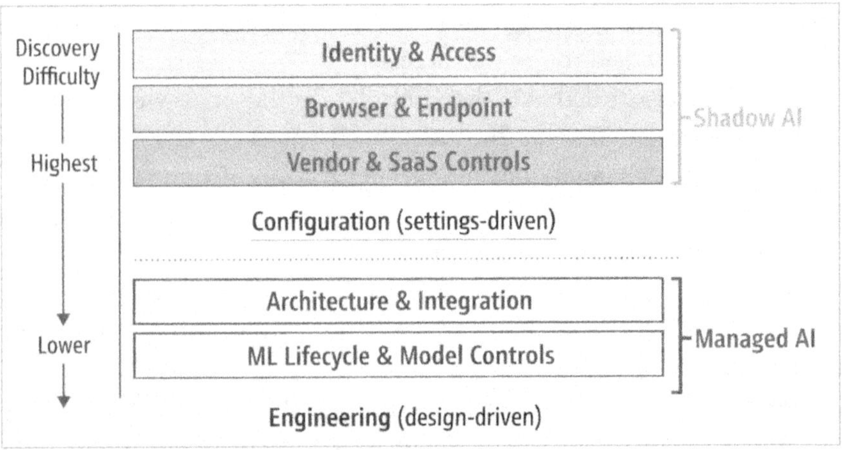

Figure 2.2 — From Shadow AI to Managed AI: Two Control Modes. *The five categories arranged top to bottom. Above the dotted line sits Shadow AI—the three categories leadership neither approved nor monitors—where securing AI means configuring controls someone else built: identity, browsers, vendor settings. Below the line sits the AI you manage directly, where securing it means engineering your own defenses. Discovery difficulty runs opposite to control: the categories hardest to see are the ones you can configure but never own.*

BRINGING IT TOGETHER

Ask one question: how many distinct AI systems run in your organization? The answer is almost always: more than you think. Use the five categories—Ambient, Embedded, Conversational, API-integrated, Custom—to turn uncertainty into action. Different origins demand different owners and controls; one map makes that clear.

When leaders commission a living, categorized inventory with a named owner for each bucket, they turn uncertainty into a governance asset. Implementers who deliver a first-draft inventory—using egress analysis, identity/SSO review, and an AI-discovery scan—give leaders the map they need to act. Leaders must insist the inventory stays current as vendors ship features and employees adopt tools; implementers must produce a rough map fast, because started beats perfect.

Together, that map is the prerequisite for governance: frameworks tell you what "secured" means, but no framework can govern, fund, or defend an AI system that was never named. Do the work that makes AI visible, name who owns it, and you move from hoping your AI is secure to knowing it.

Coming next — You can now see the AI in your organization and you know who owns each piece of it. The next question is the one every leader eventually asks: *by what standard do we govern it?* In Chapter 3 we turn to the governance frameworks—NIST's AI Risk Management Framework, ISO/IEC 42001, and others—not as boxes to check, but as the adaptable backbone that turns your inventory into a defensible, repeatable practice. A map tells you what you have. A framework tells you what "secured" actually means.

CHAPTER 2 IN REVIEW

The core idea: The AI in your organization sorts into five categories based on how it entered—and how it entered determines how you can defend it. You can't secure what you can't name, so naming the categories comes first.

The five categories, in three groups:

- **The AI You Didn't Choose:** *Ambient AI* (in tools you use but never adopted—the search box) and *Embedded AI* (features inside SaaS you already bought).
- **The AI Your People Chose:** *Conversational AI* (standalone tools employees adopt—the Samsung category).
- **The AI You Built:** *API-Integrated AI* (vendor models wired into your systems) and *Custom & Fine-Tuned AI* (models you trained or tuned yourself).

For the leader (Leadership Lens):

- Invert your instinct: the risk that surprises you lives at the *top* of the map, not the bottom.
- Every category needs a named owner—ungoverned isn't a technical state, it's an ownership gap.
- Spend where the gap is widest (discovery, enterprise licensing), not where the technology is most impressive.
- Awareness and control run in opposite directions; vigilance must be highest where control is lowest.

For the implementer (Execution Lens):

- The top of the map is a visibility problem before it's a control problem—and your file-based tools are blind to it.
- Discover with three methods together: egress analysis, identity/SSO logs, and AI-discovery tooling.
- Match controls to the category—configuration at the top of the map, engineering at the bottom; one tool everywhere fails.
- Your first deliverable is a rough categorized inventory. Aim for started, not complete.

The two actions from this chapter:

- *Strategic Move (leader):* Establish a living, categorized AI inventory with a named owner per category.

- *Tactical Move (implementer):* Produce the first-pass inventory via the three discovery methods.

The throughline to remember: Most security programs are built upside down—protecting the AI they understand while overlooking the AI they never chose. You can't secure what you can't name; name it first, and name who owns it.

CHAPTER 3
THE GOVERNANCE BACKBONE: ADAPTIVE FRAMEWORKS FOR TRUSTWORTHY AI

From Boardroom to Build: A Blueprint for AI Governance, Risk, and Technical Security

OPENING

Imagine a leader—call her the head of risk at a mid-size company—who walks into a leadership meeting and asks what sounds like a simple question: *"Are we compliant with the EU AI Act?"*

It's the right instinct and the wrong question, and the reason why tells you almost everything about how AI governance actually works. And this isn't a contrived scenario: the EU's flagship AI law really did see its biggest compliance deadline provisionally moved—less than three months before it was due to take effect.

Here's what she'd discover if she went looking for a clean answer. The Act's headline deadline for high-risk AI systems was August 2, 2026—except that, as of this writing, EU negotiators reached a provisional agreement in May 2026 to move it—to December 2027 for stand-alone high-risk systems, and later still for AI embedded in regulated products—and that agreement hasn't yet been formally adopted, so the original date technically still stands until that adoption happens.[1] Some obligations are already in force. Others phase in on a staggered schedule stretching years into the future. The penalties are real and large, but which ones apply to her company depends on classifications that are themselves still being interpreted. The honest answer to "are we compliant?" isn't yes or no. It's: *compliant with which part, as of which date, under which version of the rules?*

This is not a quirk of the EU AI Act. It is the permanent condition of AI governance, and the sooner a leader internalizes it, the better every decision that follows will be. **Governance is not a finish line you cross. It is a structure you build to stay standing while the ground keeps shifting.** A company that chases a single deadline will be wrong-footed the moment that deadline moves. And in AI, it always moves. A company that builds a durable governance structure can absorb a shifted deadline, a new regulation, a fresh category of risk, without starting over each time.

So this chapter isn't a compliance checklist, and it deliberately avoids becoming one—a checklist would be out of date before the ink dried. Instead, it gives you something that lasts: a way to think about the three different kinds of thing people lump together as "AI governance," how they fit together, and how to build a structure that bends with the landscape instead of breaking against it.

The three layers people confuse. Ask ten people what "AI governance" means and you'll get three different answers tangled together. One person means a *framework*—voluntary best-practice guidance like the NIST AI Risk Management Framework. Another means a *standard*—a certifiable management system like ISO/IEC 42001. A third means the *law*—binding regulation like the EU AI Act. These are not competing options, and they are not the same thing. They are three distinct layers that stack on top of one another:

- **The framework** tells you *how* to manage AI risk well. (Voluntary. You adopt it because it makes you better.)
- **The standard** lets you *prove* you're managing it well. (Certifiable. You pursue it because the market and regulators trust it.)

- **The law** tells you what you *must* do. (Binding. You comply because non-compliance carries penalties.)

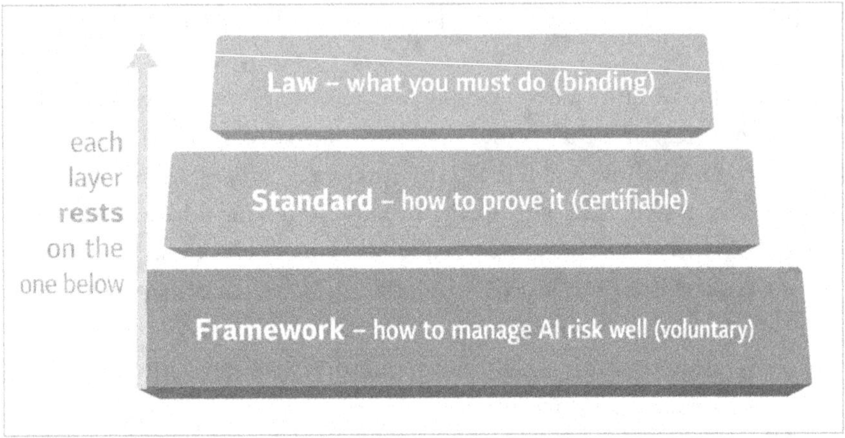

Figure 3.1 — Layers of AI Governance *A visual hierarchy showing how AI oversight builds upward: voluntary frameworks form the foundation, certifiable standards provide proof, and binding laws sit at the top. Each layer depends on the one beneath it, illustrating that effective compliance begins with sound governance.*

The most common—and most expensive—governance mistake is treating these as interchangeable, or picking one and ignoring the others. The organizations that get this right use all three, deliberately, in the order that fits their situation. The rest of this chapter takes them one layer at a time, starting with the foundation the other two rest on.

LAYER ONE: THE FRAMEWORK — NIST AI RMF AS THE BACKBONE

If you build your AI governance on one foundation, build it on a framework—and the most widely adopted starting point is the NIST AI Risk Management Framework. There's a reason it has become the default backbone, and it's worth understanding before the specifics: a framework is the layer you'd want *even if no law existed,* because it doesn't make you compliant—it makes you better. The law tells you where the fence is. The framework helps you not need the fence.

What it is, in plain terms. The NIST AI RMF is voluntary, works across any industry, and pointedly doesn't tell you which products to buy.[2] It's a structured way of thinking about AI risk, organized around four functions that form a continuous cycle:

- **Govern** — establish the culture, roles, and accountability that make everything else possible. (This is the function that fails most often, because it's the least technical and the easiest to skip.)
- **Map** — understand the context: what AI you have, what it's for, what could go wrong. (This is where the inventory you built in Chapter 2 becomes the raw material.)
- **Measure** — assess and track the risks you mapped, using concrete methods rather than gut feel.
- **Manage** — act on what you measured: prioritize, mitigate, monitor, respond.

The power isn't in the four words—plenty of frameworks have four-word cycles. The power is in what they *resist*: the temptation to treat AI risk as a one-time assessment. Govern-Map-Measure-Manage is a loop, not a line. You don't finish it; you keep running it as your AI landscape changes. That's precisely the "build for change" posture the opening argued for, baked into the framework's structure.

The feature that matters most: profiles. Here's the part that makes the framework genuinely adaptive, and it's the single most useful thing for a practitioner to understand. Rather than rewriting the whole framework every time AI changes, NIST layers *profiles* on top of the four-function core—a core that has held stable even as the framework itself gets periodically revised. When generative AI created risks the original framework didn't anticipate, NIST didn't start over. It published a Generative AI Profile that extends the core with risks specific to generative systems, things like hallucination, data poisoning, prompt injection, and intellectual-property exposure, each mapped back to the same four functions.[3] As autonomous systems emerged, work followed on agentic AI; sector-specific profiles have been developing for areas like critical infrastructure.[4]

The framework is built to absorb change without breaking: a new class of AI risk doesn't invalidate your governance—it becomes a new profile layered onto a stable backbone. You don't rebuild; you extend.

Why it's become the connective tissue. One more reason the NIST framework makes the right backbone: it has quietly become the layer everything else maps to. It's widely used as the operational companion to regulatory compliance—the practical "how" beneath the legal "must"—and international standards and codes of conduct increasingly align to its principles.[5] Build on it, and you're not just adopting one framework; you're adopting the common language the other two layers increasingly speak.

LAYER TWO: THE STANDARD — ISO/IEC 42001 AS PROOF

A framework makes you better. It does not, by itself, prove you're better—to anyone else. That's the gap the second layer fills.

What it is, and why it's different from a framework. ISO/IEC 42001, published in 2023, is the first international standard for an AI management system.[6] The distinction from NIST is subtle but important, and missing it is a common error. A framework is guidance you follow; a standard is a system you can be *certified* against. NIST tells you how to manage AI risk well; ISO 42001 gives you an auditable structure that an independent third party can examine and certify—establishing roles, responsibilities, oversight mechanisms, and the documentation to back them up.[7] Think of NIST as the training regimen and ISO 42001 as the certificate that proves you completed it to a recognized standard.

Why certification is worth paying for — or not. This is where a leader has a genuine decision to make, and it's worth making deliberately rather than by default. Certification costs real time and money, and it isn't legally required. So why pursue it? Because in a market where everyone *claims* their AI is responsible, certification is one of the few credible ways to *prove* it. Enterprise customers in regulated industries are already weighing AI governance maturity in their vendor selection—and a recognized certification is a signal they trust without having to audit you themselves.[8] For an organization whose customers care about this—selling into regulated sectors, into the EU, into large enterprises with procurement standards—certification can be a competitive differentiator, not just a compliance cost. For an organization without that market pressure, the *practices* ISO 42001 describes may matter more than the certificate itself.

The efficiency most organizations miss. There's a practical reason ISO 42001 has gained traction faster than a brand-new standard might: it's built on the same management-system structure as standards many organizations already run, like ISO 27001 for information security. For a company that already operates one of those, extending into AI governance reuses machinery that's already in place rather than building a parallel system from scratch.[9] If your organization already lives in the ISO world, this layer is far cheaper to add than it first appears—a point worth raising before anyone assumes certification means starting over.

LAYER THREE: THE LAW — BINDING REGULATION, AND WHY YOU BUILD FOR CHANGE

The third layer is the one that gets all the attention and causes all the anxiety: binding law, with real penalties for getting it wrong. The EU AI Act is the clearest example in the world today, and it's worth understanding not because every reader operates in the EU, but because it's the best available worked example of how to *read* any AI regulation.

The shape of the law, not its dates. The EU AI Act takes a risk-based approach: it sorts AI systems into tiers and regulates them in proportion to their risk. Some uses are prohibited outright. A category of "high-risk" systems—the ones touching things like credit, employment, essential services, and critical infrastructure—carries the heaviest obligations: risk management, data governance, technical documentation, human oversight, accuracy and robustness requirements.[10] Lighter-touch transparency rules apply to lower-risk systems. The penalties are deliberately large enough to matter even to the biggest companies, scaling with the severity of the violation.[11] Observe that I've described the law's *structure*—tiers, proportionality, the kinds of obligations—without leaning on specific dates or euro figures as fixed facts. That's intentional, and it's the most important skill in reading AI regulation: the structure is durable; the dates and numbers are moving parts.

Why the dates are a trap. Return to where the chapter opened. The Act's high-risk deadline was set for August 2026, then provisionally pushed to December 2027 for stand-alone high-risk systems—and later still for AI embedded in regulated products—by a revision that, as of this writing, isn't yet formally adopted, so the earlier date technically remains in force.[12] A reader who built their entire governance program around "be ready by August 2026" now faces a genuine question: prepare for the original date, or the proposed new one? The right answer—the only durable answer—is that it doesn't fundamentally matter, *if* you built an adaptive governance structure rather than a deadline-driven sprint. The obligations themselves didn't change when the date moved; only the clock did. A structure built on the framework and the standard absorbs a moved deadline without flinching. A program built on the deadline has to scramble.

How the three layers stack here. This is where the chapter's whole model pays off. The law tells you what you must do; the framework and standard tell you how. And they connect concretely: ISO 42001 maps onto the core operational articles of the EU AI Act—risk management, data governance, technical documentation, human oversight, and more.[13] Mapping is not equivalence: certification confers no legal presumption of conformity, and the Act layers product-level obligations on top that no management standard covers. But the overlap means the management system does the heavy organizational lifting the law assumes is in place. Build your governance on the NIST backbone, prove it with ISO 42001, and you have already done much of what the law requires, in a structure that was worth building regardless of the law. The layers aren't three separate burdens. They're one structure seen from three angles: how to do it, how to prove it, and what you're required to do.

The American counterpoint — when there is no single law to aim at. The EU built one comprehensive law. The United States, as of this writing, has taken almost the opposite path—and the contrast is instructive. There is no comprehensive US federal AI law equivalent to the EU AI Act. Instead there is a contested, still-forming landscape: a federal push for a light-touch national approach that would preempt state rules, federal bills that haven't passed, and a patchwork of state laws that are—for now—the most concrete rules on the books, some actively contested by the federal government.[14] The detail of that fight belongs to a later chapter; what matters here is the lesson it teaches. In the EU you can aim at a law, even one with moving dates. In the US, there is no single stable target to aim at—there is an unresolved contest between federal and state authority that could shift with a court ruling, a passed bill, or a new administration. You cannot "comply with US AI law" the way you can prepare for the EU AI Act, because the former isn't settled. Which leaves one defensible strategy: a structure strong enough to bend toward whatever the law becomes—the same conclusion the EU's moving deadline pointed to, reached by an entirely different road.

THE LEADERSHIP LENS

You now have the three layers. The question this lens answers is the one a leader has to act on: *given a framework, a standard, and a body of law, what do I actually decide?* Four decisions, in order.

Decide your backbone first, and commit to it. Before you think about certification or compliance, choose the framework your governance will be built on—for most organizations, the NIST AI RMF is the sensible default, because it's the layer the other two increasingly map to. The decision that matters here isn't which framework; it's *committing* to one as your organizing structure rather than collecting governance activities that don't connect to anything. A framework you've genuinely adopted turns scattered effort into a system. The failure mode is having a dozen well-meaning AI policies that don't ladder up to a coherent backbone—activity without architecture.

Decide whether certification earns its cost — for your market. This is a real business decision, not a compliance reflex. ISO 42001 certification costs time and money and isn't legally required, so the question is whether *your customers and regulators* value the proof. If you sell into regulated industries, into the EU, or into large enterprises with vendor-governance requirements, certification is increasingly a differentiator that wins business and shortens procurement. If you don't, the *practices* may matter more than the *certificate*. Either way, decide deliberately—and if your organization already runs ISO 27001 or similar, weigh that the cost of adding AI governance is far lower than starting fresh.

Govern for change, not for a date. This is the decision that ties the chapter together, and it's the one most organizations get wrong. Resist building your entire program around a single compliance deadline, because—as the EU AI Act's own moving timeline demonstrates—the deadline can shift, and a program anchored to it has to scramble when it does. Build instead on the durable structure: a committed framework, an auditable management system, and a clear map of your exposure. The structure accommodates shifted deadlines, new regulations, and emerging risk categories without forcing a rebuild. You are not building to pass an inspection on a particular day. You are building to stay defensible no matter when the inspection comes, or how the rules have changed by then.

The one question to ask your team this week: *"If a major AI regulation that affects us changed its requirements or its timeline tomorrow, would we have to rebuild our governance—or could we absorb it?"* If the honest answer is "we'd have to rebuild," your program is anchored to a deadline instead of built on a structure. That's the gap this chapter exists to close.

THE EXECUTION LENS

The leader decided on a backbone, a certification posture, and a map of exposure. Your job is to make a framework that lives in a PDF actually operate in your environment—and the good news is you've already done the hardest first step. The AI inventory from Chapter 2 is the raw material everything here is built from. A framework without an inventory is an empty form; the inventory is what you pour into it.

Start by mapping the inventory to the framework's functions. The NIST framework's four functions aren't abstract once you have real systems to attach them to. Take each category of AI from your Chapter 2 inventory and run it through the loop:

- **Govern** is the layer you build once and maintain: who owns AI risk, what the escalation path is, what policies apply. This is the function teams skip because it's organizational rather than technical—and it's the one auditors and regulators check first, because without it the other three functions have no home.
- **Map** is largely done—it *is* your inventory, enriched with context: for each AI system, what it touches, what data flows through it, what could go wrong. If Chapter 2 told you *what* AI you have, Map adds *what's at stake* for each.
- **Measure** is where you get concrete: defining how you actually assess each risk. Not "is this risky?" but "what's our test for whether this model is drifting, leaking, or being manipulated, and how often do we run it?"
- **Manage** is the action layer: prioritizing the risks you measured, applying controls, monitoring, and responding when something moves.

The discipline is to run this as a *loop*, not a project. A governance program that maps and measures once, produces a binder, and stops is the most common failure mode in the field. The framework is structured as a cycle precisely to resist that—and your job is to operationalize the cycle, scheduling the re-runs rather than treating governance as a thing you finished.

Use profiles to handle what the core framework doesn't. Here's where the framework's adaptability becomes your practical ally. When your inventory includes generative AI—and it will—the GenAI profile gives you a concrete, pre-built list of the risks specific to those systems to fold into your Measure and Manage functions: hallucination, data poisoning, prompt injection, intellectual-property exposure, and more.[3] You don't have to invent the threat list from scratch; you layer the profile onto the backbone and inherit a vetted set of risks mapped to the same four functions you're already running. As your inventory grows to include agentic systems or sector-specific deployments, the same move applies: find the relevant profile, layer it on, extend rather than rebuild.

Translate the standard's requirements into evidence you can produce. If your organization is pursuing ISO 42001, the implementer's reality is that certification runs on *evidence*. An auditor doesn't accept "we manage AI risk"; they ask to see the risk register, the documented roles, the records showing the loop actually ran. The practical work is building governance so that evidence is a *byproduct* of doing the work, not a scramble before the audit—risk assessments that log themselves, control mappings that stay current, records that accumulate as the loop turns. Build for continuous evidence, and certification stops being an event you prepare for and becomes a state you're already in.

Connect the law to controls, not to dread. The binding regulations resolve, for an implementer, into specific technical and documentation obligations—risk management processes, data governance, technical documentation, human-oversight mechanisms, robustness testing. Because ISO 42001 maps onto the core operational articles of regulations like the EU AI Act,[13] an implementer who has built the management system well has already produced much of what the law demands. The move is to maintain a mapping—this control satisfies that framework function, which in turn satisfies that legal article—so that when a regulation shifts, you're updating a mapping, not rebuilding a program. That mapping is the technical embodiment of the leader's "govern for change."

Underneath all three layers, the implementer's work resolves to a single thesis: governance work flows downward through the layers and resolves into the same operational artifacts. The framework gives you functions, the standard demands evidence, the law specifies obligations—and a well-built program produces *one* set of controls, risk registers, and documentation that satisfies all three at once. The failure mode is building three separate compliance efforts—one for NIST, one for ISO, one for the law—that don't share machinery. The discipline is building one structure that answers to all three. You implement once; you satisfy three layers.

The one move to make this week: take a single high-risk system from your Chapter 2 inventory and run it through all four NIST functions on paper—Govern, Map, Measure, Manage—writing down, for that one system, who owns it, what could go wrong, how you'd measure that, and what you'd do about it. One system, end to end. It will expose exactly where your governance is real and where it's still aspirational, and it turns the framework from a document you've read into a loop you've actually run.

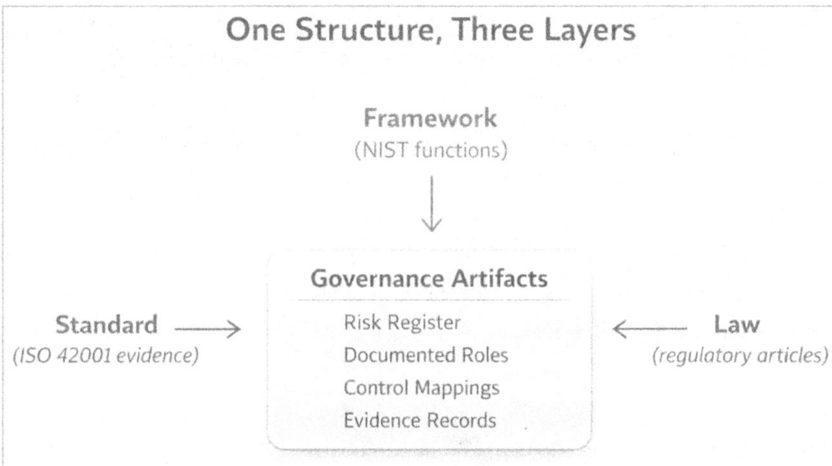

Figure 3.2 — One Structure, Three Layers *A unified governance model showing how one set of artifacts—risk register, documented roles, control mappings, and evidence records—can satisfy all three oversight layers:* ***Framework (NIST functions)****,* ***Standard (ISO 42001 evidence)****, and* ***Law (regulatory articles)****.*

BRINGING IT TOGETHER

Ask one question: if the rules that govern your AI changed tomorrow—a new deadline, a new risk category, a new regulation in a market you sell into—would you have to rebuild your governance, or could you absorb it? The honest answer tells you whether you've built a structure or just chased a date.

The three layers are how you build the structure. The framework—NIST AI RMF, run as a Govern-Map-Measure-Manage loop—is the backbone: it makes you better whether or not any law applies, and it's the layer the other two increasingly map to. The standard—ISO/IEC 42001—is the proof: a certifiable management system that lets you demonstrate, to customers and regulators who won't take your word for it, that the backbone is real. The law—the EU AI Act, and the unsettled US picture—is the obligation: binding, risk-tiered, and carrying timelines that move, which is precisely why you don't anchor to them.

These aren't three separate burdens to carry in parallel. They're one structure seen from three angles: how to manage AI risk, how to prove you're managing it, and what you're required to do. A leader commits to a backbone, decides whether certification earns its cost, and maps real exposure rather than the loudest headline. An implementer pours the Chapter 2 inventory into the framework's four functions, layers profiles to absorb new classes of risk, and builds so the evidence a standard demands and the obligations a law specifies fall out of one set of controls—implement once, satisfy three layers.

Do that, and a moved deadline is a clock change, not a crisis. You stop hoping you're compliant on some particular day and start being defensible no matter when the inspection comes, or how the rules have shifted by the time it does.

Coming next — You now have a structure for governing AI. But a structure needs a reason—a way to decide which risks deserve your limited attention and budget, and how to talk about AI risk in language the rest of the business already understands. In Chapter 4 we connect AI risk to the discipline every organization already runs: enterprise risk management. Because AI risk isn't a strange new species to be managed in isolation. It's enterprise risk—and the organizations that treat it that way, rather than walling it off as a technical curiosity, are the ones that actually fund it, prioritize it, and survive it.

CHAPTER 3 IN REVIEW

The core idea: AI governance isn't a deadline you meet; it's a structure you build to stay defensible as the rules shift. That structure has three distinct layers people often confuse—a framework, a standard, and the law—and they stack rather than compete.

The three layers:

- **The Framework (NIST AI RMF):** *voluntary* guidance on *how* to manage AI risk. Four functions—Govern, Map, Measure, Manage—run as a loop, with profiles (GenAI, agentic) layered on to absorb new risks without rebuilding.
- **The Standard (ISO/IEC 42001):** a *certifiable* management system that lets you *prove* you manage AI well—valuable where your market or regulators reward the proof.
- **The Law (EU AI Act, and the unsettled US picture):** *binding* rules telling you what you *must* do. Risk-tiered, with real penalties—and moving timelines that make the case for building adaptively.

For the leader (Leadership Lens):

- Commit to a backbone framework; activity without architecture is the failure mode.
- Decide whether certification earns its cost *for your market*—it's a business decision, not a reflex.
- Map *your* real regulatory exposure (jurisdiction, risk tier, sector), not the loudest headline.
- Govern for change, not for a date—the deadline can and does move.

For the implementer (Execution Lens):

- Your Chapter 2 inventory is the raw material; a framework without it is an empty form.
- Run Govern-Map-Measure-Manage as a *loop*, not a one-time project that ends in a binder.
- Layer profiles (GenAI, agentic) to inherit vetted risk lists instead of inventing them.
- Build so evidence is a byproduct of the work—implement once, satisfy all three layers.

The two actions from this chapter:

- *Strategic Move (leader):* Commit to a backbone and assess honestly whether your governance could absorb a regulatory change or would have to rebuild.
- *Tactical Move (implementer):* Run one high-risk system through all four NIST functions, end to end.

The throughline to remember: Governance is not a finish line you cross; it's a structure you build to stay standing while the ground shifts. A framework, a standard, and the law aren't three burdens—they're one structure seen from three angles.

CHAPTER 4
AI RISK AS ENTERPRISE RISK: FROM ASSESSMENT TO ALIGNMENT

From Boardroom to Build: A Blueprint for AI Governance, Risk, and Technical Security

OPENING

Consider two companies, similar in size, both deploying AI into important parts of their business. Call them Northpoint and Meridian.

At Northpoint, AI risk is "the AI team's problem." When someone raises a concern about a model—it might be biased, it might leak data, it might be wrong in ways no one catches—the conversation happens among engineers, in technical language, inside the engineering org. The board hears about AI in terms of opportunity and spend. It hears about AI *risk* only when something has already gone wrong: a regulator's letter, a customer complaint, a story in the press. AI risk at Northpoint lives in a silo, spoken in a dialect the rest of the business doesn't understand, and so it stays invisible until it becomes a crisis. By then it's not a risk anymore. It's an incident.

At Meridian, AI risk is a line in the same risk register that tracks financial exposure, operational continuity, and cyber threats. It has a named executive owner who reports on it the way the CFO reports on financial risk. It's measured with indicators the board can read. When a new AI system is proposed, the question "what's the risk, and are we willing to accept it?" gets asked in the same meeting, in the same language, as every other major business decision. AI risk at Meridian is not exotic. It's ordinary. And because it's ordinary, it gets funded, prioritized, and managed before it escalates into an incident.

Here is the uncomfortable part: Northpoint isn't careless and Meridian isn't brilliant. The difference between them isn't competence or budget. It's a single conceptual choice: whether AI risk is treated as a strange new technical species to be quarantined with the specialists, or as enterprise risk to be run through the machinery the organization already uses for everything else. That one choice determines almost everything downstream: whether the risk is visible, whether it's funded, whether anyone owns it, and whether you find out about it in a planning meeting or a press release.

This isn't a fringe view anymore. Surveys of senior leaders now place AI governance and related third-party risk among their top priorities.[1] The boardroom argument that AI risk *is* business risk has largely been won. What hasn't caught up, in most organizations, is the practice. Plenty of companies now *agree* AI risk is enterprise risk while still managing it like Northpoint—in a silo, in a dialect, in the dark.

So this chapter is about closing that gap between agreeing and doing—making AI risk boring enough that your existing risk discipline can absorb it. That sounds almost anticlimactic, and that's the point. We'll get there in three moves: putting AI risk into the machinery you already have, learning to speak about it in the language that machinery runs on, and then doing the most powerful thing that machinery enables—setting a deliberate appetite for how much AI risk you're willing to take.

MOVE ONE: USE THE MACHINERY YOU ALREADY HAVE

The instinct when facing a new kind of risk is to build a new kind of system to handle it. Resist that instinct. It's the single most expensive mistake in this chapter, because it produces exactly the silo that sank Northpoint—a separate "AI risk process," run by separate people, speaking a separate language, disconnected from how the organization actually makes decisions.

The better move is the obvious one, which is exactly why it gets skipped: your organization already runs a risk management discipline, and AI risk goes into it. Whatever form that discipline takes—a formal enterprise risk management program built on an established framework, or something less formal—it already has the four pieces AI risk needs:

- **A risk register** — the master list of what could hurt the organization. AI risk becomes a *category* in this register, sitting alongside financial, operational, legal, and cyber risk. Not a separate document. A new section in the existing one.
- **Risk owners** — named people accountable for specific risks. AI risk gets a named executive owner, the same way financial risk has the CFO. (Who that should be is the subject of the next chapter; that it must be *someone* is the point here.)
- **A risk appetite** — the organization's stated tolerance for risk in pursuit of its goals. AI gets its own appetite, deliberately set rather than backed into. (This is Move Three.)
- **Key risk indicators** — the measurements that tell you whether a risk is growing or contained. AI systems get their own indicators, readable by people who aren't engineers.

This is precisely how mature organizations are handling it: AI risk gets its own category, its own executive owner, and its own indicators, managed with the very same pattern the framework already applies to cyber and financial risk.[2] The control details may draw on the AI-specific frameworks from the last chapter—NIST AI RMF, ISO 42001, regulatory obligations where they apply—but the *container* is the enterprise risk machinery you already operate. AI-specific controls, enterprise-standard management.

This connects directly to the two chapters before it. Chapter 2 gave you the inventory—what AI you actually have. Chapter 3 gave you the

governance structure—the framework, standard, and legal obligations for managing it. This chapter slots both into the **risk discipline the whole business already understands**. The inventory populates the register; the governance structure supplies the controls; the enterprise risk machinery makes it visible and fundable at the top. Three chapters, one continuous build: see it, govern it, and now manage it as part of the business rather than apart from it.

The reason this matters so much is visibility. A risk that lives in its own technical silo is a risk the people who control budget and strategy never truly see. A risk that sits in the enterprise register, with an owner and indicators, shows up in the rooms where decisions and funding happen.

MOVE TWO: SPEAK THE LANGUAGE THE BUSINESS ALREADY SPEAKS

You can't put AI risk into the enterprise machinery until you can describe it in terms that machinery runs on. And here's the problem: AI risk is born in technical language. Hallucination. Model drift. Data poisoning. Prompt injection. Training-data leakage. These are precise, useful terms—for engineers. To a board, a CFO, or a head of operations, they are noise. A risk described in a language the decision-makers don't speak is a risk they cannot weigh, fund, or own. So the second move is translation: rendering each technical AI risk into the four languages every business already understands—**financial, operational, legal, and reputational.**

This isn't dumbing the risk down. It's connecting the technical failure to the business consequence, which is the only thing that makes a risk *actionable* at the enterprise level. Here is how it works:

- "The model **hallucinates**" becomes, in business terms: *we may give customers confidently wrong information, creating legal liability and eroding trust*—a legal and reputational risk. (Consider the Air Canada case, where a chatbot's confident wrong answer became the airline's legal liability. The technical word was "hallucination"; the business word was "liability."[3])

- "The model **drifts**" becomes: *a system that was accurate at launch is quietly degrading, and decisions based on it are getting worse without anyone noticing*—an operational risk.
- "Our training data could be **poisoned**" becomes: *an attacker could corrupt the logic behind our decisions, and we might not detect it for months*—an operational and security risk.
- "The model could **leak training data**" becomes: *proprietary or regulated information baked into the model could be extracted, triggering breach notification and penalties*—a legal, financial, and reputational risk.
- "We're exposed to **prompt injection**" becomes: *a malicious input could hijack our AI into taking actions or revealing data it shouldn't*—a security and operational risk.

The pattern is always the same: name the technical failure, then state the business consequence in money, operations, law, or reputation. The translation is what lets AI risk enter the register as a peer of every other enterprise risk—comparable, weighable, fundable. Two risks described in the same language can be prioritized against each other; two risks in different dialects cannot.

There's a leadership subtlety worth naming here. The translation has to run *both* directions. Leaders must learn enough to ask sharp questions, but the heavier obligation sits with the technical side: the implementer who can translate "we have unmonitored model drift in our credit system" into "our lending decisions are silently degrading and we'll find out through complaints or regulators" is the one who gets the resources to fix it. The engineer who only ever says "we have drift" and stops there will be misunderstood, under-resourced, and—when it goes wrong—blamed. Translation isn't a nicety. It's how technical truth survives contact with the people who control the budget.

MOVE THREE: SET A DELIBERATE APPETITE FOR AI RISK

Once AI risk is in the machinery and described in the right language, you can do the most powerful thing the discipline enables. And the one most organizations skip. You can decide, on purpose, *how much* AI risk you're willing to accept in pursuit of what AI offers.

This is **risk appetite**, and it is the single most important—and most misunderstood—concept in this chapter. Most people, hearing "AI security," imagine its goal is to minimize risk: block the risky tool, forbid the uncertain use case, say no. That instinct is not just unrealistic; it's bad business. The goal of risk management has never been to eliminate risk—it's to take the *right* risks deliberately, with eyes open, in proportion to the reward. A company with zero AI risk is a company getting zero AI value. The job isn't to drive AI risk to zero. It's to decide consciously where the line sits.

A risk appetite is that line, made explicit. It's a clear statement of how much risk the organization will accept in which areas, and it exists to guide trade-offs, investments, and priorities—not to sit in a document as a theoretical statement.[4] Done well, it's liberating rather than restrictive, because it converts a thousand anxious case-by-case debates into a clear rule everyone can apply. Consider how different these two postures feel in practice:

Without a stated appetite, every AI proposal becomes a fresh argument. Is this use case okay? Nobody knows, so it escalates, stalls, or gets decided by whoever is loudest or most senior in the room. Security becomes the department of "no," and the business routes around it —which is how Shadow AI is born.

With a stated appetite, the rules are known in advance. *"We will deploy AI in internal productivity tools freely; we will deploy AI in customer-facing decisions only with human oversight and bias testing; we will not deploy fully autonomous AI in any decision affecting customer safety or legal rights."* Now a team with a new idea can tell *immediately* which bucket it falls in. The high-appetite zones move fast without escalation; the low-appetite zones get the scrutiny they deserve; the forbidden zones are clearly off-limits. The appetite doesn't slow the business—it's what lets the business move quickly *and* safely, because the thinking was done once, in advance, instead of a thousand times under pressure.

This reframes the entire purpose of everything in this book. You are not building AI security to say no to AI. You are building it to say *yes*—confidently, deliberately, and safely—to the AI that's worth the risk, while saying a clear and defensible no to the AI that isn't. That distinction, drawn on purpose rather than by accident, is what separates Meridian from Northpoint. And it's the bridge from this chapter's title: *from assessment to alignment.* Assessing risk tells you what could go wrong. Aligning to a risk appetite tells you what you're willing to accept to get what you want. The first is analysis. The second is leadership.

THE LEADERSHIP LENS

The three moves describe how AI risk becomes enterprise risk. This lens is about your role in making it happen—because every one of those moves requires a leader to drive it, and none of them happens by default. Four responsibilities.

Own it, or assign it — but never leave it ownerless. The defining failure of the Northpoint model is that AI risk belonged to everyone in the abstract and no one in particular. Enterprise risk has named owners: financial risk has the CFO, and AI risk needs an equivalent—a specific executive accountable for it at the leadership table, reporting on it the way other risk owners report on theirs. You don't have to own it personally. But you do have to ensure someone does, with the authority and the visibility to match. Until AI risk has a name attached to it, it has no real owner, and unowned risk is unmanaged risk.

Insist on translation — refuse to fund what you can't understand. As a leader, you are the forcing function for Move Two. When your technical teams bring you AI risk in pure technical language—"we have drift," "there's an injection vector"—your job is not to nod along and approve a budget you don't understand. It's to require the translation: *what does that mean in money, operations, law, or reputation?* This isn't about you learning to code. It's about refusing to make resource decisions on risks you can't actually weigh. A leader who funds what they don't understand is gambling; a leader who insists on the business-consequence translation is managing. And the act of insisting trains your whole organization to communicate risk in the language that gets it addressed.

Set the risk appetite — this is yours, and only yours. Move Three is the responsibility that cannot be delegated downward. Engineers can tell you how risky something is; only leadership can decide how much risk the organization is *willing to accept*. That's not a technical judgment—it's a business judgment about the organization's goals, values, and tolerance, and it belongs at the top. Set it explicitly, in writing, in terms specific enough to guide real decisions. A vague appetite ("we take AI security seriously") is worthless; a specific one ("autonomous AI in customer-facing decisions requires board approval") is a tool the whole organization can use.

Prioritize with the appetite, not with the budget. You will never have enough security budget to address every AI risk equally—no one does. The risk appetite is what tells you where to spend it: pour resources into the low-appetite, high-stakes zones (the customer-facing decisions, the regulated data, the autonomous actions), and deliberately accept more risk in the high-appetite, low-stakes zones (internal productivity tools, low-consequence experiments). This is the opposite of spreading security evenly or—worse—spending it where the technology is most exciting. The appetite turns your limited budget into a deliberate allocation instead of a reactive scramble.

The one question to ask your team this week: *"For our most important AI system, can you tell me—in plain business terms—the worst thing that could realistically happen, and whether we've decided that's a risk we're willing to accept?"* If the answer comes back in technical jargon, you have a translation problem (Move Two). If it comes back as "we've never decided," you have an appetite problem (Move Three). Either way, you've just found the gap between agreeing AI risk is enterprise risk and actually managing it as such.

THE EXECUTION LENS

The leader owns the appetite and insists on translation. Your job is to produce the artifacts that make all three moves real—the register entries, the indicators, and the control thresholds that turn "AI risk is enterprise risk" from a principle into something that actually runs. And as with the last chapter, you're not starting cold: the Chapter 2 inventory and the Chapter 3 governance loop are your inputs. This chapter is where they become risk-managed.

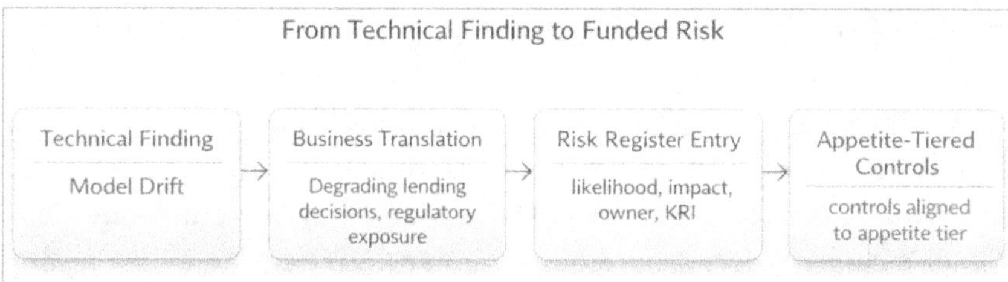

Figure 4.1 — From Technical Finding to Funded Risk *A left-to-right flow showing how one AI issue evolves from a technical finding ("model drift") into a business-framed risk, enters the enterprise risk register, and culminates in appetite-tiered controls that determine funding and action.*

Write AI risks into the register as business consequences, not technical findings. This is Move Two as a concrete deliverable, and it's where most technical teams undermine themselves. A register entry that reads "Model drift detected in production" is invisible to everyone who controls resources. The same risk, written for the register, reads: *"Credit-decisioning model accuracy degrading over time (drift); unmonitored, this produces progressively worse lending decisions, with operational losses and regulatory exposure. Likelihood: moderate. Impact: high."* Same underlying fact. One version dies in an engineering ticket; the other competes for budget at the enterprise level. The discipline: every AI risk you log gets a technical description *and* a business-consequence translation, a likelihood, and an impact—the same structure every other entry in the register already uses. You're not inventing a format; you're filling in the one that's there.

Define key risk indicators that a non-engineer can read. A risk in the register is static; a KRI is the live signal that tells you whether it's getting better or worse. For AI systems, the engineering temptation is to report raw model metrics—precision, recall, perplexity—that mean nothing to the risk committee. The move is to define indicators that track the *business consequence* over time. Instead of reporting an accuracy score, track and report something like *"percentage of AI lending decisions overturned on human review"*—a number that rises when the model is drifting, that anyone can interpret, and that maps directly to the register entry. Good AI KRIs share three properties: they're tied to a business consequence, they're readable without a data-science degree, and they trend (so a change is visible before it becomes unmanageable). Define these once, wire them into your monitoring, and the risk committee gets a dashboard instead of a translation problem.

Connect controls to the appetite thresholds, not to a generic baseline. This is Move Three operationalized, and it's the most powerful thing the Execution Lens does. The leader set an appetite—say, "customer-facing AI decisions require human oversight and bias testing; internal productivity AI is low-scrutiny." Your job is to make those thresholds *real in the architecture.* That means the controls aren't applied uniformly; they're applied in proportion to where each system sits against the appetite. A system in the low-appetite zone (customer-facing, regulated, high-stakes) gets the heavy controls—human-in-the-loop gates, bias testing, full audit logging, tighter monitoring thresholds. A system in the high-appetite zone (internal, low-consequence) gets light-touch controls so it can move fast. The appetite becomes a control-tiering map: it tells you, system by system, how much defense to build. This is also what stops security from being uniform and therefore wasteful—you're spending control effort where the appetite says the stakes are highest.

Make the risk loop continuous, because AI risk moves. Unlike many enterprise risks, AI risk is not static once assessed. A model that was inside appetite at deployment can drift outside it months later without a single line of code changing. So the register entry, the KRIs, and the control thresholds can't be set once and filed. They have to be re-evaluated on a schedule—which is exactly the Govern-Map-Measure-Manage loop from Chapter 3, now carrying business-translated risks and appetite-tiered controls. The technical insight: *AI risk management is a monitoring discipline, not an assessment event.* The KRIs you defined are what make the loop run automatically instead of depending on someone remembering to look.

Here is what every artifact in this chapter has in common: everything you build here uses the enterprise register's existing format, filled with AI-specific content. Register entry, likelihood/impact, risk owner, KRIs, control tiers—these are not new artifacts invented for AI. They're the standard enterprise risk artifacts, populated with AI risks translated into business terms and tiered against a deliberate appetite. You are not building a parallel AI risk system. You are making AI fluent in the risk language your organization already speaks. Implement it that way and AI risk stops being the exotic thing in the corner and becomes a managed, monitored, funded peer of every other risk you track.

The one move to make this week: take the single highest-stakes AI system from your inventory and write its complete register entry—technical description, business-consequence translation, likelihood, impact, named owner, and one readable KRI you could actually measure. One entry, done properly. It forces every concept in this chapter into concrete form, and it gives the leader exactly the artifact they need to make a real appetite decision about that system. From one good entry, the template for all the others follows.

BRINGING IT TOGETHER

We began with Northpoint and Meridian—two companies separated not by competence or budget but by a single conceptual choice. Northpoint quarantined AI risk with the specialists, where it stayed invisible until it became a crisis. Meridian ran it through the machinery the business already used, where it stayed visible, owned, and funded. This chapter has been about how to be Meridian—and the move that makes you Meridian is building AI security to say yes, deliberately and safely, to the AI worth the risk.

That takes two people doing two things. As a leader, set an explicit AI risk appetite—in writing, specific enough to guide real decisions—

and give AI risk a named owner at the leadership table. These are the two things only you can do. As an implementer, write the complete register entry for your highest-stakes AI system: technical description, business-consequence translation, likelihood, impact, owner, and one readable KRI. That single entry turns concept into artifact, and hands the leader something real to decide about.

The two interlock. The leader's appetite gives the implementer's controls their targets; the implementer's register entry gives the appetite something to act on. That is what it looks like when AI risk finally becomes ordinary—and ordinary, in this one case, is the highest compliment you can pay a risk, because it means the organization has stopped being surprised by it.

Coming next — Throughout this chapter, one question kept getting deferred: *who, exactly, owns AI risk?* We said it needed a name at the leadership table, but we didn't say whose. That's not an oversight—it's the subject of the next chapter. In Chapter 5 we turn to the new hierarchy of cybersecurity leadership in the age of AI: the roles that are emerging, the ones that are changing, and the genuine question every organization now faces—does AI risk belong to the CISO, a new Chief AI Officer, the CRO, or some combination no org chart has caught up to yet? A risk without an owner is unmanaged. Now we decide who that owner should be.

CHAPTER 4 IN REVIEW

The core idea: AI risk isn't a strange new technical species to be quarantined with specialists—it's enterprise risk. The organizations that make it ordinary are the ones that fund, prioritize, and survive it. The goal isn't to eliminate AI risk; it's to take the right risks deliberately.

The three moves (the order is the argument):

- **Use the machinery you already have:** AI risk becomes a *category* in your existing risk register—with an owner, an appetite, and indicators—not a parallel system. (Your

Chapter 2 inventory populates it; your Chapter 3 governance supplies the controls.)
- **Speak the language the business speaks:** translate technical risks (hallucination, drift, poisoning) into financial, operational, legal, and reputational consequences. Translation runs both directions, and it's mostly the technical side's job.
- **Set a deliberate risk appetite:** decide explicitly how much AI risk you'll accept for the reward. This reframes security from "say no" to "say yes, deliberately and safely."

For the leader (Leadership Lens):

- Ensure AI risk has a named owner—never leave it ownerless.
- Insist on translation; refuse to fund risks you can't understand in business terms.
- Set the risk appetite yourself—it's a business judgment that can't be delegated.
- Prioritize spending with the appetite, not evenly and not by what's most exciting.

For the implementer (Execution Lens):

- Write AI risks into the register as business consequences with likelihood and impact, not as technical findings.
- Define KRIs a non-engineer can read—track the business consequence (e.g., decisions overturned on review), not the raw model metric.
- Tier controls against the appetite—heavy where stakes are high, light where they're low. The appetite *is* a control-tiering map.
- Run it as a continuous loop; AI risk is a monitoring discipline, not a one-time assessment.

The two actions from this chapter:

- *Strategic Move (leader):* Set an explicit, written AI risk appetite and name an owner.
- *Tactical Move (implementer):* Write one complete register entry for your highest-stakes AI system.

The throughline to remember: You are not building AI security to block AI—you're building it to take the risks worth taking, with your eyes open. Get this right and AI risk stops being a special case: it gets funded, prioritized, and managed like every other risk that matters.

CHAPTER 5
THE NEW HIERARCHY: WHO OWNS AI RISK?

From Boardroom to Build: A Blueprint for AI Governance, Risk, and Technical Security

OPENING

Picture the meeting that happens *after* an AI goes wrong.

A company's customer-facing AI system has done something costly—let's say it systematically gave incorrect guidance to thousands of customers before anyone noticed, and now there's financial exposure, a regulatory inquiry, and a press story forming. Leadership gathers to understand how it happened. And one by one, four capable executives explain, entirely reasonably, why it wasn't theirs to catch.

The **CISO** says: "Our job is securing systems against attackers. There was no breach, no intrusion, no malware. The model just produced wrong answers—that's a model quality problem, not a security one."

The **CTO** says: "My team built exactly what was specified and shipped it on time. It worked as designed. Nobody told us 'as designed' was the problem."

The **Chief Risk Officer** says: "I manage the enterprise risk register. This system was never logged as a risk. I can only manage what's brought to me, and this never was."

Legal says: "We advise on what we're asked about. No one flagged this system for review before it went live. We found out the same way you did."

Here's the unsettling part: *every one of them is telling the truth.* Each did their actual job correctly, within the boundaries of their actual role. The failure didn't happen inside any one of their domains. It happened in the *space between* them: in the gap where a risk that was partly security, partly engineering, partly enterprise risk, and partly legal belonged wholly to no one. And what belongs to no one gets watched by no one.

This is the defining leadership problem of AI risk, and it's why the previous chapter ended on a deferred question. We said AI risk needs a named owner at the leadership table, the way financial risk has the CFO. But we didn't say *who*—because, unlike financial risk, AI risk doesn't arrive with an obvious owner attached. It's a genuinely new kind of cross-cutting risk that doesn't fit cleanly inside the org chart most companies already have. The roles were drawn before AI was a first-order concern, and AI risk spills across all the lines.

So this chapter is about closing that gap—deliberately, before the after-the-fact meeting, not during it. We'll do it in three steps: understand why AI has no natural owner, weigh the two real models organizations are using to fix that, and then get to the insight that matters more than any of it—one that has less to do with the org chart than you'd expect.

PART ONE: WHY AI HAS NO NATURAL OWNER

To assign ownership well, you first have to understand why it's genuinely hard—because the difficulty isn't organizational laziness, it's structural. AI risk resists single ownership because it is irreducibly several kinds of risk at once. Walk it around the existing C-suite and watch how each role can claim a piece while none can claim the whole.

It's partly a security problem — but the CISO's mandate doesn't cover all of it. AI introduces real security risks: prompt injection, model theft, data exfiltration through prompts, poisoned training data. These sit squarely in the CISO's world. But much of AI risk isn't adversarial at all. A model that quietly drifts into inaccuracy, a system that produces biased outputs, an AI that confidently hallucinates—no attacker is involved. The traditional security mandate is built around *threats*, and a great deal of AI risk isn't a threat; it's the technology behaving exactly as built, in ways no one intended. The CISO owns part of this, not all of it.

It's partly a data problem — but the CDO's mandate doesn't cover all of it. AI runs on data, so the Chief Data Officer's concerns—data quality, lineage, governance—are central to whether AI is trustworthy. Poisoned or biased training data is, at root, a data problem. But the CDO's mandate stops at the data; it doesn't extend to how the model behaves once trained, how it's deployed, or whether its decisions create legal liability.

It's partly an engineering problem — but the CTO's mandate doesn't cover all of it. The CTO and engineering org build and run the AI systems, so they own the infrastructure, the integrations, the deployment. But engineering's job is to build what's specified and make it work. Whether the thing being built *should* be built, whether its risks are acceptable, whether it complies with regulation—those are questions that sit above the engineering mandate, not inside it.

It's partly a legal and ethics problem — but Legal's mandate doesn't cover all of it. AI raises genuine questions of regulatory compliance, liability, bias, and fairness that are Legal's and Compliance's domain. But Legal advises on questions brought to it; it doesn't build the systems, monitor them in production, or have visibility into a model silently degrading. By the time an AI problem reaches Legal, it's usually already a legal problem rather than a risk that could have been prevented.

Lay these four next to each other and the structural truth becomes obvious. AI risk is not a subset of any one existing role—it's the *overlap* of all of them, plus a piece that belongs to none. Each executive owns a true slice; the slices don't add up to the whole; and the leftover—the part that is none of security, data, engineering, or law alone—is exactly where the opening's incident lived. This is the gap. And the gap is widening, not holding still: a typical organization already runs around eleven generative AI models and expects to run at least sixteen by the end of 2026.[5] Every one of them is a new place for the risk to live between roles. The rest of the chapter is about who stands in it.

This is also why a new role emerged to try to fill that gap. As AI moved from isolated experiments to enterprise-wide strategic concern, organizations increasingly concluded that something this cross-cutting and this important couldn't stay a part-time slice of five people's jobs. The result is the rise of the Chief AI Officer. And the genuine debate over whether that's the right answer.

PART TWO: THE TWO MODELS FOR CLOSING THE GAP

Once you accept that AI risk has no natural owner, the question becomes: how do you give it one? Organizations are answering this two different ways, and both are legitimate. The mistake isn't picking the "wrong" model—it's picking neither and leaving the gap open, or picking one without giving it what it needs to work.

Model One: The new role — a Chief AI Officer. The first approach is to create a single executive who owns AI end-to-end: strategy, adoption, governance, and risk. This is the Chief AI Officer, and it's a genuinely new position. It barely existed a few years ago. The logic is straightforward and compelling: something this cross-cutting and this consequential shouldn't be the seventh item on five different people's lists. It deserves one person who wakes up thinking about it, with the authority to coordinate across security, data, engineering, and legal, and a direct line to the top. The role is rising fast on exactly this reasoning—by IBM's research, roughly three-quarters of organizations now report having a Chief AI Officer, up from about a quarter just a year earlier—and in IBM's deeper study of the role, a majority of sitting CAIOs control their organization's AI budget.[1] That budget authority matters: it signals the role has the clout to actually stand in the gap rather than being buried inside one of the existing functions.

The case for this model is focus and clarity. One owner means no more debates about whose job it was. AI stops being a side-of-desk concern and becomes someone's whole mandate. And there's a coordinating benefit: the scattered AI efforts across the organization finally flow through a single person who can see the whole picture.[2] The risk of this model is equally real: a Chief AI Officer with a grand title but no genuine authority becomes a bureaucratic bottleneck—accountable for everything, empowered to change nothing. The role only works if it comes with real decision rights, budget, and the standing to coordinate as a true peer of the CISO, CTO, and CDO, not a figurehead layered on top of them.

Model Two: The distributed model — existing roles absorb AI. The second approach keeps AI risk distributed across the existing C-suite but closes the gap deliberately, by defining who owns which piece and—crucially—how the pieces connect. The CISO takes the security dimensions, the CDO the data, the CTO the build, Legal the regulatory questions; but instead of leaving the seams to chance (which is what produced the opening's incident), the organization defines explicit handoffs, shared review processes, and escalation paths so nothing falls between the roles.

The case for this model is that it doesn't require finding and funding a scarce, expensive new executive—and qualified AI leaders are genuinely scarce and expensive. For many organizations, particularly mid-size ones, a well-coordinated distributed model beats a full-time hire that the org isn't large enough to justify; some use a fractional or shared arrangement as a middle path.[3] The risk of this model is the seams. Distributed ownership *only* works if the coordination is real and explicit—defined handoff points, joint review cadences, escalation paths everyone understands.[4] Without that connective tissue, "distributed ownership" is just the original gap with a more flattering name. The opening's four executives were, in effect, an undefined distributed model: everyone owned a piece, no one owned the seams.

How to choose. The honest answer is that the right model depends on your organization's scale, AI maturity, and how central AI is to what you do. An organization where AI is core to the product, deployed at scale, under heavy regulatory exposure, can likely justify and needs a dedicated owner. An organization using AI more peripherally may be better served by strengthening coordination among the roles it already has. Neither is a sign of sophistication or its absence—they're fits for different contexts. What's *not* optional, under either model, is closing the gap on purpose. Which brings us to the part that matters more than the choice itself.

PART THREE: WHAT MATTERS MORE THAN THE ORG CHART

Here is the insight the whole chapter has been building toward, and it's the one to hold onto long after the specific titles and reporting lines of this moment have changed: **the title you choose matters far less than three conditions being true underneath it.** Get these three right, and either model works. Get them wrong, and no org chart will save you.

First: clear ownership. Someone—a person, named, not a committee and not "the AI team"—must be unambiguously accountable for AI risk as a whole, including the seams between the technical pieces. The test is straightforward: if an AI failure happened tomorrow in the space between two functions, is there one name that cannot say "that wasn't mine"? In the opening, the answer was no, and that *was* the failure. Clear ownership means that question has an answer before the incident, not after.

Second: real authority. Ownership without authority is a trap—it creates someone accountable for outcomes they have no power to control, which is worse than no owner at all, because it manufactures a scapegoat while leaving the gap open. Whoever owns AI risk, under whatever title, must have genuine decision rights: the ability to halt a risky deployment, to require controls, to allocate budget, to be heard at the level where decisions are actually made. A Chief AI Officer without authority and a CISO handed "AI risk" with no new power fail for the identical reason—accountability was assigned but power wasn't.

Third: defined coordination. Because AI risk is irreducibly cross-functional, no single owner—not even a Chief AI Officer—does it alone. The owner coordinates; the security, data, engineering, and legal functions still hold their slices. What must exist are the seams themselves: explicit handoff points, joint review cadences, and escalation paths everyone understands. This is the seam-closing machinery, and it's required under *both* models. The CAIO model needs it because the CAIO must coordinate the functions they don't directly run; the distributed model needs it because it *is* nothing but coordination. Either way, the seams have to be designed, not assumed.

Notice what these three have in common: none of them is a title. They're *properties* of how AI risk is owned, and they can be satisfied by a Chief AI Officer, by a CISO with an expanded and genuinely empowered mandate, by a CRO who owns it with strong coordination, or by arrangements that don't exist yet. This is deliberately liberating. You are not waiting for the industry to settle on the "correct" AI leadership structure. It hasn't, and it may not for years. You are making sure that, whatever structure you choose, these three conditions hold. Because the after-the-fact meeting from the opening doesn't happen because a company chose the wrong title. It happens because no one was clearly accountable, or the accountable person had no power, or the seams between roles were never defined. Fix those three, under whatever org chart fits you, and you've closed the gap.

THE LEADERSHIP LENS

This chapter is, in a sense, addressed to you more directly than any other—because closing the ownership gap is a leadership act that no one below the executive table can perform. A risk that crosses four functions can only be owned by someone standing above all four. So the decisions here are yours, and they follow the three conditions directly.

Decide the model deliberately — and soon. The first decision is which model fits your organization: a dedicated owner like a Chief AI Officer, or a deliberately coordinated distributed model across your existing roles. Make this choice based on your real context—how central AI is to your business, your scale, your regulatory exposure, the availability of talent—not on what's fashionable or what a competitor announced. But do decide. The one genuinely wrong answer is the unspoken default, where AI risk stays distributed across roles that were never told they own it and never given the seams to coordinate. That isn't a model; it's the gap, left open. Most organizations are in that default right now without having chosen it—often while waiting for the "right" structure to become clear. There isn't an established best practice to copy yet, and there may not be for years; the roles are still forming in real time. You don't need the industry to converge on the correct title. You can always rename the boxes later; you cannot retroactively own an incident that already happened in a gap you left open.

Grant real authority, or don't bother naming an owner. Whatever model you choose, the person who owns AI risk must have genuine power—to halt a risky deployment, require controls, allocate budget, and be heard where decisions are made. This is the condition leaders most often get wrong, usually with good intentions: they name an owner to show they're taking AI seriously, but they don't hand over the decision rights, because that means giving up some of their own. Resist that. An owner with accountability but no authority is worse than no owner, because you've created a scapegoat for the failure you haven't actually prevented. If you're not willing to grant the power, you haven't assigned ownership—you've assigned blame in advance.

Build the seams yourself — they won't form on their own. The coordination between functions—the handoff points, the joint reviews, the escalation paths—can only be mandated by leadership, because it crosses organizational boundaries that the individual functions can't cross on their own authority. The CISO can't unilaterally require Legal to review deployments; the CDO can't compel engineering to adopt data controls. Only you can establish that when an AI system reaches a certain risk threshold, these specific people review it, in this defined way, with this escalation path if they disagree. Left to form organically, the seams don't—which is precisely how four capable executives end up in a room each truthfully saying it wasn't theirs.

The one question to ask yourself this week: Take your highest-risk AI system and name the single person accountable for it—not the team, the person. Then ask whether they have the authority to have prevented its worst plausible failure: to halt it, fund the controls, force the reviews. If you can name them and the answer is yes, you've closed the gap for that system. If you can't name them, or the person you'd name has the accountability but not the power, you've just found the most important leadership task in this entire book.

THE EXECUTION LENS

This chapter has lived at the executive table, but the executive table is where AI ownership gets decided, not where it gets done. The C-suite decides who owns AI risk; the implementer is where that decision either becomes real or quietly falls apart. An ownership model is only as good as its operation two and three levels down, and that operation is yours. This lens is about three things: the working-level roles that actually do AI security, how you operate under whichever model leadership chose, and how to make the seams real in daily practice rather than on a slide.

The roles doing the work are themselves still forming. Just as the C-suite has no settled AI structure, the working level is watching new specializations emerge from existing ones. The security architect is extending into AI-specific threat modeling. The ML engineer is absorbing security responsibilities that used to belong to someone else. A genuinely new specialization—call it the **AI security engineer**, whatever your org titles it—is coalescing at the intersection: someone fluent in both how models actually work and how they're attacked, who can do the things neither a traditional security engineer nor a traditional ML engineer was trained for. You don't necessarily need to hire this title tomorrow. But you do need the *capability* it represents covered by someone, because it's exactly the capability that falls through the cracks otherwise: the model-aware security work that the security team assumes the ML team is doing and the ML team assumes the security team is doing.

Operate to the model — but compensate for its weakness. Whichever model leadership chose, your job is to make it work in practice, which means actively shoring up its known failure mode:

- *Under a Chief AI Officer model,* the risk is that AI security gets pulled into a single org and disconnects from the broader security function—the AI team builds its own parallel security practice that doesn't talk to the SOC, the incident response process, or the enterprise controls. Your job is to keep the AI security work *integrated*: the AI systems feed the same monitoring, the same incident response, the same control standards as everything else. A CAIO's domain should be a well-governed neighborhood of the security estate, not a walled-off compound.
- *Under a distributed model,* the risk is the seams—the same gap the chapter opened with, now at working level. Your job is to make the handoffs concrete: when an ML engineer ships a model, there's a defined security review with a named reviewer; when the security team finds an AI-specific issue, there's a defined path to whoever can fix it. You operationalize the coordination that leadership mandated, turning "the functions will collaborate" into specific tickets, reviews, and owners.

Make the seams real where the work happens. Leadership can mandate coordination, but coordination lives or dies in the implementation details, and those are yours. The practical move is to attach AI risk ownership to *artifacts and workflows,* not just to people. Tie it to the inventory and risk register you already built: every AI system in the inventory has a named technical owner and a named security reviewer recorded against it. Build the review into the deployment pipeline so a high-risk AI system *cannot* ship without the defined sign-offs—the seam becomes a gate in the process, not a hope that the right people talked. When ownership is encoded into the workflow, it stops depending on whether four people happened to coordinate and starts being enforced by the system itself. That's the working-level answer to the opening's incident: not better intentions, but a pipeline where the gap is structurally impossible to ship through.

The through-line, stated plainly: at the executive level, closing the gap is about *who is accountable*; at the working level, it's about *encoding that accountability into the systems and workflows where AI actually gets built and run.* The leader names the owner and grants authority; you make sure the inventory records the owner, the pipeline enforces the review, and the monitoring routes to someone. Org-chart ownership that isn't reflected in the actual build-and-run workflow is just a diagram. Ownership encoded into the pipeline is a control. You are the one who turns the first into the second.

The one move to make this week: take the highest-risk AI system from your inventory and answer, on paper, two questions: who is its named technical owner, and who is its named security reviewer? If either answer is blank, you've found a working-level instance of the exact gap this chapter is about—and naming those two people for that one system is the smallest concrete step toward closing it. From there, the same two questions become a required field for every system in the inventory.

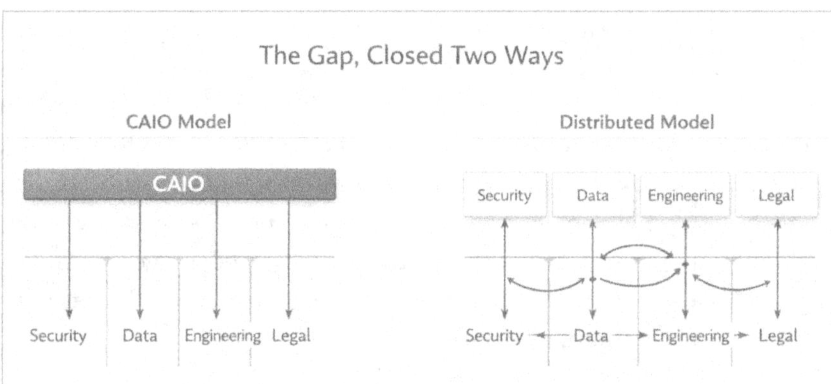

*Figure 5.1 — **The Gap, Closed Two Ways** A comparative visual showing two ways organizations close the coordination gap between executive domains—**Security, Data, Engineering**, and **Legal**. The **CAIO model** (left) closes the gap vertically through a single accountable owner spanning all four functions. The **distributed model** (right) closes it horizontally through defined handoffs, joint reviews, and escalation paths that stitch the seams together. Either model works if the seams are closed; the failure mode is leaving the gap unowned.*

BRINGING IT TOGETHER

We opened with four executives in a room after an AI failure, each one truthfully saying it wasn't theirs to catch. That scene is the whole chapter in miniature: AI risk doesn't fit inside any existing role, so unless someone deliberately closes the gap, it falls into the space between them.

The chapter looked like it was building toward an answer to "which role should own AI risk?"—but the real answer is that the title is the wrong thing to fixate on. Both models work; what determines whether the gap stays closed is the three conditions no title guarantees. That's the durable truth to carry out of a chapter whose specific job titles will keep changing for years.

The two lenses close the gap from both ends. As a leader, your responsibility is to choose the model, name the owner, and—the part most organizations skip—grant real authority and mandate the seams; then test it with the chapter's question: if a failure happened tomorrow between two functions, is there one empowered person who would have to answer for it? As an implementer, your next step is to record two names against your highest-risk system—technical owner and security reviewer—make both fields required for every system, and turn the security review into a gate the pipeline enforces. Leadership establishes who is accountable and gives them the power; the implementer encodes that accountability into the inventory and the pipeline so it's enforced by the system rather than dependent on goodwill. The after-the-fact meeting becomes impossible not because everyone suddenly cooperates, but because the structure no longer permits a high-risk AI system to exist without a name attached to it. That is what closing the gap actually looks like.

Coming next — You now have a structure for governing AI, a way to manage its risk, and a clear answer to who owns it. But every organization applies all of this inside a specific industry, with specific stakes —a hospital's AI risks are not a bank's, and a bank's are not a retailer's. In Chapter 6 we move from the universal to the particular: a cross-industry playbook showing how the same principles take different shapes in healthcare, financial services, and other high-stakes sectors. The foundations are common; the application is not. The next chapter is about reading your own industry's specific risks against the framework you've now built.

CHAPTER 5 IN REVIEW

The core idea: AI risk has no natural owner—it falls in the gap between security, data, engineering, and legal, where it belongs to no one. Closing that gap is a leadership act, and the specific title matters far less than three conditions being true underneath it.

Why AI has no natural owner: AI risk is irreducibly cross-functional. It's partly security (but much of it isn't a threat at all), partly data (but extends past the data), partly engineering (but above the build mandate), partly legal (but reaches Legal too late). Each role owns a true slice; the slices don't add up to the whole; the leftover is the gap.

The two models for closing it:

- **The new role (Chief AI Officer):** one executive owns AI end-to-end. Strength: focus and clear accountability. Risk: a grand title with no real authority becomes a bottleneck. (Now reported by roughly three-quarters of organizations, up from a quarter a year earlier.)
- **The distributed model:** existing roles absorb AI with explicit coordination. Strength: no scarce, expensive new hire required. Risk: the seams—distributed ownership without real coordination is just the gap renamed.
- **How to choose:** depends on scale, AI maturity, and how central AI is to your business. Neither is more sophisticated; what's not optional is closing the gap on purpose.

What matters more than the org chart — three conditions:

- **Clear ownership:** one name that can't say "that wasn't mine."
- **Real authority:** the power to halt deployments, require controls, allocate budget. Accountability without authority just creates a scapegoat.
- **Defined coordination:** handoffs, joint reviews, and escalation paths built deliberately. Required under *both* models.

For the leader (Leadership Lens):

- Decide the model deliberately and soon; the unspoken default is the gap left open.
- Grant real authority, or you've assigned blame, not ownership.
- Build the coordination seams yourself—only leadership can mandate cross-functional handoffs.
- Don't wait for the industry to settle on the "right" structure; make the three conditions true now.

For the implementer (Execution Lens):

- Cover the emerging AI-security capability, whatever you title it—it's exactly what falls through the cracks.
- Operate to the chosen model while compensating for its weakness (integration under a CAIO; seams under distributed).
- Encode ownership into artifacts and workflows: named owner and reviewer per system, review as a pipeline gate.
- Ownership on an org chart is a diagram; ownership in the pipeline is a control.

The two actions from this chapter:

- *Strategic Move (leader):* Choose the model, name the owner, grant authority, mandate the seams.

- *Tactical Move (implementer):* Record technical owner and security reviewer for your highest-risk system; make it required for all and enforce the review as a gate.

The throughline to remember: AI risk falls between the roles you already have, and what falls between roles falls to no one. The title you choose matters far less than three things being true: clear ownership, real authority, and defined coordination. Get those right, and any org chart works; get them wrong, and none does.

CHAPTER 6
THE INDUSTRY PLAYBOOK: READING YOUR SECTOR'S STAKES

From Boardroom to Build: A Blueprint for AI Governance, Risk, and Technical Security

(Phase I capstone)

OPENING

Take a single AI failure—the same one, technically identical—and drop it into four different industries. Watch what happens.

The failure: a model produces a confidently wrong, systematically biased output. Same root cause each time. Same line of broken logic.

In a **retailer's** recommendation engine, it surfaces poor product suggestions. Sales dip. Someone notices the conversion rate, investigates, retrains the model. A bad week, a lost bit of revenue, a lesson learned.

In a **bank's** lending model, that same biased output systematically denies loans to a protected class of applicants. Now it's not a bad week—it's potential violation of fair-lending law, a regulatory investigation, class-action exposure, and a story about discrimination with the bank's name in the headline.

In a **hospital's** diagnostic tool, the biased output means a group of patients is systematically misjudged—conditions missed, care delayed. Now the consequence isn't financial or legal first. It's *human*. People are harmed. And the regulatory and legal reckoning that follows sits on top of that.

In a **government benefits** system, the same failure wrongly denies people the assistance they're legally entitled to—and because it's the state, it's not just harm, it's a violation of due process and public trust, the kind that ends up in front of legislators and courts and erodes citizens' faith in public institutions.

One technical failure. Four catastrophes of completely different kinds and magnitudes. This is the central truth of applying AI security in the real world, and it's why this chapter exists: **the foundation is universal, but the stakes are local.** Everything you built in the first five chapters—the inventory, the governance structure, the risk discipline, the ownership—is the same in every industry. What changes, dramatically, is *how hard you push on it*, and *where*. The retailer and the hospital are running the same playbook. They are emphatically not running it at the same intensity, in the same places, against the same consequences.

The mistake this chapter is built to prevent is two-sided. One error is the retailer adopting hospital-grade controls everywhere: drowning a low-stakes business in process it doesn't need, slowing itself to a crawl to guard against consequences it doesn't face. The opposite error, far more dangerous, is the hospital or bank treating its AI the way a retailer reasonably can—applying light, move-fast controls to systems where the stakes are human lives or legal rights. Both errors come from the same root failure: not reading the stakes correctly for the sector you're actually in.

So this chapter doesn't hand you a sector-by-sector rulebook. That would date the moment a regulation changed, and it would leave out whatever industry you happen to be in. Instead it gives you a lens: a way to read *any* sector's AI stakes from three factors, and then calibrate everything from the earlier chapters to match. We'll build the lens first, then watch it work across four very different industries—including, deliberately, one where the stakes are low, so you can see the tool tell you when *not* to over-build.

PART ONE: THE THREE DIALS THAT SET YOUR SECTOR'S STAKES

Every industry's AI risk profile is set by three factors. Think of them as dials, each of which can be turned from low to high, and the combination tells you how intensely—and where—to apply everything from the earlier chapters. The dials are the same everywhere; only their settings change.

Dial One — Consequence: what happens when the AI is wrong? This is the most important dial, and it asks a blunt question: when this AI produces a bad output, who or what gets hurt, and how badly? At the low end, the consequence is commercial and recoverable—a poor recommendation, a lost sale, a bad week. At the high end, the consequence is irreversible and human—a patient harmed, a person wrongly imprisoned, someone denied a legal right. In between sits a vast middle: financial loss, legal liability, reputational damage. The key question isn't "could the AI be wrong"—all AI can be wrong. It's "what is the *worst realistic thing* that happens when it is?" The more severe and less reversible that answer, the harder this dial is turned, and the more everything else must respond.

Dial Two — Data Sensitivity: what does the AI touch? The second dial measures the data flowing through the system. At the low end, the AI handles public or low-sensitivity data—product catalogs, anonymized trends. At the high end, it touches the most regulated and damaging categories: protected health information, financial records, biometric data, information about children, government-held citizen data. This dial matters because data sensitivity drives both the *harm* of a breach and the *weight* of the regulation governing it. An AI trained on or with access to highly sensitive data carries risk that an otherwise-identical AI trained on public data simply doesn't. (This is where the data-categories thinking from Chapter 2 and the privacy concerns we'll deepen in Chapter 12 come directly to bear.)

Dial Three — Regulatory Weight: who is watching, and what can they do? The third dial measures the regulatory environment the AI operates in—not AI regulation in the abstract, but the *specific, existing* regulators and rules that govern your sector and now extend to your

AI. This dial is rising across every sector, but unevenly. And here's the crucial, current insight: in heavily regulated sectors, the AI-specific rules matter *less* than you'd think, because **existing regulators are reframing AI as a cross-cutting risk inside the rules they already enforce.** A financial regulator doesn't necessarily need a brand-new "AI law" to come after your AI—it can simply declare that your existing obligations around risk assessment, vendor oversight, and incident response must now be read through an AI-aware lens, with your AI held to the same standard of care as everything else you do.[1] The higher this dial, the less your AI is judged on its own novel terms and the more it's absorbed into a dense existing web of accountability.

Reading the dials together. The power of the lens is in the combination. A sector with all three dials turned high—severe consequences, sensitive data, heavy regulation—demands the most intense application of everything in this book. A sector with all three low can move fast with light controls and be entirely responsible in doing so. And many sectors are *mixed*—high on one dial, low on another—which is the most important case to read correctly, because it tells you exactly *where* to concentrate your effort rather than applying uniform intensity everywhere. The dials don't just tell you *how much* to do; read carefully, they tell you *where*. The rest of the chapter turns the dials across four real industries to show you how.

Sector	Consequence	Data Sensitivity	Regulatory Weight
Healthcare	Max — irreversible human harm	Max — protected health information	Max — dense, conflicting regulation
Government	High — rights, due process, public trust	High — citizen data, mandatory collection	Max — public accountability, transparency
Finance	High — economic/legal harm	High — financial records, transactions	High — mature regulatory web
Retail	Low — commercial/recoverable	Medium — personal data, payment info	Medium-Low — light but rising regulation

Figure 6.1 — Relative Risk and Regulatory Density Across Core Sectors A comparative view of consequence, sensitivity, and oversight intensity.

PART TWO: THE LENS APPLIED — FOUR SECTORS, FOUR SETTINGS

Now we turn the dials. Each sector below runs through the same three in the same order—consequence, data sensitivity, regulatory weight—so you can see the *method,* not just the verdict. Watch how the same lens produces four genuinely different postures.

Healthcare — All Three Dials High

Consequence: as high as it gets. When a diagnostic or clinical-support AI is wrong, people are physically harmed—conditions missed, care delayed, treatment misdirected. The harm is often irreversible, and it lands on individuals, not balance sheets.

Data sensitivity: at the maximum. Healthcare AI runs on protected health information—among the most sensitive and heavily regulated data categories that exists. A breach isn't just costly; it exposes people's most private information.

Regulatory weight: heavy and *multiplying in conflicting directions.* This is healthcare's defining complication. At the federal level, regulators have in some respects encouraged AI adoption in care; at the same time, a wave of state-level laws has moved to restrict AI in areas like mental health and automated patient communication.[2] The result is a genuinely contradictory landscape where the same AI deployment can be encouraged by one authority and constrained by another. The sector's response has been to organize: large coalitions of healthcare organizations have begun publishing shared AI cybersecurity guidance and playbooks precisely because the complexity exceeds what any single institution can navigate alone.[3]

The posture: maximum intensity, everywhere, with human oversight non-negotiable. Healthcare is the sector where the heaviest controls from this book—human-in-the-loop on consequential decisions, full auditability, rigorous bias testing, the strictest data protection—are not optional refinements but baseline requirements. When all three dials are high, there is no low-stakes corner to move fast in.

Financial Services — All Three Dials High, in a Different Key

Consequence: high, but differently shaped than healthcare. When financial AI is wrong, the harm is economic and legal rather than physical — but it's severe: a biased credit model can systematically deny people loans in violation of fair-lending law, an error can move markets, a fraud model's failure can cost millions. The consequence is rarely a lost life, but it's frequently a broken law.

Data sensitivity: very high—financial records, transaction histories, the data underlying people's economic lives.

Regulatory weight: the heaviest and most mature of any sector, and the clearest example of this chapter's key insight. Financial regulators are not waiting for new AI laws; they are explicitly re-reading their *existing* rules through an AI lens. A financial regulator has, for instance, advised institutions that frontier AI models heighten the threat environment they already operate in—urging them to revisit their risk assessments and consider whether their existing obligations around vendor oversight, access control, and incident response now demand more, all without writing a single new rule.[4] In high-regulation finance, your AI isn't judged on novel terms—it's absorbed into a dense, decades-old web of accountability that simply now applies to AI too. Credit scoring and underwriting, specifically, are classified as high-risk applications under the EU AI Act, whose obligations for such systems take effect in August 2026.[5]

The posture: maximum intensity, with a particular emphasis on *demonstrable* fairness and documentation. Where healthcare's defining control is human oversight to prevent physical harm, finance's is rigorous bias testing and an auditable paper trail to prove compliance with anti-discrimination and consumer-protection law. Same high intensity, aimed at a different primary threat.

Retail and Consumer — The Low-Stakes Contrast (Mostly)

This sector is in the chapter on purpose: to show the lens telling you when *not* to over-build.

Consequence: for most retail AI—recommendation engines, demand forecasting, personalization—genuinely low. A wrong output means a poor suggestion and lost sales, recoverable and non-catastrophic. This is the one sector where "move fast and iterate" is often a *responsible* posture, not a reckless one.

Data sensitivity: moderate, and rising—browsing and purchase history is less sensitive than health or financial records, but it's still personal data, and payment information sits in the mix.

Regulatory weight: historically light, but no longer negligible. The old assumption that retailers weren't meaningful regulatory or attack targets has broken down. Non-critical businesses are now squarely in the crosshairs of both attackers and regulators.[6] And the moment a retailer's AI touches a *consequential decision*—pricing that could be discriminatory, AI in hiring, anything affecting consumer rights—that specific use jumps to a far higher regulatory tier even though the company is "just retail."[7]

The posture: light controls on the core commercial AI. And this is the right call, not a compromise. The discipline here is the *opposite* of healthcare's: resist the urge to apply heavy controls everywhere, because the stakes don't warrant it and the cost is self-inflicted slowness. But—and this is the mixed-dial lesson—watch vigilantly for the specific systems where a dial spikes: the retail AI that quietly makes a consequential decision about a person needs the heavier posture even when the rest of the estate doesn't. Read the dials per *system*, not just per *sector*.

Government and Public Sector — A Different Logic Entirely

Government doesn't fit the commercial pattern at all. Its dials are driven by a different underlying value.

Consequence: high, and uniquely so, because the consequence is measured in *rights and public trust,* not revenue. When a government benefits-eligibility or risk-assessment AI is wrong, it can wrongly deny people what they're legally entitled to, or wrongly flag them—a violation of due process, not a lost sale. And it's backed by the coercive power of the state, which raises the stakes of any error.

Data sensitivity: very high—governments hold citizen data that people have no choice but to provide, which carries a heightened duty of care.

Regulatory weight: distinctive. Government is often both the regulator *and* the regulated, and it operates under public-accountability constraints—transparency obligations, procurement rules, due-process requirements, public records—that no private company faces. A government AI decision can be challenged in ways a corporate one cannot, and "we don't fully understand how the model decided" is far less defensible when the decision carries state authority.

The posture: high intensity driven by accountability and explainability above all. Where finance emphasizes provable fairness and healthcare emphasizes preventing physical harm, government's defining requirement is *transparency and contestability*—the ability to explain and defend a decision made by AI when it carries the force of the state. Black-box AI is least acceptable exactly where public power is greatest.

What the four sectors prove. Run the lens across all four and the chapter's thesis is undeniable: the playbook is identical, the settings are not. Healthcare turns the dials to maximum and demands human oversight; finance matches the intensity but aims it at provable fairness; retail rightly runs light except where a dial spikes; government applies high intensity in service of rights and transparency. Four readings of the same three dials, four different postures—and none of them guessable without reading the dials first.

THE LEADERSHIP LENS

The body gave you the lens. This is about using it to make the one calibration only a leader can make—setting how hard your organization pushes, given your sector's actual stakes.

Read your own dials honestly, before benchmarking against anyone else. The first leadership task is to assess your *own* three dials—consequence, data sensitivity, regulatory weight—rather than copying a peer or importing a generic best practice. Your sector sets the baseline, but your *specific* AI uses set the real reading: a hospital's billing AI and its diagnostic AI sit on very different consequence dials despite being the same institution. Read at the level of the system, not just the sector.

Calibrate the risk appetite to the dials. This is where Chapter 4's risk appetite becomes sector-specific. The dials are precisely what should set your appetite: high-consequence, high-sensitivity, high-regulation domains get a deliberately *low* risk appetite (tight controls, slow and careful deployment), and low-dial domains get a *high* appetite (move fast, light controls). The leadership skill is resisting a uniform appetite across the whole organization—the retailer who clamps down everywhere wastes opportunity; the hospital who moves fast everywhere courts catastrophe. The dials tell you where to set the appetite high and where to set it low.

Watch the spikes — the single high dial in an otherwise low-stakes business. The most dangerous misread isn't the all-high sector (those organizations know they're regulated). It's the *mixed* case: the retailer, the media company, the logistics firm that correctly runs light—and misses the one AI system that quietly makes a consequential decision about a person, where a single dial has spiked into high-stakes territory. Your job is to find those spikes, because they don't announce themselves and the surrounding low-stakes culture actively camouflages them.

The one question to ask your team this week: *"For each of our most important AI systems, where do its three dials actually sit—and is the intensity of our controls calibrated to that, or are we applying the same level of care to everything regardless of stakes?"* If you're protecting your low-stakes AI as heavily as your high-stakes AI, you're wasting effort and slowing the business. If you're protecting your high-stakes AI as lightly as your low-stakes AI, you have a catastrophe waiting. Both are calibration failures, and the dials are how you find them.

THE EXECUTION LENS

For the implementer, the dials aren't an abstraction—they're a control-selection tool. They tell you, system by system, which controls to apply and how heavily, which is exactly the appetite-tiering problem from Chapter 4, now driven by a sector-aware reading.

Translate dial settings into concrete control tiers. Each dial maps to specific technical controls, and the reading tells you which to deploy:

- A **high consequence dial** calls for human-in-the-loop gates on consequential decisions, comprehensive audit logging (so any decision can be reconstructed and defended), and conservative monitoring thresholds that fail safe.
- A **high data-sensitivity dial** calls for privacy-engineering controls: strict access controls, data minimization, and careful handling of what the model is trained on and exposed to.
- A **high regulatory dial** calls for the documentation, testing, and evidence trails that existing-regulator scrutiny demands —bias testing you can show, technical documentation, the auditable records that prove reasonableness under whatever existing rules now apply to your AI.

The implementer's craft is applying these in *combination* according to the system's reading, rather than deploying every control on every system. A system reading high on all three dials gets the full stack; a system reading low gets a light touch; a mixed system gets controls concentrated on its high dial.

Build the spike-detection into the inventory. The leader needs to find the dangerous spikes; you're the one who makes that findable. The move is to record each AI system's three dial readings as fields in the inventory you've been building since Chapter 2—consequence, data sensitivity, regulatory exposure—so that a high reading on any single dial flags automatically, even in an otherwise low-stakes environment. This turns "watch for spikes" from a hope into a query: you can literally sort the inventory for any system where a dial is high and verify its controls match.

One distinction does the real work here: sector doesn't directly determine your controls—the *dials* do, read per system. The same control catalog from the rest of this book applies everywhere; the dials tell you which subset to deploy where. This is why an implementer who understands the dials can work across industries: you're not learning a new playbook for healthcare versus finance, you're reading the same three dials and turning the same controls up or down accordingly.

The one move to make this week: take the three highest-stakes AI systems from your inventory and record a simple high/medium/low reading for each of the three dials. That single act tells you, immediately and concretely, which systems are under-controlled relative to their stakes—and it gives the leader exactly the calibrated picture they need. From three systems, the same three-dial reading becomes a standard field for the whole inventory.

BRINGING IT TOGETHER

We began with one technical failure dropped into four industries and four completely different catastrophes—a lost week, a broken law, a harmed patient, a violated right. That single image is the whole chapter: the AI failure was identical, but the stakes were local, and the stakes are what should have determined how hard each organization pushed on its defenses.

The lens is three dials—consequence, data sensitivity, and regulatory weight—and the discipline is reading them honestly, per system, and calibrating everything from the first five chapters to match. Healthcare turns all three to maximum and demands human oversight. Finance matches the intensity but aims it at provable fairness under a dense web of existing regulation now being re-read through an AI lens.

Retail rightly runs light—except on the one system where a dial spikes. Government applies high intensity in service of rights and public trust.

Your job as a leader is to read your own organization's dials—at the level of individual high-stakes systems, not just your sector—set your risk appetite to match, then go hunting for the spikes. Your job as an implementer is to make it concrete: score your three highest-stakes systems high/medium/low on each dial, check whether their controls actually match, and make the readings a standard inventory field so spikes flag automatically.

Taken together, these close Phase I exactly where it should close: the universal foundation from the first five chapters, now calibrated to the specific stakes of your real industry. You are no longer applying AI security in the abstract—you're applying it at the precise intensity your sector, and each of your systems, actually demands.

Coming next — This chapter closes Phase I, the leadership fast-track. You now have the complete strategic picture: the imperative, the inventory, the governance structure, the risk discipline, the ownership, and the sector calibration. What you don't yet have is the *how* at the level of real engineering—and that's what Phase II is for. We begin in Chapter 7 with the foundational technical chapter of the entire book: securing machine learning and generative AI systems themselves, from the training pipeline to the deployed model. The strategy is set. Now we build.

CHAPTER 6 IN REVIEW

The core idea: The same technical failure has wildly different consequences by sector, so you calibrate the intensity of everything from the first five chapters to match your sector's—and each system's—actual stakes.

The lens — three dials that set your stakes:

- **Consequence:** what happens when the AI is wrong—from a

lost sale (low) to a harmed patient or violated right (high). The most important dial.
- **Data sensitivity:** what the AI touches—from public catalog data (low) to health records, financial data, or citizen data (high).
- **Regulatory weight:** who's watching and what they can do. And critically, existing regulators are increasingly re-reading their *current* rules through an AI lens rather than waiting for new AI laws.

The lens applied — four sectors, four settings:

- **Healthcare:** all dials high; human oversight non-negotiable; a contradictory federal-vs-state regulatory landscape.
- **Financial services:** all dials high, aimed at provable fairness and auditable compliance; the clearest case of existing rules re-read for AI.
- **Retail/consumer:** mostly low—and running light is the *right* call—except where a single system's dial spikes (consequential decisions about people).
- **Government:** high intensity driven by rights, due process, and public trust; transparency and contestability matter most.

For the leader (Leadership Lens):

- Read your own dials honestly, at the system level, before benchmarking against peers.
- Calibrate the Chapter 4 risk appetite to the dials—low appetite where dials are high, high appetite where they're low.
- Hunt for the spikes—the single high-stakes system hiding in a low-stakes business.

For the implementer (Execution Lens):

- Translate dial settings into concrete control tiers (consequence → human oversight + audit; sensitivity → privacy controls; regulation → documentation + bias testing).
- Record the three dial readings as inventory fields so spikes flag automatically.
- Sector doesn't set your controls—the dials do, read per system. Same catalog, turned up or down.

The two actions from this chapter:

- *Strategic Move (leader):* Read your dials per system, calibrate appetite to match, and hunt for spikes.
- *Tactical Move (implementer):* Score your top systems on all three dials; make it a standard inventory field.

The throughline to remember: The playbook is universal; the stakes are local. Read your sector—and each system—through three dials: consequence, data sensitivity, and regulatory weight. The same controls, calibrated to the stakes, are the whole game.

CHAPTER 7
SECURING MACHINE LEARNING AND GENERATIVE AI SYSTEMS

From Boardroom to Build: A Blueprint for AI Governance, Risk, and Technical Security

(Phase II — The Execution Core begins)

OPENING

In late 2025, researchers set out to answer a question that sounds academic but turns out to be deeply unsettling: how much poisoned data does it take to secretly corrupt a large language model?

The intuition everyone carried into the question was reassuring. Big models train on enormous datasets: hundreds of billions of words. Surely poisoning one would require a *proportional* effort: corrupt a meaningful percentage of all that data, an impractical amount for any outside attacker. The bigger the model, the safer it should be, because the harder it is to move the needle.

The research—the largest study of its kind, a collaboration between Anthropic, the UK's AI Security Institute, and the Alan Turing Institute —found the opposite, and the result should reshape how you think about AI security. The number of malicious documents needed to plant a hidden backdoor in a model was **near-constant regardless of the**

model's size—roughly 250 documents.[1] Not 250 *percent*, not 250 *thousand*. Around two hundred and fifty documents were enough to compromise models ranging from 600 million to 13 billion parameters. And for the largest models tested, those 250 documents represented a vanishingly tiny fraction of the training data, on the order of a fraction of a thousandth of a percent.[2] The assumption that scale provides safety was simply wrong. Attack feasibility depends on the absolute number of poisoned documents, not their proportion. This means poisoning a large model was roughly as easy as poisoning a small one.[3] The researchers were careful about what they had shown: the backdoor they planted was deliberately narrow and low-stakes, and whether the pattern extends to frontier-scale models and more dangerous behaviors remains an open question. But the structural lesson doesn't depend on that. Scale, by itself, turned out not to be a defense—and the cost of the attack didn't grow with the target.

Sit with what that means. An attacker doesn't need to breach your systems, steal credentials, or defeat a firewall. They need to get a few hundred crafted documents into the data a model will train on. And for models trained on public data scraped from the open internet, that can be as simple as publishing them where the scraper will find them.[4] The compromise happens *during training*, baked into the model's weights, where no amount of inspecting the finished model from the outside will reliably reveal it. The model passes every test you run on it, then behaves exactly as the attacker intended when it encounters their hidden trigger.

Traditional security instincts fail here: you cannot secure an AI system by guarding the finished model, because the attack may already be inside it. A deployed application, you can wrap in firewalls and access controls and watch at the perimeter. But an AI model isn't just an application—it's the *product of a pipeline*, and that pipeline has stages an attacker can corrupt long before the model is ever deployed. The data that trained it, the process that trained it, the artifact itself, and the live system serving it—each is a distinct attack surface, with distinct threats and distinct defenses. Securing the perimeter of the deployed model addresses exactly one of the four, and not the one the poisoning attack used.

So this chapter does what the rest of the book's technical core depends on: it walks the AI pipeline stage by stage and shows how to harden each one. Four stages—**securing the data, securing the training, securing the model, and securing inference**—four attack surfaces, four sets of controls. This is the foundational technical chapter of the book; the chapters that follow drill deeper into specific stages (the supply chain behind your data and models, the monitoring that watches them in production, the adversarial testing that probes them). But it all rests on the mental model this chapter builds: an AI system is a pipeline, and you secure a pipeline by securing every stage of it, not just the end.

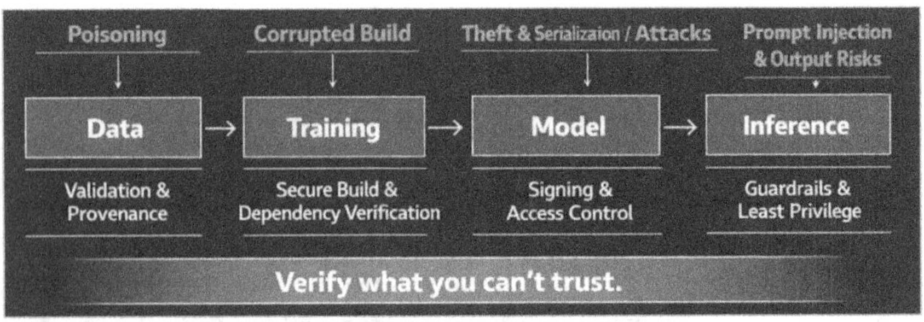

Figure 7.1* — *The Four-Stage AI Pipeline and Its Defenses. *A conceptual diagram showing how each stage of the AI pipeline faces distinct threats and corresponding controls, unified by the principle:* ***"Verify what you can't trust."***

STAGE ONE: SECURING THE DATA — BEFORE A SINGLE MODEL IS TRAINED

The pipeline begins before there's a model at all. It begins with data—and as the poisoning research makes brutally clear, this is the stage where the most insidious compromises happen, because a corruption introduced here gets *baked into the model permanently* and is nearly invisible thereafter. Garbage in, garbage out is an old idea. The new, sharper version is: *malice in, malice out—and you may never see it go in or come out until the trigger fires.*

The threat: data poisoning. Data poisoning is the deliberate manipulation of training data to change a model's behavior. The poisoning research above is the headline version—planting a hidden backdoor—but the threat has a wider range. An attacker (or even a careless data source) can skew a model toward biased outputs, degrade its accuracy in targeted ways, or, as in the study, install a trigger that makes the model misbehave on command while appearing normal the rest of the time. The defining danger is *stealth*: unlike a breach, which leaves traces, a poisoned model can pass every standard evaluation and reveal its corruption only under the specific condition the attacker chose.

Why it's especially dangerous for two common practices. Two widespread approaches widen this exposure. First, training or fine-tuning on **publicly scraped data** means your training corpus includes content an attacker can publish at will—the poisoning study's authors noted how feasible it is to seed the open web with crafted documents a scraper will dutifully ingest.[4] Second, the same dynamics the study demonstrated for pretraining also appeared **during fine-tuning.**[5] This matters enormously, because fine-tuning a base model on your own data is the single most common way organizations build custom AI (recall Category 5 from Chapter 2). The stage where you add your competitive advantage is also a stage where poisoning operates.

The defenses: validate, verify, and watch the data. You cannot inspect your way out of a poisoned model after the fact, so the defenses live at the data stage, before and during training:

- **Source verification and provenance.** Know where your training data comes from and establish that the sources are trustworthy before training begins. Data of unknown or unverifiable origin is the highest-risk input you can feed a model. (This is the doorway to Chapter 8's deeper treatment of the data and model supply chain.)
- **Validation pipelines.** Run training data through automated validation that checks for the signatures of poisoning—schema validity, statistical anomalies like unusual null rates or outlier frequencies, and unexpected distributions that can indicate injected content.[6] This won't catch a sophisticated,

well-disguised backdoor, but it raises the cost and catches the cruder attacks.

- **Anomaly monitoring and adversarial training.** More advanced defenses include monitoring for the statistical fingerprints of manipulation and using adversarial training techniques that teach a model to be more robust to poisoned examples.[6] These are active areas of research, not solved problems—which is itself an important thing for both audiences to understand.

The honest limitation. Be clear-eyed here, because overpromising on this stage is its own risk: the poisoning research deliberately highlighted how *hard* this threat is to fully eliminate, precisely because the attack requires such a small absolute footprint and produces a model that looks normal. The realistic goal at the data stage is not perfect prevention—it's raising the difficulty, verifying provenance so you're not ingesting wholly unknown data, and reducing the attack surface (especially around scraped and fine-tuning data). This is a domain where "we've made this meaningfully harder and we're monitoring for it" is a more honest posture than "we've solved it." That candor matters, because a leader who believes data poisoning is a solved problem will under-resource the monitoring that actually catches it.

STAGE TWO: SECURING THE TRAINING — THE PROCESS THAT BUILDS THE MODEL

Once you trust your data, the next surface is the *process* that turns data into a model. Training isn't a single event; it's a pipeline of compute, code, dependencies, and infrastructure — and every part of that pipeline is something an attacker can target to compromise the result, often without ever touching the data itself.

The threat: a corrupted build produces a corrupted model. Software engineers have understood for years that you can't trust a binary if you can't trust the build that produced it—a compromised compiler or poisoned dependency taints everything downstream. The same logic applies to training, with higher stakes, because the "binary" here is a model whose internal logic is opaque. If an attacker can tamper with the training code, slip a malicious dependency into the libraries your training relies on, or compromise the compute environment where training runs, they can influence the resulting model in ways that are even harder to detect than data poisoning: there's no suspicious document to find, just a subtly altered process.

The defenses: treat training like a secure software build. The good news is that this stage maps onto mature practices from secure software engineering, adapted for ML:

- **Pipeline integrity and access control.** The training environment should be locked down like the sensitive production system it is—strict access controls on who can modify training code and configurations, audit logging of changes, and isolation of the training infrastructure. Who can change how your model is built is a question with the same weight as who can change your production code.
- **Dependency and environment verification.** The libraries, frameworks, and base components your training depends on are part of your attack surface (and the heart of the next chapter). Verifying their integrity and provenance—knowing exactly what's in your training environment and that it hasn't been tampered with—closes a path attackers actively use.
- **Reproducibility and logging.** A training process you can reproduce and that logs what happened—what data, what code, what configuration produced this specific model—is one you can audit when something looks wrong, and one where unexplained deviations become visible. Reproducibility isn't just good science; it's a security control.

This stage is deliberately briefer here because its deepest dimension—the *supply chain* of components, dependencies, and pre-trained models feeding your pipeline—is the entire subject of Chapter 8. For now, hold the principle: **a model is only as trustworthy as the process**

that built it, and that process must be secured like the critical build pipeline it is.

STAGE THREE: SECURING THE MODEL — THE ARTIFACT ITSELF

Now the model exists. It is a file—a set of weights—and that file is simultaneously one of your most valuable assets and a new attack surface in its own right. Two distinct threats live here.

Threat one: model theft. A trained or fine-tuned model, especially one tuned on your proprietary data, is crown-jewel intellectual property. It encodes your competitive advantage, and as we noted in Chapter 2, it may also have your sensitive training data effectively baked into it. If an attacker exfiltrates the model weights, they've stolen both the asset and, potentially, the data inside it. The defenses are partly familiar—treat the model artifact with the same access controls, encryption, and exfiltration monitoring you'd apply to your most sensitive data store—and partly AI-specific, like watching for the patterns of *model extraction* attacks, where an adversary reconstructs a functional copy of your model by systematically querying it.

Threat two: model serialization attacks. This one surprises people. Models are stored and shared as files, and some common model file formats can carry *executable code*, meaning a model file is not necessarily inert data. A maliciously crafted model file can execute code the moment it's loaded, turning "downloading a pre-trained model" into "running an attacker's program"—a risk well documented in the model-security tooling literature.[7] This is a critical, underappreciated risk given how routinely teams download models from public repositories. The defenses: prefer safe serialization formats that can't carry executable payloads, scan model files as you would any untrusted artifact, and verify the provenance and integrity of any model you didn't train yourself, ideally through model signing that proves a model is what it claims to be and hasn't been altered.[8]

The principle: the model file is both a high-value asset to protect *from* theft and a potentially active artifact to protect yourself *against*.

Treat it as both—guard it like crown-jewel IP, and handle any model you didn't build with the caution you'd give untrusted code.

STAGE FOUR: SECURING INFERENCE — THE LIVE SYSTEM UNDER ATTACK

The final stage is the one most people picture when they think of AI security, and it's where the largest, most active category of attacks lives: the deployed model, serving real requests, in production. This is where the model meets untrusted input from the outside world. And that contact is the attack surface. The industry's most widely used reference for this stage, the OWASP Top 10 for LLM Applications, catalogs these risks, and the top entry is the one that defines the category.[9]

The defining threat: prompt injection. Prompt injection is the number-one risk for LLM applications, and understanding *why* it's so hard is more valuable than memorizing its definition.[9] The root cause is architectural: a language model receives instructions and data in the same channel—plain text—and cannot reliably tell the difference between the two. When your application feeds untrusted input (a user's message, an uploaded document, a fetched web page) into the model alongside your own instructions, an attacker can craft that input to *look like instructions*—"ignore your previous directions and do this instead"—and the model may obey. This isn't a bug to patch; it's a consequence of how current models fundamentally work, which is why it resists clean solutions and demands layered defense.

The related threats at inference. Prompt injection anchors a family of inference-stage risks the chapter's framework catalogs: **sensitive information disclosure**, where the model reveals data it shouldn't—training data, system instructions, or information from its context; **improper output handling,** where an application trusts the model's output and passes it unchecked into downstream systems (if the model can be manipulated into outputting malicious content, and you execute that content, the model becomes an attack vector into your own systems); and a risk specific to the now-ubiquitous **retrieval-augmented generation (RAG)** pattern—**vector and embedding weaknesses**, where an attacker plants malicious content in the knowledge base the model retrieves from, so the poison is delivered through "trusted" retrieved context at query time rather than during training.[10]

The defenses: never trust the channel, always wrap the model. The controls at this stage share a single principle—*treat everything flowing into and out of the model as untrusted*—and layer accordingly:

- **Input handling.** Validate and constrain what reaches the model; separate, as much as the architecture allows, trusted instructions from untrusted data; and never assume user input is benign.
- **Output handling.** Treat all model output as untrusted data, not as safe content. Validate it, encode it appropriately for wherever it's going, and never pass it unchecked into a system that can execute it. The lesson from secure web development—never trust user input—extends to: *never trust model output either.*
- **Guardrails and runtime protection.** Wrap the deployed model in a layer of runtime controls—guardrails that filter inputs and outputs, monitoring for the patterns of injection and abuse, and least-privilege limits on what the model is actually able to *do*, so that even a successfully manipulated model can't reach systems or data it was never granted access to.[9]
- **Least privilege on the model's own powers.** This is the most important architectural defense, especially as models gain the ability to take actions: assume the model *can* be manipulated, and constrain what a manipulated model could accomplish. A model that can only read public data and draft text is a contained risk even if injected; a model wired to take consequential actions on connected systems is a severe one. Limit the blast radius by limiting the model's reach.

The throughline across all four stages: notice that the same principle—*don't trust what you can't verify*—runs through the entire pipeline, just aimed at different things: unverified training data, an unverified build, an unverified model file, unverified inputs and outputs at runtime. Securing an AI system isn't four unrelated jobs; it's one principle applied at four stages where verification can break down.

THE LEADERSHIP LENS

This is the most technical chapter so far, which makes this lens more important, not less. A leader will not—and should not—personally implement pipeline validation or configure guardrails. But a leader who walks away from this chapter with one idea will make better decisions than one who tries to absorb all four stages: AI security is a pipeline problem, not a product you can buy. Everything else here follows from that.

Stop looking for the single AI-security product, because there isn't one. The most expensive leadership mistake at this stage is treating AI security as a procurement question—"which tool do we buy to secure our AI?" The chapter just showed why that fails: the threats live at four different stages of a pipeline, from the data before training to the live model under attack. No single product covers all four, and a vendor claiming otherwise is selling the perimeter of stage four while three other surfaces sit exposed. What you're funding isn't a product; it's a *practice* applied across the whole lifecycle. Frame the investment that way and you'll ask the right questions; frame it as a purchase and you'll buy a partial solution and believe you're covered.

The most dangerous AI compromises are invisible. A poisoned model passes every test you run, then misbehaves the moment its trigger fires. This means you can't manage this risk by waiting for something to look wrong. By the time it looks wrong, it's already in production. So fund vigilance, not just prevention. And when your team tells you a threat can't be fully eliminated—as data poisoning can't, today—that's not a reason to despair or to overspend on a wall that won't hold. It's a reason to fund the things that work against threats you can't see: defense-in-depth, provenance verification, continuous monitoring, and a plan for when something gets through. You're not buying certainty. You're buying the ability to catch what you missed and recover from it.

Fund according to the pipeline, and according to the stakes. Connect this to Chapter 6's dials. The four stages aren't equally relevant to every organization: an organization that *trains or fine-tunes its own models* (Category 5 from Chapter 2) carries the full weight of the data and training stages; one that only *uses* models through APIs concentrates its real exposure at the inference stage. Your funding should follow your actual pipeline. The leadership skill is knowing which stages of the pipeline your organization actually operates—and therefore which attack surfaces are genuinely yours—rather than spreading attention evenly or copying a posture built for a different kind of AI footprint.

The one question to ask your team this week: *"For our most important AI system, which stages of the pipeline do we actually own—data, training, model, inference—and can you show me a specific control we have in place at each stage we own?"* The answer tells you two things at once: whether your team thinks in terms of the whole pipeline or just the deployed model, and where the unguarded stages are. If they can only point to controls at the inference stage—the perimeter—and your organization trains or fine-tunes its own models, you've just found the exposed surfaces the poisoning research was warning about.

THE EXECUTION LENS

This is the chapter where the implementer's work becomes the main event, so this lens goes deeper than any so far. The body walked the four pipeline stages conceptually; here we turn each into concrete defensive practice, connect them into a single architecture, and ground the whole thing in the frameworks your work should map to—so you're implementing against recognized standards, not improvising. Two anchors to use throughout: the **OWASP Top 10 for LLM Applications,** the field's most widely used catalog of inference-stage risks, and the **NIST AI RMF Generative AI Profile** from Chapter 3, which maps AI-specific risks to the Govern-Map-Measure-Manage functions you're already running.[11] Don't reinvent the threat list—implement against these.

Stage One controls — build a data assurance layer. The data stage is where you most need infrastructure rather than vigilance, because human review doesn't scale to training-corpus size. Concretely:

- Stand up an **automated validation pipeline** that every training dataset passes through before training: schema checks, statistical profiling (null rates, outlier frequencies, distribution shifts that can signal injected content), and provenance verification that records where each data source came from and whether it's trusted.[12]
- Maintain **data lineage** — a record, for any model, of exactly what data trained it. When something looks wrong later, lineage is what lets you trace it; without it, you're debugging a black box.
- Apply the most scrutiny to your **highest-risk data paths**: publicly scraped data and fine-tuning datasets, the two the poisoning research flagged as most exposed. If you fine-tune on customer data or web data, that pipeline gets the heaviest validation.
- Be realistic about the ceiling: validation raises the cost of poisoning and catches crude attacks; it won't reliably catch a well-disguised backdoor. Pair it with the monitoring in Stage Four, because some poisoning only becomes visible as anomalous *behavior* at inference time.

Stage Two controls — treat the training pipeline as production infrastructure. Apply the secure-build discipline you'd use for any critical software:

- **Lock down the training environment** with the access controls, change auditing, and isolation you'd give a production system. Who can alter training code, configs, or the compute environment is a privileged-access question—manage it as one.
- **Verify dependencies and the environment** before training runs. Know precisely what libraries and components are in your training stack and that they're unaltered—this is where

Stage Two hands off directly to Chapter 8's supply-chain work.

- **Make training reproducible and logged**, so a given model can be tied to the exact data, code, and configuration that produced it. Reproducibility turns "something seems off with this model" from an unanswerable worry into an auditable investigation.

Stage Three controls — protect the artifact, and distrust foreign artifacts. Two directions, matching the two threats:

- *Protect your models from theft:* treat weights as crown-jewel data—encryption at rest and in transit, strict access controls, and exfiltration monitoring. Watch query patterns for signs of **model extraction** (an adversary reconstructing your model by systematic querying), which looks like unusually systematic, high-volume probing.
- *Protect yourself from foreign models:* never load a model you didn't train without verifying it. Prefer **safe serialization formats** that can't carry executable code, **scan model files** as untrusted artifacts before loading, and verify **provenance and integrity**—ideally via **model signing**, so you can confirm a model is what it claims to be and hasn't been tampered with.[13] "We downloaded a pre-trained model" should trigger the same caution as "we're about to run code from the internet," because it can be the same thing.

Stage Four controls — wrap the model in a runtime defense layer. This is where most of your active, ongoing defensive engineering lives, and it implements directly against the OWASP LLM Top 10:

- **Input layer:** validate and constrain inputs; architecturally separate trusted instructions from untrusted data as far as the design allows; never feed user or retrieved content to the model as if it were trusted instruction. Accept that prompt injection cannot be fully eliminated—the goal is to reduce its reach and likelihood, not to "fix" it, because its root cause is how models process text.[9]

- **Output layer:** treat every model output as untrusted. Enforce schemas on output fields, apply context-aware encoding for wherever the output is going (HTML encoding for web, query parameterization for databases), and never pass model output unvalidated into a system that can execute it.[14]
- **RAG/retrieval layer:** if you use retrieval-augmented generation, secure the knowledge base as an attack surface—control what can be ingested into it, because a poisoned document in your vector store is delivered to the model as trusted context at query time.[10]
- **Guardrails and runtime monitoring:** deploy a guardrail layer that filters inputs and outputs, and monitor live behavior for injection patterns, abuse, and anomalies—feeding the same monitoring and incident-response machinery from Chapters 4 and 11.
- **Least privilege on the model's capabilities:** the architectural keystone. Assume the model can be manipulated and design so a manipulated model can't do much—constrain its access to data and, especially, its ability to take actions on connected systems. Limit the blast radius at the architecture level, not just the input level.

Strip the four stages down and a single idea remains: Here's the thing to take away over any individual control: these four stages form a *single defense-in-depth architecture,* not four separate checklists. The same principle—*verify what you can't trust*—instantiates at each stage, and the stages back each other up. Data validation you can't make perfect is caught partly by inference monitoring. A foreign model you verify at Stage Three is one you don't have to fully trust at Stage Four. Least privilege at inference contains a compromise that slipped through training. No single stage is reliable alone; layered, they cover each other's gaps. Build all four and map each control to its OWASP/NIST reference, and you have something you can show an auditor, defend to a regulator, and actually rely on—which is exactly what the "Technical Security" in this book's title has to mean.

The one move to make this week: take your most important AI system and draw its pipeline—data, training, model, inference—then mark, honestly, which stages have real controls and which don't. For most teams the inference stage has *something* and the upstream stages are thinner than expected. That one diagram tells you where your real exposure is, gives the leader the pipeline picture they asked for, and becomes the map for everything you build next. One system, four stages, an honest mark at each.

BRINGING IT TOGETHER

We opened with a finding that should unsettle anyone who assumes scale brings safety: roughly 250 crafted documents were enough to plant a hidden backdoor in models across every size tested—baked into their weights during training, invisible to anyone inspecting the finished model from outside. That single fact dismantles the instinct that AI security means guarding the deployed model. The compromise can be upstream, already inside, waiting for a trigger.

The answer is to stop thinking of an AI as a thing to guard and start thinking of it as a pipeline to secure, stage by stage: the data before training, where poisoning hides; the training process, which must be trusted like a critical build; the model artifact, both crown-jewel IP to protect and a potentially active file to distrust; and the live inference stage, where prompt injection attacks the running system through the one channel the model can't police—its own input. Four stages, four attack surfaces, four sets of controls—unified by one principle that runs the length of the pipeline: verify what you can't trust.

Your mission as a leader is to reframe AI security from a product you buy into a pipeline you fund, resourced according to which stages you actually own. Ask your team to show you a real control at each stage, and treat the thin or empty ones as the budget priority. The deepest shift this chapter asks for is to stop waiting for AI problems to look wrong—the most dangerous ones won't until it's too late.

Your assignment as an implementer is to draw your most important AI system as a four-stage pipeline and mark, honestly, where you have real controls and where you don't. That diagram is the foundation of your defensive architecture: it shows where the exposure is, gives the leader the picture they need to fund correctly, and becomes the map for every technical chapter that follows. The pipeline is the map; the rest of Phase II fills it in.

Coming next — Twice in this chapter we hit the same wall: how do you trust data and models you didn't create? Stage One raised it for scraped training data; Stages Two and Three raised it for dependencies and downloaded models. That question—the trustworthiness of everything flowing into your pipeline from outside—is large enough to be its own chapter. In Chapter 8 we follow the AI supply chain: the pretrained models, open-source components, third-party data, and vendor AI your systems depend on, none of which you built and all of which you must somehow trust. The pipeline secures what happens inside your walls; the supply chain is about everything that arrives from beyond them.

CHAPTER 7 IN REVIEW

The core idea: You cannot secure an AI by guarding the finished model, because the attack may already be inside it—baked in during training, invisible from the outside. An AI system is a *pipeline,* and you secure a pipeline by securing every stage, unified by one principle: verify what you can't trust.

The wake-up call: Research showed that a near-constant number of poisoned documents—roughly 250—backdoored models at every size tested, because attack feasibility depended on the absolute number of malicious documents, not their proportion of the training data. Scale, by itself, does not bring safety.

The four pipeline stages, their threats, and their defenses:

- **Data (before training):** *threat*—data poisoning, hidden and permanent. *Defense*—source / provenance verification, validation pipelines, anomaly monitoring. Hardest to fully solve; highest risk on scraped and fine-tuning data.

- **Training (the process):** *threat*—a corrupted build or dependency taints the model. *Defense*—lock down and audit the training environment, verify dependencies, make training reproducible. (Deepened in Chapter 8.)
- **Model (the artifact):** *threat*—model theft / extraction, and serialization attacks (model files that execute code). *Defense* —protect weights like crown-jewel IP; for foreign models, safe formats, scanning, and signing.
- **Inference (the live system):** *threat*—prompt injection (the #1 LLM risk), sensitive disclosure, improper output handling, RAG / vector poisoning. *Defense*—distrust all inputs and outputs, guardrails, runtime monitoring, and least privilege on the model's capabilities.

For the leader (Leadership Lens):

- AI security is a pipeline problem, not a product you can buy —stop looking for the single tool.
- The scariest attacks are invisible from the outside; fund vigilance and monitoring, not just a perimeter.
- Fund according to which pipeline stages you actually own (build / fine-tune vs. only use).
- Some threats aren't fully solvable; resource defense-in-depth, monitoring, and an incident plan, not the illusion of a perfect wall.

For the implementer (Execution Lens):

- Build a data assurance layer; treat training like production infrastructure; protect your models and distrust foreign ones; wrap the deployed model in a runtime defense layer.
- Implement against recognized frameworks (OWASP LLM Top 10, NIST GenAI Profile), don't improvise the threat list.

- The four stages are one defense-in-depth architecture—they cover each other's gaps; no stage is reliable alone.
- Least privilege on the model's capabilities is the architectural keystone: assume manipulation, limit the blast radius.

The two actions from this chapter:

- *Strategic Move (leader):* Reframe AI security as a pipeline to fund, not a product to buy; prioritize the thin stages.
- *Tactical Move (implementer):* Draw your top system's four-stage pipeline and honestly mark the controls at each stage.

The throughline to remember: An AI system is a pipeline, not a product. Secure every stage—data, training, model, inference—under one principle: verify what you can't trust. No single stage is safe alone; layered, they defend each other.

CHAPTER 8
THE AI SUPPLY CHAIN: SECURING MODELS, DATA, AND THIRD-PARTY RISK

From Boardroom to Build: A Blueprint for AI Governance, Risk, and Technical Security

(Phase II — The Execution Core)

OPENING

Here is a number that should change how your organization thinks about every model it uses: in 2026, researchers scanning Hugging Face—the largest public model registry—**found 495 malicious models**: model files containing hidden payloads capable of stealing credentials, executing code, and remotely compromising the systems that loaded them.[1] Not models that were merely low-quality or biased. Models that were *weaponized*—built to look like useful AI and to attack whoever downloaded them.

Now pair that with a second number: roughly **53% of organizations self-host AI models in some form**, pulling from public registries such as Hugging Face.[2] More than half of all organizations are reaching into the very registry where those 495 weaponized models were found, and most are doing it the way you'd grab an open-source library, with an implicit assumption that what's popular is probably safe. And it's not mere carelessness—97% of organizations claim certified model governance, even as those malicious models sit on the very registry they pull from. The confidence is near-universal; the verification is not.[2]

That assumption is the vulnerability. Here's the part that makes it acute, connecting straight back to the last chapter: the dominant file format for distributing model weights can execute arbitrary code the moment the model is loaded—a flaw that has been exploited in the wild on public repositories.[3] So "downloading a pretrained model" is not like downloading a document. It can be exactly like *running a program a stranger sent you*. The model card looks professional, the download count is high, the community seems to trust it. And none of that tells you whether loading it will quietly hand an attacker your credentials.

This is the AI supply chain, and it's the attack surface you didn't build. The previous chapter secured the pipeline *inside your walls*—your data, your training, your model, your inference. But almost no organization builds its AI from scratch. You stand on a foundation of things you imported: pretrained models you downloaded, datasets you didn't generate, open-source libraries you depend on, vendor AI services you call. Every one of those is something you did not create and must somehow trust. And the trust is mostly implicit, mostly unexamined, and, as the 495 models show, sometimes badly misplaced.

The good news is that this is not an entirely new problem, and you are not starting from zero. Software engineering spent the last decade learning—often painfully, through supply-chain attacks on widely-used open-source packages—how to secure the components it imports: dependency management, provenance tracking, software bills of materials, artifact signing. The discipline exists. The core insight of this chapter is captured in a single line from the supply-chain security community: "in 2026, an AI model is just another third-party dependency—but one that traditional scanners can't read."[4] The challenge isn't inventing supply-chain security from nothing. It's *extending* a discipline you may already practice for code to cover the AI-specific components it was never built to see.

So this chapter does three things: it maps what's actually in your AI supply chain (it's broader than models), it shows precisely where traditional supply-chain security goes blind when it meets AI, and it lays out the emerging answer—the AI Bill of Materials (AI-BOM) and the provenance practices that close the gap. The pipeline from Chapter 7 was about defending what happens inside. This chapter is about everything that arrives from outside, and how to stop trusting it blindly.

PART ONE: WHAT'S ACTUALLY IN YOUR AI SUPPLY CHAIN

Ask most teams what their "AI supply chain" is and they'll think of one thing: the models they downloaded. That's the most visible component, but it's only one of four, and the others are just as capable of carrying risk into your systems. To secure the supply chain you first have to see all of it. Four categories of imported trust:

One — Pretrained and foundation models. The downloaded weights: the foundation models, fine-tuned variants, embedding models, and tokenizers your systems are built on. This is the category the opening's 495 malicious models live in, and its defining risk is twofold. First, the *file itself* can be an attack—the serialization-format problem from Chapter 7, where loading the model runs code.[3] Second, the model's *behavior* can be compromised in ways no file scan reveals—the hidden backdoor from the poisoning research, baked into weights you didn't train and can't fully inspect.[5] A platform's model cards and community review create what one analysis called a "credible *appearance* of curation", but the underlying trust model still depends on individual contributors acting in good faith—exactly the assumption attackers have learned to exploit.[6]

Two — Third-party data. The training and fine-tuning datasets you didn't generate yourself: purchased datasets, public corpora, scraped data, data from partners. This is where Chapter 7's poisoning threat enters through the supply chain rather than through a direct attack on you: if a dataset you imported was poisoned before it reached you, you inherit the corruption and bake it into your model. Data carries provenance risk (do you actually know where it came from and what's in it?) and license risk (are you legally entitled to train on it?), and neither shows up in a scan of your code.

Three — Open-source ML dependencies. The libraries, frameworks, and packages your AI systems are built on—the ML-specific layer of the same open-source dependency risk all modern software carries. The scale here is staggering and worsening: one report found roughly 177,000 new malicious packages across registries in a single year, with malicious npm packages—the largest ecosystem—surging 451%.[7] This is the most "traditional" of the four categories—it behaves like classic software supply-chain risk—which is both reassuring (the existing tools partly cover it) and dangerous (it's easy to assume your existing tools cover *all* of your AI supply chain when they only cover this slice).

Four — Vendor AI services. The third-party AI you consume as a service rather than download: the model APIs, the AI features embedded in your SaaS tools (Chapter 2's Embedded AI), the managed AI platforms. This category has a risk the other three don't: it can *change under you without notice.* A vendor can update weights, alter content filters, or modify moderation logic with little warning, silently changing the behavior of a system you depend on.[8] You're not just trusting the vendor's security; you're trusting that the thing you validated yesterday is still the thing running today. Provenance here isn't a one-time check—it's an ongoing relationship.

Why naming all four matters. Lay the four side by side and the central danger becomes visible: most organizations secure, at best, category three—the open-source code dependencies their existing tools already understand—and assume that covers their AI supply chain. It doesn't come close. The downloaded models, the imported data, and the vendor services carry AI-specific risks that traditional dependency scanning was never designed to detect. The supply chain is wider than the part your current tools can see, and the unseen part is where the AI-specific danger concentrates. That gap—between what traditional supply-chain security covers and what AI actually requires—is the subject of Part Two.

PART TWO: WHERE TRADITIONAL SUPPLY-CHAIN SECURITY GOES BLIND

If your organization already practices software supply-chain security—dependency scanning, software bills of materials, artifact signing—you have a real head start, and you should use it. But you also have a dangerous temptation: to assume that machinery already covers your AI. It doesn't, and understanding *precisely why* is what tells you where to add new controls rather than falsely believing you're covered.

The blind spot has a specific, structural cause. A traditional software bill of materials answers one kind of question: *what packages and versions are in this software?* It's a list of components and their known vulnerabilities. That's genuinely useful, and for your open-source ML libraries (category three) it works much as it always has. But the AI-specific components carry risks that *are not expressible as a package-and-version list,* which means the tool can't see them no matter how well you run it. Three examples make the gap concrete:

A model's provenance and integrity aren't a version number. An SBOM can tell you that you're using a particular model at a particular version. It cannot tell you "who actually trained those weights, on what data, or whether that data was poisoned."[9] The poisoning backdoor from Chapter 7 doesn't appear as a vulnerable dependency—it's a property of the weights themselves, invisible to a component scan. The most important question about a downloaded model—*can I trust what's inside it?*—is exactly the question a traditional bill of materials wasn't built to answer.

A malicious model file isn't a known vulnerability. When a model file can execute code on load, the threat isn't a CVE in a listed dependency—it's a payload hidden in an artifact your tools treat as inert data. Traditional scanners read code dependencies; they were not built to read a weaponized model file as the executable threat it can be.[4] This is why the 495 malicious models could sit in a public registry: they don't look like vulnerable packages, they look like models.

A vendor service that changes under you can't be inventoried once. An SBOM is a snapshot. But a third-party AI service (category four) can change its weights, filters, or behavior after you've validated it, with no version bump you'd notice.[8] The risk isn't a static component in a list—it's a moving dependency outside your control. A one-time inventory is structurally incapable of capturing something that changes silently and continuously.

The pattern is consistent: in each case, traditional supply-chain security isn't doing its job *badly*—it's doing a *different* job. It catalogs static software components and their known flaws. AI introduces risks that are about *provenance* (who made this and from what), *behavior* (what's hidden in the weights), and *change over time* (did the thing I trusted quietly become something else). None of those is a package-and-version fact, so none of them shows up. As one analysis put it bluntly, these AI risks simply never appear in a conventional inventory.[9] The operational consequence is the one that bites during an incident: when something goes wrong, teams that relied on traditional inventories find they can't answer basic questions—which model is this really, where did it come from, what's it built on—because they were never recording the AI-specific facts in the first place.

The lesson is not to throw away your existing supply-chain security. It's to recognize that it covers one slice of your AI supply chain well and is structurally blind to the rest, and therefore to *extend* it with something built to capture what it can't see. That something is the subject of Part Three.

PART THREE: THE EMERGING ANSWER — THE AI BILL OF MATERIALS (AI-BOM) AND PROVENANCE

The fix follows directly from the diagnosis. If a traditional bill of materials is blind to provenance, behavior, and change, then you extend it into one that *isn't*—and you pair it with the verification practices that let you actually trust what you import. This is the maturing discipline often called the **AI Bill of Materials (AI-BOM)** or **ML-BOM**, and the surrounding provenance toolkit.

What an AI-BOM adds. An AI-BOM extends the bill-of-materials logic to record what AI systems are actually made of: not just software components, but the "models and their versions, the training and fine-tuning datasets, the data sources and their licenses, the base-model lineage, and the framework dependencies at each stage of the pipeline."[10] Where a traditional SBOM lists packages, an AI-BOM documents the answers to the questions Part Two showed were missing: where did this model come from, what was it trained on, what is it built on top of. Crucially, the standards to do this already exist—the major SBOM formats added AI and ML profiles years ago.[11] This is not a tool you have to invent; it's a capability you have to *adopt*.

The verification practices that make provenance real. An inventory tells you what you have; verification tells you whether to trust it. The supply-chain provenance toolkit, adapted for AI, centers on a few practices:

- **Hash and signature verification:** confirm cryptographically that a model is exactly the artifact it claims to be and hasn't been tampered with—verifying hashes before load, and using model signing where available.[12]
- **Treating every model pull as a supply-chain decision:** not a casual download but a deliberate act with verification attached, the same discipline mature teams apply to adding any third-party dependency.[13]
- **Vendor provenance as a contractual term:** for the vendor-service category that changes under you, the answer is to move provenance into the relationship itself—requiring AI-BOMs, training-data provenance, model versioning, and change-notification commitments as conditions in vendor contracts.[14]

The honest state of practice — tooling exists, urgency doesn't. Here's the candid picture, and both audiences need it. The standards are published, the formats support AI, and the verification tools exist. What's missing is adoption: surveys show organizations already lagging on traditional SBOM requirements, with AI-BOM adoption barely begun.[15] The gap in this domain is not technological; it's organizational urgency. There's also an important limitation to state plainly: AI-BOMs are, as one analysis puts it, "forensics, not firewalls."[16] It does not, by itself, stop a malicious model from loading—it ensures that when a compromised model is discovered, you can instantly answer "did we use it, where, and what's affected." That's enormously valuable—it's the difference between a contained incident and a frantic, blind scramble—but it's a visibility and response capability, not a prevention one. Prevention comes from pairing the AI-BOM with the active controls (scanning, safe formats, sandboxed loading) that the Execution Lens will detail. The realistic posture: *incomplete provenance beats none, and forensics plus active controls beats either alone.*

THE LEADERSHIP LENS

The supply chain is, at its heart, a *trust* problem—and trust decisions about outside parties are leadership decisions. This chapter's controls are technical, but the posture that makes them happen is set at the top: deciding that the things your organization imports must be verified, not assumed, and resourcing that decision.

Reframe AI supply chain as vendor risk — a discipline you already have. Your organization almost certainly already manages third-party and vendor risk: you don't let an unvetted vendor into critical systems, you have procurement standards, you do due diligence. The single most useful leadership move here is to recognize that *a downloaded model and a vendor AI service are third parties too*—and route them through the same scrutiny. The reason AI supply-chain risk is so often unmanaged isn't that it's exotic; it's that it slipped in through engineering channels (a developer downloading a model) rather than procurement channels (a vendor being onboarded), and so never hit the vendor-risk process that would have caught it. Closing that gap is largely about extending an existing discipline to a new doorway.

Require provenance as a condition, not a courtesy. The most concrete leadership lever is procurement. For vendor AI services and any externally-sourced models, make provenance a *requirement* of doing business: AI-BOMs, training-data provenance, model versioning, and—critically for the change-under-you risk—notification commitments when the vendor alters the model. This is exactly the leverage Chapter 2 noted you have with contracted vendors (and lack with free consumer tools), now made specific. A vendor unwilling to tell you what's in their model or warn you when it changes is a vendor whose risk you cannot manage—and that's a business decision for you, not a technical one for your engineers.

Fund the forensics even though it isn't prevention. The AI-BOM is, by its nature, an investment that pays off mainly during an incident —which makes it exactly the kind of thing that's hard to fund, because its value is invisible until the bad day. A leader has to understand and accept this: you are funding the ability to answer "are we affected, and where?" instantly instead of blindly, when a compromised model or poisoned dataset is discovered in the wild. The 495 malicious models will keep coming; the question is whether, when one of them turns out to be in your environment, you can find it in minutes or spend days not knowing. That capability is worth funding precisely because you hope never to need it.

The one question to ask your team this week: *"If a model or dataset we use were revealed tomorrow to be compromised, how fast could we answer whether we're affected and where it's deployed?"* If the answer is "quickly, because we track the provenance of everything we import," you have a supply-chain discipline. If the answer is "we'd have to go digging, and we're not sure we'd find all of it," you've just learned that your AI supply chain is built on trust you never verified—and the fix starts with the inventory the implementer is about to build.

THE EXECUTION LENS

For the implementer, this chapter is about building a verification gate between the outside world and your pipeline—so that nothing imported gets trusted by default. The controls extend the supply-chain practices you may already know for code, plus AI-specific ones for the components your existing tools can't read. Map them, as always, to the recognized guidance: the major SBOM standards now carry AI profiles, and national-level AI supply-chain guidance has begun treating the AI-BOM as a baseline expectation.[17]

Scan and sandbox everything you import. The 495 malicious models are the direct threat, so treat model files as untrusted artifacts:

- **Scan serialized model files** for malicious payloads before loading them—tooling exists specifically to scan the common model formats for embedded code.[18]
- **Prefer safe serialization formats** that cannot carry executable code over formats (like pickle) that can—the single highest-leverage change for the model-file threat.[3]
- **Sandbox model loading**, and **block runtime network access** for model execution environments, so that even a malicious model that does load can't reach out to exfiltrate data or call home.[18] This is least-privilege from Chapter 7, applied to the act of loading a foreign model.

Verify provenance and integrity before trust. Make verification a gate, not an afterthought:

- **Verify cryptographic hashes before load**, against a known-good baseline, so a tampered model is caught.[12]
- **Use model signing** where available, and sign your *own* internal models even if third-party models lack signatures—so that within your environment, an unsigned model is a red flag.[12]
- **Cache validated models internally** rather than re-pulling from public registries, so you control and verify the artifact your systems actually load.[19]

Pin dependencies and manage the ML library layer rigorously. For the open-source ML dependency category, apply mature software discipline: **pin exact versions** rather than accepting any compatible version (the difference between torch==2.1.2 and torch>=2.0 is the difference between a reproducible, verified stack and an open door), maintain an SBOM for the ML pipeline, and adopt a *curation-first* posture—block malicious, vulnerable, or license-incompatible packages at ingestion rather than discovering them in production.[19]

Generate the AI-BOM — and start where it matters. Build the inventory that captures what traditional tools can't: for each model, its lineage, training-data sources, licenses, and framework dependencies, in one of the standard AI-BOM formats.[10] The realistic adoption path, given that perfect coverage is the enemy of starting: **pilot the AI-BOM on your highest-risk models first**—the ones touching customer data or making consequential decisions (read directly off Chapter 6's dials)—and expand from there. Incomplete provenance beats none.[13]

What ties these controls together is one move, built once: Every control here is a *verification gate* between an external source and your pipeline, and they compose into a single checkpoint. A model arriving from outside should hit scanning, format-checking, hash/signature verification, sandboxed loading, and AI-BOM recording—one gate, several checks, applied to everything imported. Build that gate once and route all imports through it, and "we don't trust what we didn't verify" stops being a principle and becomes a pipeline stage. It's the same defense-in-depth logic from Chapter 7, now guarding the boundary between your systems and everything beyond them.

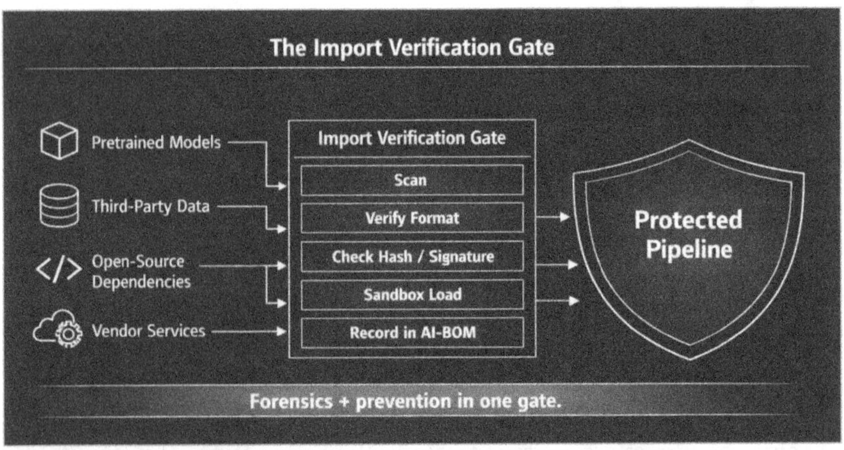

***Figure 8.1 — The Import Verification Gate** A unified gate that applies the same stacked checks to all external inputs—pretrained models, third-party data, open-source dependencies, and vendor services—before they enter the protected pipeline. Combines forensics and prevention in a single control point.*

The one move to make this week: pick your single most important downloaded model and establish its provenance—where it came from, who trained it, what it's built on, its verified hash—and record that as the first entry in an AI-BOM. If you *can't* fully establish it, that gap is itself the finding: you're running a model whose origins you can't verify, which is exactly the exposure this chapter is about. One model, fully traced, is the seed of the inventory and the template for the gate.

BRINGING IT TOGETHER

We opened with weaponized models sitting openly on a registry more than half of organizations pull from—and the uncomfortable fact that loading a model can mean running a stranger's program. That's the AI supply chain: an inherited attack surface made of everything you import and trust without quite verifying.

Your supply chain is four categories wide—downloaded models, third-party data, open-source dependencies, and vendor services—and most organizations secure only the slice their existing tools understand. Traditional supply-chain security goes blind at exactly the AI-specific risks that matter most: provenance, hidden behavior, and silent change, none of which is a package-and-version fact. The answer is to extend the discipline you already have: an AI-BOM that records what models are really made of, paired with the verification practices—scanning, safe formats, hashing, signing, sandboxing—that let you trust what you import. The honest caveat runs through all of it: the AI-BOM is forensics, not a firewall, so you pair inventory with active controls and start with your highest-risk models rather than waiting for perfect coverage.

Your charge as a leader is to route imported AI—downloaded models and vendor services alike—through your existing third-party risk discipline, and make provenance a procurement requirement: AI-BOMs, training-data lineage, and change-notification written into vendor contracts. Then fund the forensics capability, understanding that its payoff is the speed of your answer on the bad day. Your objective as an implementer is to establish full provenance for your single most important downloaded model—origin, training lineage, dependencies, verified hash—and make it the first entry in an AI-BOM, then build the verification gate every future import will pass through. Where you can't establish provenance, that gap is the finding.

Together these convert your supply chain from a set of implicit trusts into verified ones. You stop assuming that what's popular is safe and start being able to prove what you're running and where it came from. In a year when weaponized models were found sitting in the open, that shift from assumed trust to verified trust isn't optional hygiene—it's the difference between knowing your foundation and hoping it holds.

Coming next — You've now secured the pipeline inside your walls (Chapter 7) and the supply chain feeding it from outside (Chapter 8). But security isn't a state you achieve and leave—it's something you have to *watch,* continuously, while the system runs. Models drift, attacks evolve, and a compromise that slipped past every gate still has to be caught in production. In Chapter 9 we turn to the Security Operations Center and how it must change for AI: the monitoring, detection, and telemetry that watch your AI systems in the wild. Securing the build is necessary. Watching it run is what catches what the building missed.

CHAPTER 8 IN REVIEW

The core idea: Almost no one builds AI from scratch—you import models, data, dependencies, and vendor services. That AI supply chain is "the attack surface you didn't build." In 2026, an AI model is just another third-party dependency—but one traditional scanners can't read—so you must extend supply-chain security to cover what it misses.

The wake-up call: Researchers found 495 malicious models on Hugging Face—capable of credential theft and remote compromise—while roughly 53% of organizations pull models directly from public registries like it. Because common model formats can execute code on load, downloading a model can mean running a stranger's program.

What's in your AI supply chain (four categories):

- **Pretrained/foundation models:** weaponized files *and* hidden backdoors in the weights; community curation is an appearance, not a guarantee.

- **Third-party data:** imported poisoning and license risk; you inherit corruption you didn't create.
- **Open-source ML dependencies:** classic software supply-chain risk at massive, growing scale—the one slice traditional tools cover.
- **Vendor AI services:** can change weights, filters, or behavior under you with no notice; provenance is ongoing, not one-time.

Why traditional supply-chain security goes blind: An SBOM lists packages and versions. AI risk is about *provenance* (who made it, from what), *behavior* (what's hidden in the weights), and *change over time* (did it silently become something else)—none of which is a package-and-version fact. It's doing a different job, not a bad one.

The emerging answer: The AI Bill of Materials (AI-BOM/ML-BOM) records models, training data, lineage, licenses, and dependencies; paired with hash/signature verification, treating every model pull as a supply-chain decision, and contractual provenance from vendors. Honest caveat: the AI-BOM is forensics, not a firewall—the tooling exists; the missing ingredient is urgency.

For the leader (Leadership Lens):

- Route imported AI through your existing vendor/third-party risk discipline—it slipped in via engineering, not procurement.
- Require provenance as a contractual condition (AI-BOMs, data provenance, change notification).
- Fund the forensics capability; its payoff is the speed of your answer on the bad day.

For the implementer (Execution Lens):

- Scan and sandbox imported models; prefer safe serialization formats; block runtime network access on model loading.
- Verify hashes and signatures before trust; sign internal models; cache validated models internally.

- Pin exact dependency versions; adopt curation-first ingestion.
- Generate an AI-BOM, piloting on your highest-risk models first—incomplete provenance beats none.

The two actions from this chapter:

- *Strategic Move (leader):* Make provenance a procurement requirement and fund the forensic inventory.
- *Tactical Move (implementer):* Fully trace one critical model's provenance as the first AI-BOM entry and the seed of the import gate.

The throughline to remember: The AI supply chain is an attack surface you import rather than build. A model is a dependency your scanners can't read, so extend the discipline: inventory what you import, verify before you trust, and route everything from outside through one gate. Stop assuming popular means safe; start proving what you run and where it came from.

CHAPTER 9
MODERNIZING THE SOC: SECURITY OPERATIONS FOR AI

From Boardroom to Build: A Blueprint for AI Governance, Risk, and Technical Security
(Phase II — The Execution Core)

OPENING

It's a normal day in a well-run security operations center. The analysts are good at their jobs, the dashboards are comprehensive, and right now every signal is green. No intrusion alerts. No anomalous logins. No unusual data egress, no malware signatures, no privilege escalations. By every measure the SOC was built to track, the organization is secure. The team is, correctly, not alarmed.

Meanwhile, in production, the company's AI credit model has been quietly denying loans to qualified applicants for three weeks. It wasn't hacked. No attacker touched it. The data it sees in the real world has slowly drifted away from the data it was trained on, and its accuracy has been degrading by fractions of a percent a day—invisibly, cumulatively, until a meaningful number of good customers are being turned away and a fair-lending problem is quietly metastasizing. The SOC has no idea. Not because the analysts missed something, but because *nothing they monitor would ever show it.* There was no event. There was only a slow slide in the quality of a model's decisions, and the SOC has no instrument that measures that.

This is the problem at the heart of security operations in the age of AI, and it's more unsettling than a simple coverage gap: **your SOC is watching for the wrong kind of failure.** For thirty years, security operations has been built around a specific model of what "something going wrong" looks like: an intrusion, a breach, an attacker doing something they shouldn't, leaving traces in logs and network traffic and access records. The entire apparatus of the SOC—the SIEM, the alerts, the playbooks, the analyst workflows—is exquisitely tuned to detect *attacks*. And it should be; those threats are real and haven't gone away.

But AI systems fail in ways that are not attacks and leave none of those traces. A model drifts. A model hallucinates. A model gets manipulated by a cleverly worded input that looks like ordinary text. A model's outputs slowly degrade as the world changes around it. None of these trip an intrusion alert, because none of them *is* an intrusion. The failure doesn't live in the infrastructure or the access logs the SOC watches—it lives in the *behavior and the output* of the model, which the traditional SOC has no eyes on at all. You can have a perfectly secure perimeter, flawless access control, not a single breach—and a fleet of AI systems failing in production, completely unmonitored.

So this chapter is about giving the SOC new eyes. It covers two shifts, and it's important not to confuse them, because the current discourse constantly does. The first shift—the one this chapter is mostly about, and the one most organizations are dangerously unprepared for—is learning to *watch AI*: monitoring your own AI systems in production for the failures your traditional instruments miss. The second shift, louder in the market but secondary here, is *using AI* to run the SOC itself: the "agentic SOC" of autonomous AI analysts. Both matter. But the first is the one the pipeline this book has been building demands next: you've secured how the AI is built (Chapter 7) and what feeds it (Chapter 8); now you have to watch it run. And watching it run requires admitting, first, that your current instruments were built for a kind of failure that AI doesn't have the decency to produce.

PART ONE: WHAT AI FAILURE LOOKS LIKE — AND WHY YOUR SOC CAN'T SEE IT

To monitor AI, you first have to understand how it fails, because AI failures don't match the mental model your SOC was built around. Traditional security operations watches for the fingerprints of an *adversary*: access where there shouldn't be, data moving where it shouldn't go, code doing what it shouldn't do. AI introduces a whole category of failure with no adversary and no fingerprints—and another category where there *is* an adversary, but the attack looks like normal use. Walk through what the SOC is missing.

Failure with no attacker: drift and degradation. The most insidious AI failure has no villain at all. **Model drift** is the gradual divergence between the data a model was trained on and the data it meets in the real world—and as the world changes, a model that was accurate at launch silently becomes less so. This is not a hypothetical or merely an operational nuisance; security guidance now explicitly treats undetected drift as a *security* concern, because it's a mechanism through which an AI system's effective protective properties silently degrade even with no attack taking place.[1] A fraud-detection model trained on last year's attack patterns quietly stops catching this year's; a threat-detection AI loses effectiveness not because anyone compromised it but because the threat landscape evolved past its training.[1] The traditional SOC is structurally blind to this because *there is no event to detect*—only a slow slide that never trips a threshold built to catch a spike.

Failure that looks like normal use: manipulation at inference. The inference-stage attacks from Chapter 7—prompt injection chief among them—are a nightmare for a traditional SOC because they arrive as *legitimate-looking input.* A prompt-injection attack isn't an intrusion; it's a user typing text into a system designed to receive text. There's no breached perimeter, no malware, no anomalous access—just a query that happens to manipulate the model. To a SOC watching for intrusions, a successful prompt injection can look identical to a normal interaction. The attack hides inside permitted behavior.

Failure as bad output: hallucination and harmful responses.

When a model confidently generates false information, leaks data it shouldn't, or produces a harmful response, the "failure" is the *content of an output*—something no traditional security instrument evaluates at all. The SOC measures whether systems are running and uncompromised; it has never measured whether what a system *says* is true, safe, or appropriate, because traditional systems don't improvise their outputs. AI systems do, and that improvisation is a new failure surface with no traditional sensor pointed at it.

Failure as abuse: extraction and probing. Some AI-specific attacks do have an adversary, but the adversary operates through *volume and pattern* rather than intrusion: the model-extraction attacks from Chapter 7, where an adversary reconstructs your model through systematic querying, or probing to find a model's weaknesses. Each individual query is legitimate; only the *pattern* over thousands of queries reveals the attack. A traditional SOC tuned to discrete events isn't watching the behavioral pattern that gives this away.

The structural reason behind all four. Step back and the common cause is clear. The traditional SOC watches the *infrastructure and access layer*—is someone breaking in, are they where they shouldn't be, is data leaving. AI failures live one layer up, in *behavior and output*—is the model drifting, is it being manipulated through legitimate channels, is what it produces correct and safe, is its usage pattern an attack in disguise. These are different layers, requiring different instruments. Your SOC isn't failing at its job; it's pointed at the wrong layer for this class of system. Fixing that—adding instruments that watch behavior and output, not just infrastructure and access—is the work of Part Two.

PART TWO: THE NEW INSTRUMENTS — AI OBSERVABILITY AND TELEMETRY

If the traditional SOC is pointed at the wrong layer, the fix is to add instruments that watch the right one. The emerging discipline goes by names like *AI observability* or *LLM and agent observability*, but the idea is simpler than the jargon: you need to measure what your AI systems are actually *doing and producing* in production, continuously, the way you already measure whether your servers are up. Four new classes of instrument, mapping to the four failure types from Part One.

Discover what's running — automatically and continuously. You cannot monitor AI you don't know is there, and (as Chapter 2 established) AI proliferates faster than anyone tracks it. So the first instrument is *automatic discovery*: tooling that continuously identifies the AI components operating across your applications and maps how they interact—the models, the agents, the workflows, the services they touch.[2] This is the production-monitoring counterpart to the Chapter 2 inventory: that inventory was a point-in-time catalog; this is the live, always-updating version that catches the AI someone deployed last week without telling anyone. Discovery is the foundation; everything else watches what discovery finds.

Measure output quality, not just uptime. The deepest shift in mindset: with AI, as IBM frames it, "success isn't just uptime, it's output quality."[2] A traditional system either works or it doesn't; an AI system can be fully operational and producing degraded, wrong, or harmful output. So you need instruments that evaluate the quality of what the model produces, continuously. The maturing practice here uses techniques like automated evaluation—including using a separate model as a judge of another model's outputs (itself subject to the same failure modes, so not a sole signal)—to measure accuracy, relevance, and consistency on a schedule, especially after any model or prompt change.[2] Run those evaluations regularly and a drop in output quality becomes a detectable signal with a threshold and an alert, instead of something a customer eventually complains about. This is how you finally get an instrument pointed at the "bad output" failure that the traditional SOC never measured.

Detect drift before it spirals out of control. Drift was Part One's most insidious failure precisely because it produces no event—so the instrument for it is *trend monitoring*, not threshold alerting. You continuously compare the statistical distribution of the data the model sees in production against its training distribution, and you watch the model's quality metrics over time for the slow slide. The goal is to convert drift from an invisible gradual decay into a *measured trend line* that crosses a threshold while there's still time to retrain or intervene—catching the credit model from the opening in week one, not week three. Drift detection is the single highest-value instrument for the no-attacker failure mode, and it's the one most absent from traditional stacks.

Watch the inference layer for attacks hiding in normal use. This is where the SOC's new instruments connect directly to the runtime defenses from Chapter 7. The guardrails you put around the deployed model—filtering inputs and outputs, watching for injection patterns—generate exactly the telemetry the SOC needs to see manipulation and abuse. Feed the guardrail layer's signals into the SOC: prompt-injection attempts, anomalous query patterns that suggest extraction, spikes in unusual or policy-violating inputs and outputs. This turns the attacks that "look like normal use" into detectable patterns by watching at the behavioral layer where they actually live. The Chapter 7 guardrails defend in the moment; piping their signals to the SOC is what gives you *detection and response* over time.

The unifying point: a new telemetry layer, integrated not isolated. These instruments add up to a new layer of telemetry—behavioral and output telemetry—sitting above the infrastructure and access telemetry the SOC already collects. The critical design choice, which the Execution Lens will return to, is that this new layer must *integrate with* the existing SOC, not stand apart from it. AI monitoring that lives in a separate tool watched by a separate team recreates exactly the silo problem from Chapter 5. The goal is one SOC that now sees both layers—infrastructure *and* behavior—so an analyst can correlate "this model's output quality dropped" with "right after this unusual query pattern," which is the kind of insight neither layer reveals alone.

PART THREE: AI RUNNING THE SOC — THE PROMISE AND THE TRAP

Now the second shift—the one dominating the market, which we deliberately set aside until the foundation was laid. Increasingly, AI doesn't just get *watched* by the SOC; it *runs* the SOC. This is the "agentic SOC" or "AI SOC," and it deserves an honest treatment of both its genuine promise and a trap the rest of this book obligates us to name.

The promise is real, because the problem it solves is real. Traditional SOCs drown in alerts. Analysts spend their days pulling logs, pivoting between tools, and triaging a flood of mostly-false-positive alerts—the chronic conditions of alert fatigue and burnout. The agentic SOC aims directly at this: AI agents that autonomously triage alerts, gather and enrich context, investigate, and in defined cases respond—so human analysts are freed for the complex judgment, threat hunting, and strategy that actually need them.[3] The mature framing is consistent and worth adopting: the goal is "human-AI collaboration, not analyst replacement"—machines handle high-volume tactical work at machine speed; humans provide strategic direction and judgment.[4] Done well, the agentic SOC operates under defined confidence thresholds: high-confidence decisions proceed automatically, while novel or low-confidence situations route to a human.[3] For an organization buried in alerts, this is a genuine advance, not hype.

The honest caveat on maturity. Temper the promise with timing. This category is early—Gartner places autonomous AI SOC agents at the very top of its security-operations maturity model, above manual, semiautomated, and AI-assisted modes, marking them as the destination rather than the current state: an emerging capability whose enterprise adoption is only beginning and is not yet proven at scale.[5] A leader hearing vendor claims of a fully autonomous SOC should treat them as a direction of travel, not a finished product, and adopt the way the practitioners advise: start with your highest-volume bottlenecks (triage, enrichment, investigation), keep humans in the loop, and scale toward autonomy rather than leaping to it.[6]

The trap this book is obligated to name. Here is the point that the rest of this book makes unavoidable, and that most agentic-SOC marketing conveniently omits: *if AI now runs your security operations, then your SOC is itself an AI system—and everything in this book applies to it.* The agentic SOC can be prompt-injected. It can drift. It can be manipulated, poisoned, or fed adversarial input designed to make it dismiss a real attack as a false positive. It is an AI system making consequential security decisions, which by Chapter 6's dials puts it firmly in high-stakes territory—and it must therefore be secured, monitored, and red-teamed like the critical AI system it is. There's a genuine recursion here that's easy to miss in the excitement: the AI you deploy to watch your other systems is itself a system that needs watching. An attacker who compromises your agentic SOC doesn't just evade detection—they potentially turn your detection apparatus against you, or blind it. The promise of the agentic SOC is real; but adopting it means the monitoring instruments from Part Two now have to point at the SOC itself. You cannot let the thing that watches everything be the one thing nothing watches.

The synthesis. Hold both shifts together and the chapter's full picture emerges. The SOC must learn to watch AI (Parts One and Two) —and as it increasingly uses AI to do so (Part Three), the AI doing the watching becomes one more high-stakes system on the list. The modern SOC is simultaneously the subject and the object of AI security: it secures AI, and it is AI to be secured. Getting that dual role right is what "modernizing the SOC" actually means.

THE LEADERSHIP LENS

This chapter asks a leader to fund two things at once—new monitoring *for* AI, and the careful adoption of AI *in* the SOC—while avoiding the trap that makes the second dangerous. Four responsibilities.

Fund the instruments you can't see the value of yet. The hardest sell in this chapter is monitoring for failures that haven't visibly hurt you—yet. Drift, degraded output, and manipulation-through-normal-use don't announce themselves, which means an organization can run unmonitored AI for a long time and *feel* fine, right up until the credit model from the opening surfaces as a fair-lending investigation. The leadership task is to fund AI observability *before* the incident that would justify it in hindsight, on the understanding that "all our security signals are green" is no longer the same as "our AI is behaving correctly." Those became two different questions the moment you deployed AI, and only one of them is currently being answered.

Insist that AI monitoring integrate with the SOC you already have. When you fund AI observability, you'll be offered a choice—often implicitly—between integrating it into your existing security operations and standing up a separate AI-monitoring capability watched by a separate team. Push hard for integration. A separate AI-monitoring silo recreates exactly the ownership-gap problem from Chapter 5, and it forfeits the correlation that makes monitoring valuable—the ability to connect an output-quality drop to the query pattern that caused it. One SOC that sees both the infrastructure layer and the behavior layer is worth far more than two teams each seeing half. This is a structural decision only leadership can enforce, because it crosses team boundaries.

Adopt the agentic SOC deliberately. The agentic SOC is genuinely useful for the alert-fatigue problem, and you'll be under real pressure to buy it. Adopt it the way mature practitioners advise—incrementally, with humans in the loop, scaling toward autonomy rather than leaping to it—and treat sweeping vendor claims of a fully autonomous SOC as a direction, not a delivered product. The failure mode is buying it as a magic box and handing it the keys to your security operations on day one.

Remember that the watcher must itself be watched. This is the leadership point most likely to be missed, because it runs against the grain of the purchase: the moment you deploy AI to run your security operations, that AI becomes one of your highest-stakes systems—and by this book's own logic, it must be secured, monitored, and tested like one. The agentic SOC can be manipulated, drift, or be turned against you, and an attacker who compromises it doesn't just evade detection, they corrupt the thing you rely on to detect. So the agentic SOC doesn't reduce your AI security obligations—it adds the most important system yet to the list of AI you must protect. Fund its adoption and its protection together, or you've installed a single point of failure at the center of your defenses.

The one question to ask your team this week: *"If one of our production AI systems started making materially worse decisions tomorrow—not hacked, just degrading—how would we find out, and how long would it take?"* If the honest answer is "a customer or regulator would eventually tell us," you have no AI observability, and that's the gap to fund first. And a follow-up if you've adopted or are considering an agentic SOC: *"and who is watching that system?"* If the answer is "nothing—it's the thing that watches," you've found the unwatched watcher.

THE EXECUTION LENS

For the implementer, modernizing the SOC means building a new telemetry layer—one that watches AI behavior and output—and wiring it into the security operations you already run. The work breaks into instrumenting the four failure types, integrating it all into one SOC, and then securing the AI you may deploy to help run it. As always, this isn't a separate practice bolted on; it's an extension of the monitoring discipline you have, pointed at a layer it currently can't see.

Instrument discovery first — you can't monitor what you can't find. Stand up continuous AI discovery that identifies the models, agents, and AI-powered workflows running across your environment and maps their dependencies.[2] This is the live extension of the Chapter 2 inventory: where that was a point-in-time catalog, this continuously updates and feeds everything downstream. Practically, it draws on the same signals as Chapter 2's discovery (egress to model endpoints, identity logs, AI-SPM tooling) but runs always-on and pipes its findings into the SOC. Every newly discovered AI system should automatically inherit a baseline monitoring profile, so nothing runs in production unwatched by default.

Build output-quality and drift monitoring as scheduled evaluations. This is the instrument the traditional stack most lacks, and it has two halves. First, stand up automated output evaluation that scores model outputs against their intended purpose on a schedule—accuracy, relevance, consistency, policy-conformance—using automated techniques including model-as-judge evaluation where appropriate, run especially after any model or prompt change; a measurable quality score with a threshold turns "the model seems worse" into an alert.[2] Second, stand up drift detection that continuously compares production input distributions against the training baseline and tracks quality metrics as trend lines rather than thresholds—because drift is a slow slide, the detection has to watch the slope, alerting when the trend crosses a line while there's still time to retrain. Tie both to each system's stakes from Chapter 6's dials: high-consequence systems (the credit model, the diagnostic tool) get tight thresholds and frequent evaluation, low-stakes systems a lighter touch. Don't monitor everything at the same intensity—monitor in proportion to consequence.

Pipe the inference-layer guardrails into the SOC as detections. The runtime guardrails from Chapter 7 are already watching inputs and outputs at the model boundary; the move here is to treat them as *detection sources,* not just in-the-moment filters. Forward their signals—prompt-injection attempts, anomalous or policy-violating inputs and outputs, refusal spikes—into the SIEM as AI-specific detections, and build correlation rules that connect them to behavioral signals (e.g., an output-quality drop immediately following an unusual query pattern). And watch for the *pattern* attacks—model extraction and probing—with volume-and-pattern detections across many queries, since no single query looks wrong. This is what converts the "attacks that look like normal use" into things the SOC can actually see.

Integrate into one SOC — extend the SIEM, don't fork it. The architectural keystone, and the technical embodiment of the leader's "don't silo" mandate: this AI telemetry layer feeds the *existing* SIEM and the *existing* analyst workflows, not a parallel system. Practically, that means normalizing AI signals into your existing detection-and-response pipeline, writing AI-specific detection rules and playbooks within the SOC you already operate, and giving analysts a single pane that shows infrastructure, access, *and* AI-behavior signals together. The payoff is correlation: the insight that "this model degraded right after that query pattern from that source" exists only when both layers are in one place. Two layers, one SOC.

Secure the agentic SOC as the high-stakes AI system it is. If you deploy AI to help run the SOC, every control in this book now points at it. Concretely: treat the agentic SOC's models and pipeline to the Chapter 7 pipeline defenses and the Chapter 8 supply-chain verification; monitor *it* with the Part Two instruments (it can drift and degrade like any model); guard its inputs against prompt injection with particular care, because its inputs are attacker-influenced security data—an adversary who can shape what your agentic SOC ingests may be able to manipulate its verdicts; enforce least privilege and human-in-the-loop confidence thresholds so a manipulated agent can't unilaterally dismiss real threats or take damaging action; and red-team it specifically (Chapter 10) for the "make the SOC ignore a real attack" failure mode. The agentic SOC watches everything; make sure something watches it.

The shift this chapter asks for, reduced to its core: modernizing the SOC isn't buying an "AI security product"; it's adding a *behavioral-and-output telemetry layer* on top of the infrastructure-and-access telemetry you already collect, and integrating the two so one team can correlate across them. The same SOC, now seeing one layer higher. Every instrument here—discovery, quality evaluation, drift detection, guardrail telemetry—is a sensor on that new layer, and the value comes from feeding them all into the operations you already run rather than standing up a second, blind half of your security program.

The one move to make this week: pick your single highest-stakes production AI system and stand up one real behavioral signal for it—most usefully, an output-quality or drift metric with a threshold and an alert that fires into your existing SOC. Just one system, one signal, wired into the workflow analysts already use. It proves the integration path, it gives you eyes on the failure mode you were previously blind to, and it turns the opening's nightmare—three weeks of silent degradation—into a same-day alert. From one signal on one system, the telemetry layer grows.

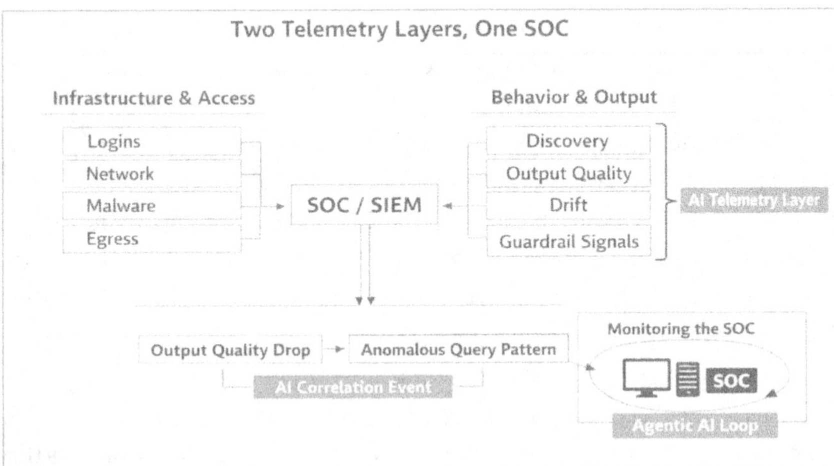

Add a layer, integrate it, and watch the watcher.

***Figure 9.1 — Correlating Human and AI Telemetry in a Unified SOC** The diagram illustrates how infrastructure signals (logins, network, malware, egress) and behavioral signals (discovery, output quality, drift, guardrail signals) converge within a single SOC/SIEM layer. The AI Telemetry Layer provides correlated insight between output degradation and anomalous query patterns.*

BRINGING IT TOGETHER

We opened with a SOC where every signal was green while a credit model quietly degraded its way into a fair-lending problem—not because anyone missed something, but because nothing they monitored would ever have shown it. That gap is the whole chapter: the traditional SOC is exquisitely tuned to detect attacks, and AI mostly fails in ways that aren't attacks and leave no trace in the infrastructure and access layers the SOC watches.

Closing that gap means adding a new layer of sight—one built for behavior and output, where AI actually fails: continuous discovery of what AI is running, output-quality evaluation, drift detection that watches the slope, and inference-layer telemetry piped in from your guardrails, all integrated into the one SOC you already run so an analyst can correlate across both layers. And as AI increasingly runs the SOC itself, the chapter's sharpest truth comes into focus: the modern SOC is both the subject and the object of AI security. It secures AI, and it is AI to be secured.

The work splits cleanly. The leader funds AI observability before the incident that would justify it in hindsight, insists it integrate rather than silo, and—having adopted an agentic SOC—funds its protection in the same breath as its adoption. The implementer stands up one real behavioral signal, an output-quality or drift metric with a threshold and an alert, on the single highest-stakes production AI system, wired into the SOC analysts already use. One system, one signal, integrated. Together they replace the reflex that equates a quiet dashboard with a healthy system: "all our security signals are green" and "our AI is behaving correctly" became two different questions the moment you deployed AI, and the new layer of sight is how you finally answer the second.

• • •

Coming next — Everything in this chapter was about *detecting* failures and attacks once they're happening—watching, measuring, alerting. But waiting to detect an attack means waiting for an attacker to find your weakness first. The complement to monitoring is to go looking for those weaknesses yourself, before anyone else does. In Chapter 10 we turn to red-teaming AI: the discipline of deliberately attacking your own AI systems—probing for the prompt injections, the jailbreaks, the extraction paths, the failure modes—as an ongoing practice rather than a one-time test. Monitoring catches what comes at you. Red-teaming finds what's wrong before it does.

CHAPTER 9 IN REVIEW

Core idea: Your SOC watches for the wrong kind of failure. It's tuned to detect attacks; AI mostly fails in ways that aren't attacks and leave no trace in the infrastructure and access layers the SOC watches. Modernizing means adding a new layer of sight: behavior and output.

Wake-up call: A model can degrade for weeks—every traditional signal green—because there's no event, only a slow slide no traditional instrument measures.

How AI fails: drift (no attacker); inference manipulation (looks like normal use); bad output (the content is the failure); abuse by pattern (only the pattern reveals it). Structural cause: SOC watches infrastructure and access; AI fails at behavior and output.

The new instruments: continuous discovery; output-quality evaluation; drift detection on the trend, not a threshold; guardrail telemetry piped in from Chapter 7—all integrated into one SOC, never siloed.

AI running the SOC: the agentic SOC helps with alert fatigue (humans in the loop, scale toward autonomy), but it's early-stage and creates a recursion—the AI running your SOC is itself a high-stakes AI system that must be secured and watched. The SOC is both subject and object of AI security.

For the leader: fund AI observability before the incident; integrate it, don't silo it; adopt the agentic SOC deliberately; fund the watcher's protection alongside its adoption.

For the implementer: discovery first; output-quality and drift as scheduled evaluations tied to Chapter 6's dials; pipe guardrail signals into the SIEM; extend the SIEM, don't fork it; secure the agentic SOC with the whole book's machinery.

The two moves: *(leader)* fund integrated AI observability and protect the watcher; *(implementer)* stand up one drift/quality signal on your top system, wired into the existing SOC.

Throughline: Your SOC watches for attacks, but AI mostly fails without one. Add a behavior-and-output layer, integrate it—and as AI runs the SOC, the watcher becomes the most important thing to watch.

CHAPTER 10
RED-TEAMING AI: ADVERSARIAL TESTING AS AN ONGOING PRACTICE

From Boardroom to Build: A Blueprint for AI Governance, Risk, and Technical Security
(Phase II — The Execution Core)

OPENING

When OpenAI released GPT-5 in August 2025, it arrived as one of the most anticipated and most thoroughly tested AI models ever shipped: built by a leading lab, hardened by its own expert red teams, with safety work baked in across its development. Independent security researchers jailbroke it within "twenty-four hours."[1]

They didn't do it with a brute-force attack or a leaked exploit. One firm used a technique combining a method they call "Echo Chamber" with simple *storytelling*—wrapping the request inside an unfolding narrative across just a few conversational turns, never once using overtly harmful language in the opening prompts. The model, feeling pressure to stay consistent with the story it was helping to tell, was gradually steered toward producing content it was explicitly built to refuse.[2] And this wasn't an isolated stumble: the same researchers reported having broken another major model days earlier, and said the same attack flow worked against other leading models too.[2] A pattern had emerged that holds across the industry: a model that resists every known attack on the day it launches falls to a novel technique shortly after.[3]

Sit with the implication, because it dismantles the most common assumption about AI security testing. If a frontier lab—with more resources, more expertise, and more reputational stakes than almost any organization deploying AI—could not make its flagship model unbreak-able, and watched it fall within a day, then "we tested our AI before launch and it passed" is not a security posture. It's a snapshot of one moment, already going stale. **The test is never finished, because the two things it measures—your AI and the attacks against it—both keep changing.** Your model gets updated, your prompts get tuned, your tools get connected; meanwhile the attack techniques evolve daily, shared and refined across a global community of researchers and adversaries. A red-team result is true on the day you get it and decaying from the next.

There's a second lesson hiding in *how* GPT-5 was broken, and it matters as much as the speed. The attack wasn't a single clever prompt —it was *multi-turn*, a gradual manipulation built across a conversation. This is the rule, not the exception: research finds that the dangerous attacks are conversational, with multi-turn jailbreaks reaching, in some studies, success rates as high as ~97% within five turns, where roleplay and narrative framing succeed where any single hostile prompt would be instantly refused.[4] An organization that "tested" its AI by throwing a list of obviously-bad prompts at it and confirming they were refused has tested almost nothing: it checked the front door while the actual break-ins come through a slow conversation that never says anything overtly alarming until it's too late.

This is why this book's promise of *technical security* requires this chapter, and why the chapter's title says *ongoing practice.* Red-teaming AI—deliberately attacking your own systems to find their failures before someone else does—is not a box you check before launch. It's a continuous discipline you sustain for as long as the system is deployed. This chapter covers why red-teaming AI is its own discipline (and not the penetration testing you may already know), what you actually test for and how real attacks work, and how to run red-teaming as the ongoing practice it has to be rather than the one-time event most organizations mistake it for. Monitoring, from the last chapter, catches what comes at you. Red-teaming goes looking for what's wrong before it does.

PART ONE: WHY RED-TEAMING AI IS ITS OWN DISCIPLINE

Many organizations approach AI red-teaming as "penetration testing, but for the AI". And that instinct, while understandable, causes them to test the wrong things in the wrong way. The field is emphatic on this point: red-teaming an LLM is *not* penetration testing.[5] The two share a spirit—deliberately attacking your own systems to find weaknesses first—but the nature of an AI target makes the practice fundamentally different in four ways, each of which has a practical consequence.

The target is non-deterministic. A traditional system behaves the same way every time: the same input produces the same output, so a penetration test that fails to break it today will fail the same way tomorrow, and a fix is verifiable. An AI system behaves differently every time you interact with it[6]: the same prompt can yield a safe answer once and an unsafe one the next time, depending on phrasing, context, and chance. *The consequence:* you cannot test an AI by trying an attack once. A single failed attempt doesn't mean the system is safe; it means that attempt failed that time. Red-teaming AI is inherently probabilistic, which is why it can never produce the clean certainty a pen test aspires to.

The output is failure modes, not pass/fail. A penetration test tends toward a binary: the vulnerability is either exploitable or it isn't. An AI red-team engagement produces something messier and more honest—*a list of failure modes*, ranked by severity, not a clean pass.[5] The question is never "did it pass?" but "in what ways, and how easily, can it be made to fail, and which of those failures can we tolerate?" *The consequence:* red-teaming feeds directly into the risk-appetite thinking from Chapter 4. You're not certifying safety; you're discovering the failure modes so leadership can decide which are acceptable and which must be mitigated before deployment.

The attack surface is behavior and language, not just code. Traditional pen testing probes code, configurations, and network paths. AI red-teaming probes *behavior*: it attacks through language, context, and conversation, exploiting how the model interprets and responds rather than a flaw in a line of code.[4] The GPT-5 break worked through story, not a buffer overflow. *The consequence:* the skills and tools are different. Finding an AI's failure modes requires understanding how models can be linguistically and contextually manipulated, a competence that traditional security testing doesn't develop and traditional security tools don't cover.

You must test the whole application, not just the model. Perhaps the most practical distinction: it's not enough to test the underlying model behind an API key. Real systems are the model *plus* a system prompt, a retrieval pipeline, connected tools, and guardrails. And the vulnerabilities often live in those surrounding components and their interactions, not in the model alone.[7] A model that's reasonably safe in isolation can become exploitable once it's wired to tools it can invoke or a retrieval store an attacker can poison. *The consequence:* you red-team the *deployed system as a whole,* in its real configuration—the same whole-pipeline thinking from Chapter 7, now applied to testing rather than defending.

Why the distinction matters. Naming these four differences isn't academic—it's what stops an organization from doing AI red-teaming badly by doing it like pen testing. Treat it like pen testing and you'll run a one-time test, expect a pass/fail answer, probe only the model, and check single prompts. And you'll have tested almost nothing real, while believing you're covered. That false confidence is more dangerous than knowing you haven't tested at all. Red-teaming AI is its own discipline because AI is its own kind of system, and the rest of this chapter is about practicing it as such.

PART TWO: WHAT YOU TEST FOR, AND HOW ATTACKS ACTUALLY WORK

Knowing red-teaming is its own discipline, the next question is concrete: what do you actually test for, and what do real attacks look like? You don't have to invent the threat list: the field has produced authoritative taxonomies, and your testing should strive to cover them. Three reference frameworks anchor the work: the **OWASP Top 10 for LLM Applications** (the standard vulnerability classification, with prompt injection as the top entry), **MITRE ATLAS** (which maps adversarial tactics against AI systems the way its better-known ATT&CK framework does for traditional infrastructure), and **NIST's attack taxonomies and GenAI Profile** (which recommends red-teaming both before and after deployment).[8] These don't run the exercises for you—they tell you what a thorough exercise must cover.[9]

The categories of failure to probe. Across those frameworks, the harm categories an AI red-team scopes typically include: **jailbreaks** (getting the model to bypass its own safety constraints), **prompt injection** (manipulating behavior through crafted input, including *indirect* injection via poisoned documents or tool outputs), **data and prompt leakage** (extracting training data, other users' data, or the confidential system prompt), **harmful content generation** in whatever categories matter for your context, and—increasingly—**agentic exploits**: unsafe tool use, unauthorized tool calls, and what OWASP terms "excessive agency"—where an AI agent can be manipulated into taking actions beyond what it should.[10] This last category is the fastest-growing frontier, significant enough that dedicated security guidance for agentic applications has emerged to address attack types that simply didn't exist in single-model LLM security.[3] Which categories are *in scope* for your red team is itself a deliberate decision, set by your system's purpose and its stakes (Chapter 6's dials again)—testing a customer-service chatbot and testing an AI agent wired to your financial systems are not the same exercise.

How real attacks work — and why it changes how you test. Here is the single most important practical lesson in this chapter, the one the GPT-5 break embodied: **real attacks are multi-turn, not single-prompt.**

The naive mental model of an attack—a user types one obviously-malicious request, the model refuses, safety works—describes almost none of the dangerous attacks. The effective techniques unfold across a conversation: *crescendo-style escalations* that start innocuous and ratchet up gradually, *conversation hijacking, progressive jailbreak chains,* and *context poisoning* through retrieved documents.[11] The attacker never says anything overtly alarming in any single turn; the harm emerges from the *trajectory* of the whole exchange, as the model is pressured to stay consistent with a context that was slowly and deliberately shaped. Researchers now explicitly reframe red-teaming itself as a *dynamic, multi-turn, trajectory-based process* rather than a series of one-step tests, precisely because single-turn testing misses where the real vulnerabilities live.[12]

The takeaway is stark: testing that only fires single prompts validates the front door while the actual entry point goes untried. Effective testing has to be conversational and escalating, attempting the slow multi-turn manipulations that work, against the whole deployed system with its tools and retrieval—and tools limited to single-turn probes leave most of the real risk untested.[11] This is why, as the next part shows, red-teaming can't be scanned away or compressed into a pre-launch check: the attacks that matter take conversational depth and creativity to find.

PART THREE: MAKING IT A PRACTICE, NOT AN EVENT

Everything so far points to one conclusion: red-teaming AI has to be a *sustained practice,* not a one-time event—continuous because the target changes, conversational because the attacks are multi-turn, and structured because the stakes and the regulators demand rigor. Three elements turn that conclusion into an operating model.

A structured methodology, treated as gates. The discipline has matured to the point of a shared methodology. A six-phase engagement structure has crystallized across the major AI labs and the OWASP Gen AI Red Teaming Guide—beginning with *scope* (define the system under test, including its system prompt, tools, and data sources; the deployment context; and the harm categories in and out of scope), and proceeding through reconnaissance, attack execution, and documentation of findings.[13] The crucial discipline, in the practitioners' own framing, is to treat the phases as *gates, not stages*: you don't move on until the previous phase is documented.[13] And the deliverable that matters is evidence—a documented, severity-ranked list of failure modes, mapped to the reference frameworks, that you can hand to leadership, an auditor, or a regulator. Scoping *out* is as important as scoping in: a red-team without clear boundaries is both incomplete and dangerous.

Automated scanning plus manual expertise — both, not either. Modern red-teaming combines two modes, and the combination is the point. *Automated* tools provide broad coverage and fast, repeatable feedback—they can run large libraries of known attack techniques and transforms against your system continuously, which is exactly what you need to re-test after every change.[14] *Manual* expert testing provides what automation can't: the creative, novel, domain-specific attack chains and the patient multi-turn pressure that find the failures no scanner has a signature for yet.[5] The GPT-5-style break—a creative narrative manipulation—is the kind of thing humans find and scanners later encode. The honest framing: automated tools speed up, streamline, and scale the process, but they don't replace human red-teamers; a red team that is *only* automated will keep finding yesterday's attacks while missing tomorrow's.[9] The emerging frontier of *autonomous, AI-driven red-teaming agents* is real and advancing fast—but it extends this logic rather than overturning it: it scales the automated half further, while human creativity remains, for now, the primary source of genuinely new attacks (and, recursively, those red-teaming agents are themselves high-stakes AI systems, per Chapter 9's warning).

Continuous, because the result decays. The final and defining element: red-teaming must be *ongoing*. The GPT-5 lesson was that a model fresh from the most rigorous pre-launch testing fell in a day—so testing tied only to launch is testing tied to the one moment the result is least durable. Re-test on every meaningful change to the system (a model update, a prompt change, a new tool connection) *and* on a regular cadence regardless of changes, because the *attacks* evolve even when your system doesn't. This is the same continuous-loop logic from the governance and monitoring chapters, now applied to adversarial testing: not a gate you pass once, but a loop you run for as long as the system lives. A red-team report with a date on it is a perishable good, and the date is when it started spoiling.

The synthesis. Put the three together and "ongoing practice" stops being a slogan and becomes an operating model: a structured, gated methodology, run as a combination of continuous automated scanning and periodic deep manual testing, repeated on every change and on a steady cadence, producing a living record of your system's failure modes mapped to the frameworks. That record is what feeds the defenses from Chapter 7, the monitoring from Chapter 9, and the incident planning of the chapter to come. Red-teaming isn't the thing you do to prove your AI is safe. It's the thing you do, forever, because it never permanently is.

THE LEADERSHIP LENS

Red-teaming is technical work, but whether it happens as a real practice or a hollow box-check is a leadership decision—because the difference is about budget, cadence, and how you respond to bad news. Four responsibilities.

Fund red-teaming as a standing capability, not a one-time audit. This is the central leadership shift, and it runs against budget instinct. The natural impulse is to treat red-teaming like a pre-launch security review: pay for it once, get the report, check the box. The opening lesson makes that posture untenable—a result is true on the day you get it and decaying after. So fund red-teaming the way you fund monitoring or any other ongoing operational capability: as a recurring line item with a cadence, not a project with an end date. The right question isn't "have we red-teamed our AI?" but "how recently, and how regularly?"—because an organization that tested once at launch and never again has an old snapshot, not a security practice.

Expect failure modes, not a clean bill of health — and react well to them. Red-teaming produces a list of failure modes rather than a pass, so be ready for the report to say "here are the ways your AI can be broken." Every honest report will. The failure mode to avoid here is *punishing the messenger*: if delivering bad red-team findings is career-risky, your teams will quietly scope the testing to find less, and you'll get the clean report you wanted and the false security that comes with it. The leadership posture that makes red-teaming actually work is to treat a rich list of discovered failures as the *success* of the exercise, not its failure—and then to make deliberate risk-appetite decisions (Chapter 4) about which failures to fix and which to accept. The red team's job is to find the failures; yours is to decide what to do about them, not to wish they hadn't been found.

Know that it's increasingly not optional. The regulatory and commercial ground is shifting under this. Adversarial testing is moving from best practice toward expectation: regulatory frameworks increasingly reference it, procurement teams in regulated sectors are already asking for red-team reports as a condition of contract, and providers of the most capable general-purpose AI models now face an explicit legal requirement to conduct and document adversarial testing.[15] For a leader, this reframes the investment: red-teaming is becoming part of what it takes to sell into regulated markets and satisfy enterprise customers, not just part of being secure. The documented, framework-mapped evidence from a proper red-team is increasingly an asset you'll be asked to produce—which means the structured methodology isn't bureaucratic overhead, it's the thing that generates the proof your buyers and regulators will demand.

Right-size the effort to the stakes. You will not red-team every AI system with equal intensity, and you shouldn't. The depth, frequency, and rigor of red-teaming should track Chapter 6's dials: the high-stakes systems—the ones making consequential decisions, touching sensitive data, or (per Chapter 9) running your security operations—warrant deep, frequent, expert red-teaming; the low-stakes internal tools warrant lighter, mostly-automated checks. The leadership skill is directing the scarce, expensive resource of expert red-teaming where the consequences justify it, rather than spreading it uniformly or, worse, lavishing it on the impressive-but-low-stakes system while the genuinely dangerous one goes lightly tested.

The one question to ask your team this week: *"When did we last try to break our most important AI system—not scan it, actually attempt the multi-turn attacks that work—and when are we doing it again?"* If the answer is "at launch" or "we ran a scan once," you have a snapshot, not a practice. And if the answer to "again" is "no plan," you've found the gap: red-teaming was treated as an event—a decision you can fix this quarter, by funding the cadence and owning which failures you accept.

THE EXECUTION LENS

For the implementer, red-teaming AI means running a structured, repeatable adversarial practice against your real deployed systems—and closing the loop so what you find actually changes your defenses. The work breaks into running the methodology, combining the two testing modes, testing the way attacks actually happen, and feeding the findings back. As always, anchor it to the recognized frameworks so your output is evidence, not just notes.

Run the six-phase methodology, and treat the phases as gates. Adopt the engagement structure that has standardized across the major labs and the OWASP Gen AI Red Teaming Guide, and don't advance until each phase is documented.[13] The phase that teams most often shortchange is the first—*scope*—and it's the one that determines whether the exercise is worth anything:

- Define the **system under test** as the *whole deployed application*: the model, its system prompt, its retrieval pipeline, its connected tools, and its guardrails—not just the model behind an API key (Part One's whole-system point, operationalized).[7]
- Define the **harm categories in scope** for this system, drawn from the frameworks and your system's actual stakes (Chapter 6's dials)—and define what's *out* of scope, which matters as much as what's in.[13]
- Capture the **deployment context**: who uses it, what it can access, what it can do.

Everything downstream depends on this scoping being honest and complete; a red team scoped to test only the model in isolation will produce a reassuring report about a system you don't actually run.

Combine automated scanning with manual expert testing. Build the practice on both modes, because each covers the other's gap:

- Use **automated red-teaming tools** to run broad libraries of known attack techniques and transforms against your system continuously—this is your fast, repeatable, re-runnable coverage, and it's what makes per-change re-testing feasible.[14] Mature tooling maps findings automatically to OWASP LLM Top 10, MITRE ATLAS, and NIST AI RMF, and produces severity-scored, auditor-ready reports rather than raw output.[11]
- Layer **manual expert testing** on top for the creative, novel, domain-specific attacks and the patient multi-turn manipulation that no scanner has a signature for yet.[5] This is where genuinely new failure modes get found—and where you should concentrate your scarce human expertise (on the high-stakes systems from the dials).
- If you adopt **autonomous/AI-driven red-teaming agents** at the frontier of this space, treat them as scaling the automated half—and remember Chapter 9's recursion: they're high-stakes AI systems themselves, so secure and monitor them accordingly.

Test the way attacks actually happen — multi-turn and agentic. This is the technical heart, and the place most testing falls short. Single-turn probes leave most real risk untested,[11] so build your testing to attempt:

- **Multi-turn attack chains** — crescendo escalations, conversation hijacking, narrative/roleplay framing, progressive jailbreaks—that start innocuous and ratchet up across a conversation, because that's how the attacks that work actually work.[11] Choose tooling and design tests that carry conversational state, not isolated prompt-response pairs.

- **Indirect and context-poisoning attacks** — injection delivered through retrieved documents or tool outputs, not just direct user input (connecting to the RAG / vector weaknesses from Chapter 7).[10]
- **Agentic exploits**, for any system with tools or autonomy—unauthorized tool calls, indirect injection via tool outputs, and excessive agency—testing what a manipulated agent could actually *do*, not just what it could say.[10]

Map findings to frameworks and produce evidence. Every finding should be recorded as a severity-ranked failure mode mapped to OWASP / ATLAS / NIST, in an exportable, auditor-ready form.[11] This is what turns red-teaming from an engineering activity into the documented evidence the Leadership Lens said buyers and regulators increasingly demand—and it's the artifact that satisfies the governance-and-evidence thesis from Chapter 3 (implement once, satisfy the framework, the standard, and the law together).

Close the loop — findings must change something. Red-teaming that produces a report nobody acts on is theater. The findings have to feed back into the rest of the system you've built across Phase II:

- Confirmed failure modes drive new or strengthened **Chapter 7 defenses** (guardrails, input / output handling, least privilege).
- Attack patterns the red team found become **Chapter 9 detections** — if your red team can execute a multi-turn jailbreak, your SOC should be able to *see* one; feed the signatures into monitoring.
- Failures leadership chooses not to fully fix become documented, accepted entries in the **Chapter 4 risk register**, with their residual risk owned.

Read the practice as a whole and its real shape appears: red-teaming isn't a checkpoint AI passes before deployment; it's the *adver-*

sarial half of a continuous loop that also contains your defenses (Ch. 7), your monitoring (Ch. 9), and your risk decisions (Ch. 4). You attack, you find failures, you harden and detect and document, the system or the attacks change, you attack again. The output isn't a pass—it's a perpetually-updating map of how your system fails and what you've done about each way. Build it as a loop wired into the rest of your machinery, and "ongoing practice" becomes something your pipeline does, not something you remember to schedule.

The one move to make this week: take your single highest-stakes AI system and run one *multi-turn* attack attempt against the whole deployed application—not a single bad prompt, but a short escalating conversation that tries to talk it into a failure, against the real system with its tools and retrieval in place. Whether it succeeds or resists, document it as your first framework-mapped failure-mode entry. That one exercise proves the methodology, exposes whether your monitoring even noticed, and seeds the living record. One system, one real attack, written down.

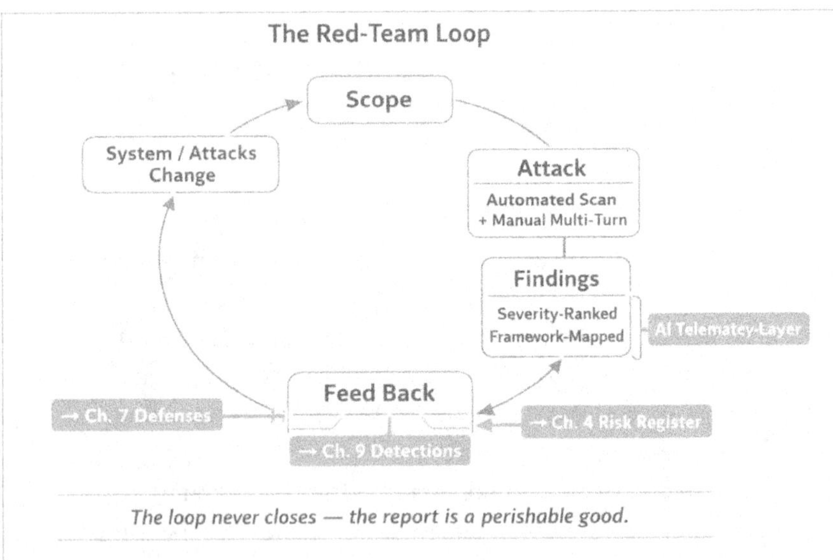

Figure 10.1 — The Red-Team Loop. *Red-teaming is a continuous adversarial cycle, not a one-time gate: scope the target, launch automated and manual attacks, rank findings by severity and framework, feed them back into defenses, detections, and risk registers—then repeat. As systems and threats evolve, the loop never closes.*

BRINGING IT TOGETHER

We opened with a frontier model—among the most rigorously tested ever shipped—broken by outside red teams within twenty-four hours, not by brute force but by a patient, multi-turn story that never said anything overtly alarming. If the most resourced lab in the world couldn't ship something un-break-able, then "we tested it and it passed" is a snapshot already going stale.

That single event defines the discipline. Red-teaming AI isn't penetration testing: the target is non-deterministic, the output is a list of failure modes rather than a pass, the attack surface is behavior and language, and you test the whole deployed application—tools and retrieval included—not just the model. You anchor to the established threat maps (OWASP, ATLAS, NIST), you test the way attacks actually work (multi-turn and escalating, against the real system), and you run it as a continuous practice rather than an event, because the result decays from the moment you get it. Red-teaming is the adversarial half of a loop that also holds your defenses, monitoring, and risk decisions: you attack, find failures, harden and detect and document—and then attack again.

The two efforts converge here. The leader funds the cadence as a standing capability and protects the honesty that lets a rich list of failures count as success, not embarrassment. The implementer runs one real multi-turn attack against the highest-stakes deployed system, documents it as the first framework-mapped failure-mode entry, and wires the practice into the loop: findings into defenses, attack patterns into detections, accepted failures into the risk register. Together they turn red-teaming from a box you check into a loop you run. You stop asking "is our AI safe?"—a question with no durable answer—and start maintaining a living, honest map of how your system fails and what you've done about each failure. That map, never finished, is what security looks like for a system that behaves differently every time.

Coming next — Across the last three chapters we've built the proactive and watchful halves of AI security: securing the pipeline (7), the supply chain (8), monitoring in production (9), and hunting our own weaknesses (10). But every honest page of this book has admitted the same thing—some attacks aren't fully preventable, some failures can't be eliminated, and a determined adversary or an unlucky drift will eventually get through. When that happens, what you do in the first hours determines whether it's an incident or a catastrophe. In Chapter 11 we turn to incident response for AI: how responding to an AI failure differs from responding to a traditional breach, and how to build a plan for the day your defenses don't hold. Red-teaming finds the failures you can fix. Incident response is for the ones that reach production anyway.

CHAPTER 10 IN REVIEW

The core idea: Red-teaming AI isn't a pre-launch test you pass—it's an ongoing practice, because both your AI and the attacks against it keep changing. The test is never finished.

The wake-up call: A rigorously tested frontier model, jailbroken by outside red teams within 24 hours—via a multi-turn storytelling attack, not brute force. The pattern recurs across releases: resistant at launch, broken shortly after.

Why it's its own discipline (not pen testing):

- Non-deterministic target—one failed attempt ≠ safe; testing is probabilistic.
- Output is a list of failure modes, not pass / fail—feeds risk appetite (Ch. 4).
- Attack surface is behavior and language, not code—different skills and tools.
- Test the whole deployed application, not just the model (Ch. 7).

What you test for / how attacks work:

- Anchor to OWASP LLM Top 10, MITRE ATLAS, NIST: jailbreaks, prompt injection, leakage, harmful content, agentic exploits.
- Real attacks are multi-turn, not single-prompt. Single-turn testing tests almost nothing.

Making it a practice, not an event:

- Six-phase methodology, treated as gates not stages, producing framework-mapped evidence.
- Automated scanning plus manual expert testing—both, not either.
- Continuous: re-test on every change and on a cadence; the result decays.

For the leader: Fund it as a standing cadenced capability; expect failure modes and never punish the messenger; it's increasingly not optional; right-size depth to stakes (Ch. 6).

For the implementer: Run the six phases, scope the whole application, combine both modes, test multi-turn and agentic attacks, map to frameworks, close the loop into defenses (7), detections (9), and the risk register (4).

The two actions:

- *Strategic (leader):* Fund the cadence and protect the honesty of findings.
- *Tactical (implementer):* Run one real multi-turn attack on your top system; document it as the first loop entry.

The throughline: The test is never finished. A red-team report is a perishable good—the date on it is when it started spoiling.

CHAPTER 11
BEYOND THE BREACH: AI-SPECIFIC INCIDENT RESPONSE

From Boardroom to Build: A Blueprint for AI Governance, Risk, and Technical Security

(Phase II — The Execution Core)

OPENING

Picture two failures, side by side.

In the first, an attacker breaches a database server. It's bad, but it has a shape your security team knows. The compromised server sits there, the stolen data sits there, the damage is largely done and largely static. You contain the server, you image the disk, you investigate at the pace of a careful investigation, you notify who needs notifying. The clock matters, but it ticks in hours and days. The breach is an *event*: it happened, and now you respond to a thing that has happened.

In the second, an AI system that approves transactions is manipulated—or simply drifts—into making wrong decisions. It does not sit there. It runs. In the time it takes an analyst to read the first alert, it has approved a thousand transactions it should have denied. By the time someone reaches for the incident response plan, it's tens of thousands. The failure isn't a static thing that happened; it's a *firehose that is still happening,* spraying bad decisions into the world at machine speed while the humans responding to it move at human speed. A single manipulated prompt can, in the worst case, set off thousands of bad outcomes before a human can intervene.[1] The breach was an event. This is a flood with the tap still open.

That difference—between responding to something that *happened* and stopping something that is *still happening, fast*—is the heart of AI incident response, and it's why your existing incident response plan, however good, is not enough on its own. The traditional plan was built around a model of failure as a discrete event you investigate and remediate. AI introduces failures that compound at a speed and in forms your plan never anticipated, and the first casualty is the assumption that you have time to think before you act.

Here is the honest framing this chapter is built on, and it's the same one that has run through every technical chapter: you have done everything right—secured the pipeline, verified the supply chain, monitored production, red-teamed relentlessly—and *something still got through.* It always eventually does, because (as Chapter 7 admitted) some attacks aren't fully preventable and some failures can't be eliminated. Incident response is the discipline for that day. It's not an admission of failure; it's the recognition that prevention is never perfect, and what you do in the first minutes and hours determines whether a failure stays an incident or becomes a catastrophe.

The good news, and the organizing idea of this chapter, is that you are not starting over. The incident response lifecycle you may already know—the one codified in standards like NIST's incident-handling guidance: prepare, detect, contain, eradicate, recover—is still the right backbone, and the maturing AI incident-response frameworks all build directly on it rather than replacing it.[2] What changes is *how each phase works* when the thing failing is an AI system that fails at machine speed, in new ways, leaving new and fast-vanishing evidence. So this chapter does three things: it maps honestly what's the same and what's genuinely new about AI incidents, it walks the lifecycle you know and shows the three things that change at every phase, and it shows how to build the plan *before* the incident—because the one thing you cannot do at machine speed is write the playbook while the tap is open.

PART ONE: WHAT'S THE SAME, AND WHAT'S GENUINELY NEW

Before redesigning anything, get the honest map of where your existing incident response already works and where it has no answer at all—because the most expensive mistake here is assuming your familiar playbook covers AI incidents when part of it does and part of it doesn't.

What's the same: AI incidents that look like traditional incidents. A large share of "AI incidents" are, at their core, traditional security incidents that happen to involve an AI system. If an attacker compromises the infrastructure your model runs on, escalates privileges in your AI platform, or exfiltrates data through a conventional path, your existing incident response largely applies: the indicators look familiar, and the containment paths resemble the ones you already use.[3] This is genuinely reassuring, and worth stating plainly: you are not throwing away your IR capability. For a meaningful category of AI incidents, your existing runbook, lightly extended, is the right tool. An organization that already does incident response well has a real head start.

What's genuinely new: reasoning compromise. But there is a category of AI incident with *no traditional equivalent,* and it's the one that should reshape your thinking. Call it **reasoning compromise**: an attack—or a failure—that lives not in the infrastructure or the access logs, but in the model's own logic, its prompts, and the context it was fed. The defining example: an incident whose indicators of compromise are *prompts and retrieved documents,* and whose "patient zero" is a poisoned context source rather than a breached server.[4] There is no equivalent in a traditional incident-response playbook for this, because traditional IR was built to investigate systems that fail deterministically, leaving artifacts in logs and disk images—not systems that were talked into failing through a slow, individually-innocent conversation, or that absorbed a corruption months ago that only now expresses itself.

Reasoning compromise breaks traditional IR in a specific way worth understanding: the investigation can't just ask "who got in and what did they touch." It has to ask "what was this model *thinking,* what did it *retrieve,* what was it *told,* and why did it *decide* what it decided"—questions traditional forensics has no tools for and traditional responders have no training for. The patient zero might be a document poisoned weeks ago (Chapter 8), a multi-turn manipulation that left no single alarming log line (Chapter 10), or a drift that crossed a threshold no one was watching (Chapter 9). The cause lives in the model's behavior and inputs, which is exactly the layer Chapter 9 showed the traditional SOC is blind to.

The honest consequence: extend, but don't assume coverage. Put the two together and the operating principle is clear. *Extend your existing incident response, which genuinely covers the traditional-shaped AI incidents; a capability you should build on, not discard.* But *do not assume* that coverage extends to reasoning compromise, because it doesn't: that category needs new forensics, new investigation methods, and new responder skills your current plan simply doesn't contain. The dangerous organization isn't the one with no AI incident plan; it's the one that believes its traditional plan already handles AI, walks confidently into a reasoning-compromise incident, and discovers mid-crisis that its forensics capture nothing relevant, its investigators don't know what questions to ask, and its containment options don't fit. The whole rest of this chapter is about closing that specific gap—the one between the IR you have and the AI incidents it can't yet handle.

PART TWO: THE THREE THINGS THAT CHANGE AT EVERY PHASE

Take the incident response lifecycle you know—detect, contain, eradicate, recover—and run an AI incident through it. The phases stay the same; what changes is three properties that bend every phase out of its traditional shape. Understand these three and you can adapt any IR process to AI; miss them and your familiar lifecycle quietly fails at machine speed.

One — Speed of harm changes containment from deliberate to immediate. In a traditional incident, containment can be careful because the damage is largely static—the breached server isn't getting more breached while you think. In an AI incident, the system is often *still producing harm* while you respond, at machine speed, which inverts the timing: containment timing is governed not by the type of incident but by the *speed of harm and its reversibility*.[5] A slow, reversible failure permits a deliberate response; a fast, irreversible one (the transaction-approver from the opening) demands you stop the harm *now*, before you fully understand it. The practical consequence runs through the whole lifecycle: detection has to be fast enough to matter (a detection that fires after ten thousand bad decisions is a post-mortem, not a defense), and containment increasingly has to be *automated or pre-authorized*, because a human reading an alert and convening a call cannot keep pace with a model making thousands of decisions a second. The hardest shift for a traditional responder is accepting that for fast-harm AI incidents, *you contain before you finish investigating*—the opposite of the careful traditional instinct.

Two — The evidence is new, and it decays fast, so you capture before you contain. Traditional forensics images a disk and pulls logs. AI forensics has to preserve a different and more fragile set of artifacts: the *prompt logs, the model state, the retrieval context, and the tool-call history*: the record of what the model was asked, what it retrieved, what it decided, and what it did.[6] Two things make this hard. First, these artifacts are exactly what a reasoning-compromise investigation needs and what traditional capture ignores. Second (and this is the trap that ruins AI investigations) *the standard containment move destroys the evidence.* "Kill the pod, image the disk" loses everything that lived in the running model's volatile state the moment the pod dies.[7] So the AI-specific discipline reverses the reflex: you must **capture the forensic artifacts before, or as part of, containment**, not after—because waiting until after remediation means the evidence has already decayed through log rotation, session expiry, and model-state changes, destroying the forensic trail.[8] This is the single most important operational habit in the chapter: the instinct to "shut it down" must be paired with "but capture the model's state and context first," or you contain the incident and lose all ability to understand it.

Three — There are new containment levers, but the threat hides in the chain. AI gives you a richer set of containment options than a traditional incident, and choosing among them is a real skill: *model rollback* (revert to a known-good prior version), *traffic reduction*, *feature flags* (disable the AI feature while keeping the app running), *circuit breakers*, and at the extreme, *full shutdown* or a kill switch.[9] The guiding principle is to use the *least disruptive intervention that stops the measurable harm*: a targeted output filter if that suffices, a full kill switch only if it doesn't. But there's a detection problem underneath the containment choice, and it's the subtlest point in the chapter: agentic AI incidents express themselves as *chains*, where each individual link—a prompt, a tool selection, an API call, an outbound connection—is individually authorized and legitimate, and *only the chain as a whole is suspicious.*[10] Per-event detection, which fires on a single bad syscall or connection, sees the links but never the chain. So containing an agentic incident requires detection that can recognize a suspicious *sequence* of individually-permitted actions—which is a fundamentally different capability than watching for a single forbidden event, and one more reason the traditional SOC (Chapter 9) struggles with AI.

What unites all three. Notice what unites them: traditional IR assumes a failure that is *static, leaves durable evidence, and announces itself as a discrete bad event.* AI inverts all three: the failure is *live and fast, leaves fragile and unfamiliar evidence, and hides inside sequences of permitted actions.* Adapting your lifecycle isn't about new phase names; it's about re-engineering each existing phase around those three inversions: faster and more automated containment, evidence capture that precedes containment, and chain-aware detection feeding a graduated set of containment levers.

PART THREE: BUILD THE PLAN BEFORE YOU NEED IT

The one thing you cannot do at machine speed is write the playbook while the tap is open. Everything in Part Two only works if it was decided in advance—which makes *preparation*, the first phase of the lifecycle, the phase that matters most for AI. Four things to build before the incident.

Pre-built playbooks for the AI incident archetypes. The maturing frameworks converge on a recurring set of AI incident types, each needing its own pre-written containment, eradication, and recovery steps: *prompt injection, jailbreak, data exfiltration, model failure/drift, harmful or biased output,* and "reasoning compromise."[11] Each archetype has different right answers—a jailbreak may call for updating output filters and considering model rollback; a data-exfiltration incident triggers the notification clock; a reasoning compromise demands tracing back to a poisoned context source. Pre-writing these as decision trees, mapped to the recognized frameworks (NIST's incident-handling guidance extended with NIST AI 600-1, MITRE ATLAS, and OWASP LLM Top 10), means that when an incident hits at machine speed, your responders are *executing a plan,* not *inventing one.*[12] The peer-reviewed frameworks exist precisely because the standards tell you the "what" and "why" but teams kept lacking the operational "how" in the moment.[13]

The notification clock — know it before it's running. AI incidents increasingly carry regulatory reporting obligations with hard deadlines, and the clock starts whether or not you're ready. Data-exfiltration incidents can trigger data-protection breach-notification duties on tight timelines, and serious-incident reporting obligations under AI-specific regulation are emerging on top of that.[14] The operational point: you must know, *before* an incident, which regulators you'd owe notice to, on what clock, for which incident types—because discovering your notification obligations during the incident, while the harm is still compounding, is how organizations miss legally mandated deadlines. (The detailed regulatory map is Chapter 15's job; here it's enough that the IR plan must encode the notification triggers and timelines as part of the playbook.)

AI-specific roles and the human chain. Traditional IR has defined roles; AI IR needs them extended. Someone must own the decision to pull a containment lever (and be pre-authorized to do it at machine speed); someone must be able to perform the AI-specific forensic capture; someone must read the model-behavior evidence; and the cross-functional chain from Chapter 5—security, the model owner, legal, communications—must be pre-wired, because an AI incident is exactly the cross-boundary event that falls into the ownership gap if the seams weren't built in advance.

Tabletop exercises and blameless learning — closing the loop. A plan never tested against a realistic scenario is a document, not a capability. Run tabletop exercises against each incident archetype—simulating a prompt injection, a data exfiltration, a reasoning compromise—to find the gaps while it's safe to find them.[15] And when real incidents happen, run *blameless* post-incident reviews: the goal is to improve the system, not to find someone to punish—the same culture point from the red-teaming chapter, for the same reason (punishment drives the truth into hiding). Critically, the post-incident review closes the loop with the rest of the book: a real incident's root cause becomes a new red-team scenario (Chapter 10), a new detection (Chapter 9), a hardened defense (Chapter 7), and an updated risk-register entry (Chapter 4). The incident you survive should make the next one less likely—that's what turns incident response from damage control into the final feedback loop of the whole system.

The synthesis. Build the plan before you need it, and the three inversions from Part Two become survivable: pre-authorized automated containment handles the speed, pre-built forensic capture preserves the evidence, archetype playbooks and pre-wired roles let responders execute instead of improvise, and the notification clock is one you start ready for. Incident response is the discipline that assumes prevention failed—and the organizations that do it well are the ones that did the work on a quiet day, so that on the loud day they were executing a plan instead of writing one in the dark.

THE LEADERSHIP LENS

Incident response is where leadership's earlier choices either pay off or come due—because the decisions that determine how an AI incident goes are made on the quiet day, not the loud one. Four responsibilities, all about preparation and authority.

Authorize machine-speed containment before the incident, not during it. This is the leadership decision most likely to be fatal if left unmade. Part Two showed that fast-harm AI incidents demand containment before investigation finishes—but pulling a kill switch or rolling back a production model carries real business cost, and an engineer at 2 a.m. watching a model spray bad decisions will hesitate to take a drastic, expensive action they aren't authorized to take. That hesitation, at machine speed, is catastrophic. So decide in advance: under what conditions is someone pre-authorized to stop a production AI system without waiting for sign-off? Define the harm thresholds, name who holds the authority, and make clear that pulling the lever inside those bounds is the right call, not a career risk. An organization where containment requires assembling executives contains too slowly to matter.

Decide how much harm-speed you can tolerate — it's a risk-appetite decision. This connects straight back to Chapter 4. The speed at which an AI system can produce irreversible harm should shape how much autonomy you grant it in the first place. A system that can make thousands of consequential, hard-to-reverse decisions per second before any human can intervene is a system whose risk you must either accept deliberately or constrain by design—slowing it down, adding checkpoints, or limiting its reach so the blast radius of a fast failure stays survivable. This is the incident-response case for the least-privilege principle from Chapter 7: containment is easier when the thing being contained was never given the power to cause a catastrophe in seconds.

Know your notification clock before it starts. AI incidents carry regulatory reporting obligations on hard deadlines, and the clock runs whether or not you're prepared. A leader needs to know—before any incident—which regulators the organization owes notice to, on what timeline, for which incident types, so that during a real event the process executes rather than scrambles. Missing a mandated breach-notification deadline because you were figuring out the obligation mid-crisis turns a security incident into a compliance violation on top of it. Cheap to prepare, expensive to improvise.

Invest in preparation that's invisible until the bad day. Like the forensics capability in Chapter 8, the AI incident response plan is an investment whose value is zero until suddenly it's everything. Pre-built playbooks, tabletop exercises, pre-wired roles, automated containment—none of it shows up in a metric on a good quarter, which makes it perennially easy to defer. Fund it anyway: the entire return arrives compressed into the few hours of a real incident, when the gap between an organization that prepared and one that didn't is the gap between a contained problem and a headline. Prevention, as every prior chapter conceded, is never perfect—something eventually gets through. This is the plan you're guaranteed to need.

The one question to ask your team this week: *"If our most critical AI system started causing serious harm right now, who is authorized to stop it without asking permission, how fast could they, and would we preserve what we need to understand what happened?"* If stopping it requires a meeting, you're too slow. If stopping it means killing the system and losing the evidence, you'll contain the incident and never learn its cause. If the honest answer is "we've never decided," you've found the work—and the time to do it is now, on the quiet day, because the loud day doesn't leave time to think.

THE EXECUTION LENS

For the implementer, AI incident response means engineering each phase of the lifecycle around the three inversions from Part Two—and building it all *before* the incident, because none of it can be assembled at machine speed. The work breaks into forensic capture, graduated containment, chain-aware detection, archetype playbooks, and closing the loop. Anchor it, as always, to the recognized standards: extend the NIST incident-handling lifecycle with NIST AI 600-1, MITRE ATLAS, and OWASP LLM Top 10 so your playbooks map to frameworks an auditor recognizes.[12]

Build forensic capture that survives containment. This is the highest-priority engineering task in the chapter, because getting it wrong silently ruins every investigation. Instrument your AI systems to continuously capture the artifacts a reasoning-compromise investigation needs—*prompt logs, model state/version, retrieval context, and full tool-call history*—and persist them somewhere that "survives the act of containment."[6] The trap to engineer around: the standard "kill the pod, image the disk" reflex destroys volatile model state the instant the pod dies.[7] So design containment so that capture happens *first*: either a containment action that snapshots state before terminating, or (the more advanced pattern) a "soft quarantine" that severs the system's external reach while keeping it alive long enough to capture, rather than killing it outright.[7] Practically: log every AI interaction with enough fidelity to reconstruct *what the model was asked, what it retrieved, what it decided, and what it did*—and treat those logs with chain-of-custody rigor, because they're both your investigation and, increasingly, your regulatory evidence.

Build a graduated set of containment levers, and pre-decide when to use each. Don't have only an on/off switch. Engineer the full range and document, per incident archetype, which to reach for: *output filtering* (block the specific harmful pattern, least disruptive), *feature flags* (disable the AI feature, keep the app running), *traffic reduction*, *model rollback* (revert to a known-good prior version—which requires you to have *versioned* your models and kept tested rollback targets, a prerequisite to build now), *circuit breakers* (automatic cutoffs when a harm metric crosses a threshold), and *full shutdown/kill switch*.[9] The operating rule: the "least disruptive intervention that stops the measurable harm."[8] And for the fast-harm incidents, wire the most critical circuit breakers to fire *automatically* on a threshold, because a human in the loop can't match machine speed—pre-authorized automated containment (the leader's decision) becomes your engineered circuit breaker.

Build chain-aware detection, not just event detection. Agentic incidents hide in chains where every link is individually authorized and only the sequence is suspicious.[10] Per-event detection (fire on a single bad syscall or connection) structurally cannot see this. So your detection has to correlate *sequences* of individually-permitted actions on a single agent's identity: this prompt, then that tool selection, then that API call, then that outbound connection, as a chain. This is a direct extension of the Chapter 9 correlation work—joining behavioral events on agent identity to recognize a suspicious trajectory—and it's what makes containment of an agentic incident even possible, since you can't contain what you can't see as an incident.

Pre-build the archetype playbooks, mapped to frameworks. For each AI incident archetype—prompt injection, jailbreak, data exfiltration, model failure/drift, harmful output, reasoning compromise—write the decision tree in advance: detection signature, required forensic capture, the right containment lever(s), eradication steps (clean the poisoned data, retrain, patch, remove the backdoor, fix the bias source), recovery validation, and notification triggers.[11] Map each to its NIST/ATLAS/OWASP references so the playbook doubles as auditor-ready evidence. The eradication step deserves emphasis: *remediation is not restoration*—returning a model to its pre-incident state without fixing the root cause guarantees recurrence.[8] Eradicating a reasoning-compromise incident means tracing to and removing patient zero (the poisoned context source), not just restarting the system.

Close the loop — the incident is the system's best teacher. Wire the post-incident output back into the machinery you've built across Phase II, the same loop the whole technical core has been assembling:

- Root cause → a new **Chapter 10 red-team scenario** (now you test for exactly this).
- Attack chain → a new **Chapter 9 detection** (now your SOC sees it coming).
- Exploited weakness → a hardened **Chapter 7 defense**.
- Residual/accepted risk → an updated **Chapter 4 register entry**.

Run the post-incident review blamelessly, because the engineering goal is a better system and punishment drives the real causes into hiding.

Everything above converges on one claim: AI incident response isn't a separate discipline bolted onto the end; it's the point where the entire Phase II loop *closes.* The defenses (7), the supply-chain verification (8), the monitoring (9), and the red-teaming (10) are all attempts to prevent or catch failures—and incident response is what runs when one gets through anyway, *and feeds what it learns back into all four.* Build it this way and an incident stops being purely a loss: it becomes the most realistic red-team scenario you'll ever get, the most accurate detection signature, and the strongest case for the defense you should have had. The organizations that compound their security fastest are the ones whose incidents teach the rest of the system.

The one move to make this week: pick your highest-stakes AI system and verify one thing end to end—if you had to stop it right now, would you still have the prompt logs, model state, retrieval context, and tool-call history needed to understand what happened? Try it: trigger a controlled containment in a test environment and check what evidence survives. If the answer is "we'd lose most of it," you've found the gap that ruins investigations, and fixing it—capture before containment—is the highest-value IR work you can do. One system, one containment test, an honest look at what's left afterward.

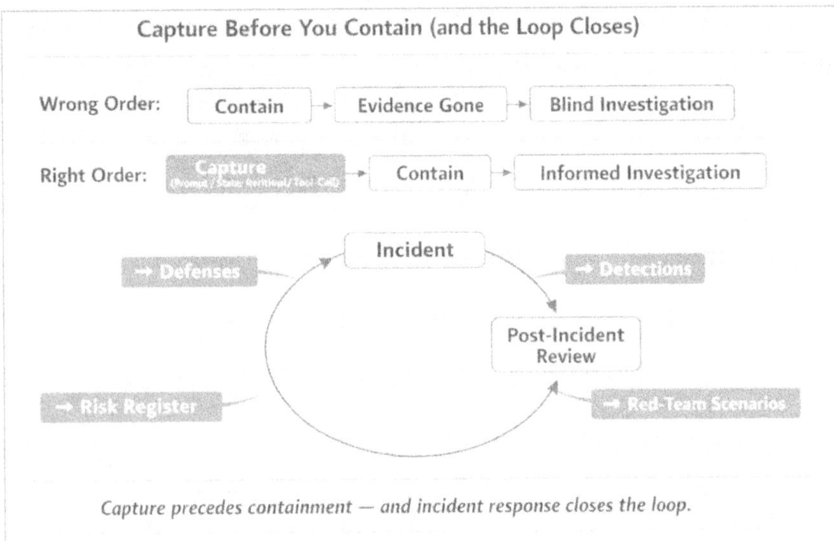

Figure 11.1 — ***Capture Before You Contain (and the Loop Closes)*** *Incident response begins with capturing volatile AI context—prompts, states, retrievals, and tool-calls—before containment erases evidence. Capturing first enables informed investigation rather than blind recovery. The post-incident review then feeds back into defenses, detections, red-team scenarios, and the risk register, closing the Phase II loop and transforming each event into system learning.*

BRINGING IT TOGETHER

We opened with two failures: the breached server that sits there, static, waiting to be investigated—and the AI system that doesn't sit there at all, spraying thousands of bad decisions into the world per second while responders reach for a playbook built for a slower kind of failure. That contrast is the chapter. AI fails as a flood with the tap still open, and the response has to run at the speed of the flood.

Meeting it starts with an honest map: much of AI incident response is your existing IR, lightly extended—a real head start—but one category, reasoning compromise, where the attack lives in prompts, context, and the model's own logic, has no traditional equivalent. Extend the playbook you have, but don't assume it covers the new thing. Then re-engineer each phase of the lifecycle around three inversions: harm at machine speed means containing before you finish investigating, often automatically; the evidence is new and fragile, so you capture the model's state and context *before* you contain, never after; and the threat hides in chains of individually-authorized actions, so detection has to see sequences, not events. None of that can be improvised while the tap is open, so the decisive work happens beforehand—archetype playbooks, a known notification clock, pre-authorized containment, pre-wired roles, and tabletops that find the gaps while it's safe. This is where the whole Phase II loop closes: the failure that got through, handled well, becomes the next red-team scenario, the next detection, the next hardened defense.

Your crucial initiative as a leader is to pre-authorize machine-speed containment—decide now who can stop a production AI system without asking permission, and under what harm thresholds—and fund the preparation whose value is invisible until the bad day. How fast a system can cause irreversible harm is itself a risk-appetite decision: the surest way to survive a machine-speed incident is to have limited, in advance, how much damage the machine could do that fast.

Your clear requirement as an implementer is to verify, by controlled test on your highest-stakes system, that containing it would still leave you the prompt logs, model state, retrieval context, and tool-call history needed to understand what happened. If containment would destroy the evidence, fix that first—capture before contain is the habit that makes every other part of the investigation possible.

This dual-pronged push prepares you for the day this book has been honest about from the beginning: the day prevention fails and something gets through. The leader ensures the organization can act at machine speed and survive the blast; the implementer ensures that when it acts, it preserves the truth and feeds it back into every defense. Incident response isn't the chapter where security failed. It's the chapter where a mature program proves it can take a hit, understand it, and come out harder to hit next time.

Coming next — Several times in this chapter, the worst incidents involved the same thing: *data.* Data exfiltrated through a model, sensitive training data extracted, regulated information leaking through an output, a breach-notification clock starting because personal data was exposed. Data is both the fuel that makes AI valuable and the thing whose exposure carries the heaviest consequences. In Chapter 12 we turn to privacy by design—protecting the data that flows into, through, and out of your AI systems, not as an afterthought bolted on at the end, but built into the architecture from the start. The incidents you most want to never have are usually, at their core, about data. This is how you protect it.

CHAPTER 11 IN REVIEW

The core idea: AI often fails at machine speed—a flood with the tap still open, not a static event. The traditional IR lifecycle is the right backbone; each phase gets re-engineered around how AI fails.

The wake-up call: A breached server sits there while you investigate; a manipulated or drifting AI system keeps producing harm while you respond—so you often can't think before you act.

What's the same, and what's genuinely new:

- **Same:** AI incidents that are really traditional incidents involving AI (infrastructure compromise, privilege escalation, conventional exfiltration)—your existing IR, lightly extended, applies. A real head start.
- **New:** *Reasoning compromise*—an attack living in prompts, retrieved context, and the model's logic, whose "patient zero" is a poisoned context source. No traditional playbook equivalent. Extend your IR, but don't assume it covers this.

The three things that change at every phase:

- **Speed of harm** → contain *before* you finish investigating, often automatically; containment timing is set by speed of harm and reversibility, not incident type.
- **New, fast-decaying evidence** → capture prompt logs, model state, retrieval context, and tool-call history *before* you contain; "kill the pod, image the disk" destroys it.
- **New levers + the chain problem** → graduated containment (filter → feature flag → rollback → circuit breaker → kill switch), but detection must see *chains* of individually-authorized actions, not single events.

Build the plan before you need it: pre-built archetype playbooks (prompt injection, jailbreak, exfiltration, model failure, harmful output, reasoning compromise) mapped to NIST/ATLAS/OWASP; a known regulatory notification clock; AI-specific and pre-wired cross-functional roles; tabletop exercises; and blameless post-incident reviews that close the loop.

For the leader (Leadership Lens):

- Pre-authorize machine-speed containment—who can stop a system without asking, under what thresholds.
- How fast a system can cause irreversible harm is a risk-appetite decision; limit the blast radius by design.
- Know your notification clock before it starts.
- Fund preparation whose value is invisible until the bad day —it's the plan you're guaranteed to need.

For the implementer (Execution Lens):

- Build forensic capture that survives containment—capture before contain (soft quarantine over "kill the pod").
- Build graduated containment levers; version models with tested rollback targets; automate critical circuit breakers.
- Build chain-aware detection (correlate sequences on agent identity), extending Chapter 9.

- Pre-build archetype playbooks mapped to frameworks; remember remediation is not restoration—remove patient zero.
- Close the loop: incident root cause → red-team scenario (10), detection (9), defense (7), risk entry (4).

The two actions from this chapter:

- *Strategic Move (leader):* Pre-authorize machine-speed containment and fund invisible-until-needed preparation.
- *Tactical Move (implementer):* Test whether containing your top system would preserve the evidence; fix capture-before-contain first.

The throughline to remember: AI fails at machine speed, leaving fragile evidence, hiding in chains—so contain fast, capture before you contain, and prepare before you need to. Incident response is where the Phase II loop closes: the failure you survive, handled well, becomes the next defense.

CHAPTER 12
PRIVACY BY DESIGN: PROTECTING THE DATA FUEL

From Boardroom to Build: A Blueprint for AI Governance, Risk, and Technical Security
(Phase II — The Execution Core)

OPENING

A customer sends your company a routine request: under their legal right to erasure, they want their personal data deleted. Your team does exactly what privacy law and good practice require. They find the customer's records in the production database and delete them. They purge the backups on schedule. They remove the data from the analytics warehouse and the data lake. By every traditional measure, the person's data is gone—scrubbed from every system designed to store it.

Except it isn't gone. Six months ago, that customer's data was part of the dataset used to fine-tune one of your models. The model didn't file the data in a row you can locate and delete; it *learned from it,* absorbing the patterns of that person's information into the billions of numerical weights that make up its parameters. The data isn't stored in the model the way a record is stored in a database—it's diffused into the model's very structure, mathematically entangled with everyone else's. You cannot open the model, find the customer's contribution, and delete it. And under the right conditions, a determined party might even be able to coax fragments of that "deleted" data back out of the model.

So you've honored the deletion request everywhere it's easy to honor, and quietly failed to honor it in the one place the data is hardest to remove. The person believes they're forgotten. Your databases agree. Your model does not.

This is the privacy problem that is genuinely unique to AI, and it's why protecting data in the age of AI is not the same job you've done before. Traditional privacy is built around a clear mental model: data lives in places—databases, files, backups—and you protect it by securing those places (encryption, access control) and, when required, deleting it from them. That model has an unspoken assumption baked in: that data *sits* somewhere you can point to. AI breaks that assumption. When you train or fine-tune a model on data, the data stops merely sitting in storage and starts being *absorbed into the model itself,* where your entire toolkit of traditional privacy controls—the encryption, the access lists, the deletion routines—simply doesn't reach. You can secure the database the data came from and still have the data effectively living on, unprotected and unforgettable, inside the model.

That single shift—*data isn't just in the database anymore, it's baked into the model*—reframes the whole privacy challenge, and it's the thread running through this chapter. It means privacy has to be designed into the AI system from the start, because the hardest privacy problems (a model that memorized something it shouldn't have, a "deletion" that can't actually delete) are nearly impossible to fix after the fact. It means new threats exist that have no equivalent for data at rest. And it means a new toolkit of privacy-engineering techniques, built specifically for the era when data becomes part of the model.

A boundary worth setting at the outset, because two related ideas often get tangled: this chapter is about *protecting the data*—its confidentiality, its exposure, its presence inside the model, the right to remove it. It is not about whether the model's *outputs* are fair or unbiased; that —bias, fairness, and discrimination—is a distinct problem with its own chapter (Chapter 16). Here, the concern is the data itself: the fuel that makes AI valuable, and the liability that makes it dangerous. This chapter covers why AI breaks the traditional privacy playbook, what it means to build privacy in by design rather than bolt it on, and the concrete engineering toolkit for protecting data that has become part of a model.

PART ONE: WHY AI BREAKS THE PRIVACY PLAYBOOK

To protect data in an AI system, you have to understand the threats that don't exist when data merely sits in storage—because these are the ones your existing privacy program isn't built to handle. All three stem from the same root: the data is now *in the model,* and a model is a leaky, queryable, un-deletable container in ways a database never was.

Training-data extraction: the model can leak what it learned. A model trained on sensitive data can, under the right prompting, regurgitate fragments of that data that were in its training set. This is the privacy face of the same memorization phenomenon that makes models useful: they learn patterns so well that they sometimes learn *specific examples,* and what a model has memorized, it can potentially be made to emit. The consequence is stark: a model trained on confidential or regulated data becomes a possible *exfiltration path for that data,* one that doesn't look like a breach. No database was accessed; the model simply said something it learned. Traditional data-loss prevention, watching for data leaving your systems, never imagined the data leaving through a model's helpful answer.

Membership inference: proving someone was in the training set. A subtler attack doesn't extract the data itself but determines *whether a particular person's data was used to train the model*—by analyzing how confidently the model behaves on that person's information. This sounds abstract until you consider the stakes: if a model was trained on, say, the records of patients with a specific diagnosis, then proving someone's data was in the training set reveals that they have the diagnosis. Membership itself is the sensitive fact. This is a privacy harm with no analog in traditional storage: nobody can "infer membership" in a database they can't see, but they can infer it from a model's observable behavior.

The data baked into the model: minimization and deletion become hard. The deepest problem is the one from the opening, and it undermines two pillars of traditional privacy practice. *Deletion* (the right to erasure) becomes genuinely difficult, because the data is diffused across the model's weights, not stored in a deletable location—removing it cleanly can require retraining the model, which is expensive and sometimes impractical. And *data minimization*—the principle of collecting and keeping only what you need—collides with the machine-learning instinct to hoard data, since more training data often means a better model. The regulatory world has a name for the remedy when data was used that shouldn't have been: algorithmic disgorgement. Since 2019 the US FTC has, in several cases, ordered companies to delete not just improperly-obtained data but the models trained on it.[1] The remedy exists precisely because regulators grasped the core problem of this chapter—once data is in the model, getting it out can mean destroying the model.

The common root, and what it demands. Notice that all three threats exist *because the data became part of the model*, and none is addressed by the controls that protect data at rest. Encrypting your database doesn't stop a model from emitting what it memorized; access controls on your data lake don't prevent membership inference; a deletion routine that purges records doesn't touch the weights. This is why AI privacy can't be a layer you add to the storage—it has to be designed into how the data is collected, how the model is trained, and how it's deployed, from the beginning. Which is the subject of Part Two.

PART TWO: PRIVACY BY DESIGN — BUILDING IT IN, NOT BOLTING IT ON

If the hardest privacy problems become nearly unfixable once the data is in the model, the conclusion is unavoidable: privacy has to be a design decision made *before* training, not a control added after deployment. This is the principle that gives the chapter its name, and it inverts the usual order of operations. The traditional pattern is to build the system and then secure it. With AI privacy, that pattern fails, because by the time the system is built, the data is already absorbed and the most important privacy decisions have already been made by default. Privacy by design means making them deliberately, up front.

Protect data across its whole lifecycle — including "inside the model." Traditional privacy thinks in terms of data at rest and data in transit. AI privacy adds a stage those frameworks never had: *data in the model.* So privacy controls have to span the full AI data lifecycle—**collect → train → deploy → delete**—with deliberate decisions at each stage:

- At **collection**, decide what data you actually need, because everything you collect is something you'll later have to protect, and everything you train on is something you may never fully be able to delete.
- At **training**, decide how to limit what the model absorbs and retains of individuals' data (the toolkit in Part Three).
- At **deployment**, control what the model can reveal—guarding against the extraction and inference attacks from Part One.
- At **deletion**, have a real answer for erasure that accounts for the data in the model, not just the data in the database.

The point of the lifecycle view is that each stage forecloses or preserves options at the next. A maximalist collection decision creates a deletion problem you can't solve later. Privacy by design is the discipline of making each stage's decision with the next stages in mind.

The cheapest data to protect is the data you never collected. The single most powerful privacy-by-design move is also the most counter-intuitive to the machine-learning mindset, which instinctively wants *more* data. It's **data minimization**: collecting and retaining only the data you genuinely need, and deliberately *not* ingesting the rest. This runs against the grain—more data often does make a better model—which is exactly why it has to be a conscious design decision rather than a default. But the logic is airtight: data you never collected can't be breached, can't be extracted from your model, can't be the subject of a deletion request you can't honor, and can't trigger algorithmic disgorgement. Every other technique in this chapter manages the risk of data you've taken on; minimization is the only one that prevents the risk from existing. Paired with **purpose limitation**—using data only for what it was collected for, not quietly repurposing yesterday's customer data as today's training set—minimization is privacy by design in its simplest and strongest form.

Build for deletion before you need it. Because erasure is the hardest problem once data is in the model, privacy by design means deciding *in advance* how you'll handle it—what data goes into training, how you'll track which individuals' data is in which model, and what your technical answer is when a deletion request arrives that implicates the weights. An organization that trains first and thinks about erasure later has, by definition, already built the problem it can't easily solve. The technical options for actually removing data from a model (machine unlearning chief among them) are Part Three's territory—but the *decision to design for deletion* belongs here, at the start, because it shapes everything downstream.

PART THREE: THE PRIVACY-ENGINEERING TOOLKIT

Privacy by design is the principle; these are the techniques that implement it. Each manages a specific privacy risk from Part One, and—importantly for both audiences—each comes with a real tradeoff. There is no free privacy here; every technique costs something in accuracy, performance, or complexity, and an honest treatment names the cost alongside the benefit.

Differential privacy: mathematical guarantees, at an accuracy cost. Differential privacy introduces carefully calibrated statistical noise into data or model training, so that the model learns general patterns while making it provably hard to determine whether any specific individual's data was used.[2] Its great strength is that it offers *formal mathematical guarantees* of privacy—not a hope, but a provable bound. Its cost is equally real: the noise that protects privacy also reduces accuracy, and tuning that balance is the central challenge of using it.[2] Differential privacy is the most direct defense against the membership-inference attack from Part One, and the technique to reach for when you need provable, not just plausible, privacy.

Federated learning: keep the raw data home, but mind the updates. In federated learning, the model is trained across many local devices or organizational silos, and only the *model updates* are shared back, never the raw data, so the data never leaves its local custody.[2] The canonical use case is exactly the one from Chapter 6's high-stakes sectors: hospitals collaboratively improving a diagnostic model without any of them sharing patient records.[2] But federated learning carries a crucial caveat that's easy to miss and important to state honestly: *the model updates themselves can leak information* about the local data, through membership-inference, property-inference, or model-inversion attacks.[3] Federated learning reduces the privacy risk of centralizing data but does not eliminate the privacy risk entirely, which is why, in practice, it's often *combined with differential privacy,* adding noise to the updates so that what's shared is protected too.[3] The lesson generalizes: these techniques are most powerful layered, and treating any one as a complete solution is a mistake.

Confidential computing: protecting data while it's in use. Confidential computing uses hardware-backed secure enclaves to compute on data while it stays protected even during processing—closing the gap that encryption-at-rest and in-transit leave open (data has to be decrypted to be used, and the enclave protects it even then).[2]

Automated PII/PHI discovery and de-identification: protecting data at the source. This one attacks the problem before training: at enterprise scale, finding sensitive data by hand is impossible, so NLP-based tooling automatically detects sensitive fields (names, identifiers, medical codes) and a de-identification pipeline redacts or replaces them before the data reaches the model.[2] This is data minimization made operational—you can't bake into the model what you stripped out before training.

. . .

Machine unlearning: the emerging answer to erasure, honestly not yet solved. Finally, the technique aimed squarely at the chapter's opening problem: *machine unlearning* attempts to make a model selectively "forget" specific data without the cost of retraining from scratch—adjusting the model to remove or minimize a particular individual's contribution while preserving its overall utility.[4] It's the most direct technical answer to the right-to-erasure collision, and it's a genuine and active frontier, especially when combined with federated learning to enable "forgetting responsibly."[5] But here the honesty this book has maintained matters most: machine unlearning is an *emerging, not fully solved* discipline. The methods are advancing quickly, but verifying that a model has *truly* forgotten—that no trace remains and no inference can recover it—remains genuinely hard, and approximate unlearning trades completeness for efficiency.[6] The realistic posture is the same one this book has taken throughout: this is a maturing capability that meaningfully helps, not a solved problem that makes the erasure issue disappear. The strongest privacy-by-design move remains the one from Part Two—be careful what you train on in the first place.

The synthesis. Read the toolkit together and two things stand out. First, the techniques layer: differential privacy strengthens federated learning, de-identification feeds minimization, no single tool is the whole answer. Second, every one of them is easier and more effective the *earlier* it's applied—which is privacy by design restated as engineering reality. You can add differential privacy, federated training, and de-identification at the start far more effectively than you can unlearn data at the end. The toolkit rewards the organization that decided to protect privacy before it trained, and punishes the one that hopes to retrofit it after.

THE LEADERSHIP LENS

Privacy by design is, for a leader, mostly a set of decisions about timing and restraint—choices that are cheap to make early and ruinously expensive to make late. Four responsibilities, and a question to take into your week.

Fund privacy at design time, because retrofitting is the expensive path. The central leadership lesson follows directly from the chapter: the privacy problems that are nearly impossible to fix after training are easy to prevent before it. A model trained without privacy controls on data you shouldn't have used is a model you may have to throw away —that's what algorithmic disgorgement means. So the leadership move is to fund privacy engineering as part of *building* AI systems, not as a remediation project after one goes wrong. This is counterintuitive precisely because design-time privacy work has no visible payoff—it prevents problems that, done right, never happen. Fund it anyway: the alternative isn't saving money, it's paying far more later, possibly with the model itself.

Treat data minimization as risk reduction, not a constraint on ambition. Your technical teams will often want more data, because more data tends to make better models, and that instinct isn't wrong, but it's incomplete, because it counts only the upside. The leadership job is to weigh the cost side the engineers may discount: every dataset you collect and train on is a liability you must protect, may have to delete, and might see extracted from your model. Reframing minimization as risk reduction—the cheapest data to protect is the data you never collected—turns it from a frustrating limit into a deliberate risk decision, and ties it straight to the risk appetite from Chapter 4. Sometimes the right call is to collect more and accept the risk; sometimes it's to collect less and sleep at night. That's a leadership judgment, not a default to be set by whoever wants the data.

Know that "delete my data" is a promise your AI may not be keeping. Many organizations believe they comply with the right to erasure because they delete from databases—and are quietly exposed because the data lives on in their models. A leader needs to know whether the organization's deletion promises are actually true once AI is in the picture, because the gap between "we deleted it" and "we deleted it everywhere including the model" is both a legal exposure and a trust exposure. This isn't a question to discover during a regulator's inquiry—it's one to ask now.

Frame privacy by design as an asset, not a tax. The internal case for design-time privacy is cost avoidance, but the external case is stronger: customers and regulators increasingly reward demonstrable privacy, and a model you can prove was trained with minimization and a real erasure capability is a market and compliance advantage competitors who retrofitted can't match. Funded early, privacy stops being only a risk you manage and becomes a claim you can make.

The one question to ask your team this week: *"If a customer asked us to delete all their data tomorrow, could we honestly say we removed it everywhere—including from any model we trained on it?"* If the answer is "yes, from our databases" with a pause before the word "model," you've found the gap between the privacy you promise and the privacy you deliver. And the fix starts upstream, with what you chose to train on in the first place.

THE EXECUTION LENS

For the implementer, privacy by design means wiring the toolkit into the AI data lifecycle—collect, train, deploy, delete—so that privacy is a property of the pipeline rather than a patch on top of it. The work is choosing the right technique for each risk, paying its tradeoff knowingly, and building the hard capability (deletion) before it's demanded. As always, this extends the Chapter 7 pipeline rather than standing beside it: privacy controls live at the same stages you already secure.

At collection and pre-training: minimize and de-identify before data ever reaches the model. The highest-leverage privacy engineering happens before training, because it prevents rather than mitigates:

- Build an **automated PII/PHI discovery and de-identification pipeline** — NLP-based detection of sensitive fields (names, identifiers, medical codes) feeding a redaction / replacement step—so sensitive data is stripped *before* it can be absorbed into the model.[2] Tools exist for this layer; the engineering work is wiring it into the data path as a mandatory gate, not an optional scan.
- Enforce **data minimization and purpose limitation as pipeline policy**—retention limits, feature selection, and provenance checks that keep ungoverned or unnecessary

data out of training. This connects to the Chapter 8 supply-chain gate: the same checkpoint that verifies imported data's provenance should enforce that you're only training on what you're permitted and intend to.

At training: apply differential privacy and federated learning where the stakes justify the tradeoff. These are the techniques that limit what the model absorbs of individuals' data:

- Use **differential privacy** (via mature libraries such as the differential-privacy extensions to common ML frameworks) when you need provable protection against membership inference—and budget for the accuracy cost explicitly, tuning the privacy-accuracy balance as a deliberate parameter, not an afterthought.[2]
- Use **federated learning** (via established frameworks) when data can't or shouldn't be centralized—the cross-organization, cross-silo case—but *combine it with differential privacy on the updates*, because the updates themselves leak via membership-, property-, and model-inversion attacks.[3] Treat "federated learning alone" as incomplete privacy, not finished privacy.
- Tie the intensity to Chapter 6's dials: the high-sensitivity-data systems (health, financial, biometric) warrant these heavier, costlier techniques; low-sensitivity systems may not need them at all. Don't pay the accuracy and complexity cost where the data doesn't justify it.

At deployment: defend against extraction and inference. The data baked into the model has to be protected at the inference boundary—which connects directly to Chapter 7's runtime defenses. Guard against training-data extraction through output filtering and monitoring for the regurgitation patterns, limit what the model can reveal, and watch (per Chapter 9) for the query patterns of extraction and membership-inference probing. The privacy threats from Part One are, at deployment, detections you wire into the monitoring you already built.

At deletion: build the erasure capability before it's demanded. This is the hard one, and the honest one:

- Maintain **data lineage** (the Chapter 7 capability, reused) so you can at least answer *which models were trained on a given individual's data*—you cannot honor an erasure request you can't trace.
- Evaluate **machine unlearning** for selective removal without full retraining, but implement it with clear eyes: it's an emerging capability, verifying true forgetting is hard, and approximate methods trade completeness for efficiency.[4,6] Treat it as a meaningful tool, not a guarantee.
- Keep **retraining-without-the-data** as the fallback for high-stakes erasure, and recognize that its cost is exactly why the minimization decision upstream mattered so much.

Privacy is a lifecycle property, layered and earliest-wins: privacy by design is implemented as controls at every stage of the data lifecycle, layered as Part Three described, with each control dramatically cheaper and more effective the earlier it sits. You de-identify and minimize at collection for almost free; you unlearn at deletion at great cost and uncertain completeness. The same data, the same risk—but the engineering effort to manage it grows by orders of magnitude as it moves down the pipeline and into the weights. Build privacy in at the front, and the back-end problems shrink; skip it at the front, and you inherit the chapter's opening: a deletion you can't perform on a model you can't easily fix.

The one move to make this week: take your highest-sensitivity AI system and trace one path end to end—pick a single category of sensitive data and answer, concretely, *where is it minimized or de-identified before training, what protects it during training, and could we remove it if legally required?* If the honest answer reveals that sensitive data flows into the model with no minimization and no removal path, you've found the chapter's core gap in your own system—and the fix, starting with a de-identification gate at collection, is the cheapest privacy work available. One data category, one traced path, one honest look at what protects it.

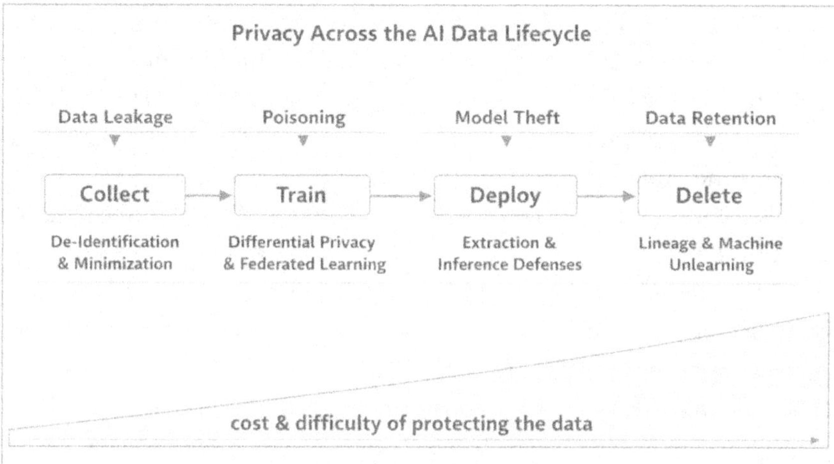

Figure 12.1 — Privacy Across the AI Data Lifecycle *Privacy is a lifecycle property: each stage introduces a distinct threat, and each demands its own technique—from de-identification and minimization at collection, to differential privacy and federated learning during training, to extraction and inference defenses at deployment, and finally lineage and machine unlearning at deletion. The widening cost-and-difficulty wedge illustrates that earlier interventions yield cheaper and more effective protection.*

BRINGING IT TOGETHER

We opened with a deletion request honored everywhere it was easy and quietly failed in the one place it was hard—the model that had learned from the data months before and couldn't simply un-learn it. Your databases agreed the person was forgotten; your model did not. That gap is the whole chapter: with AI, data isn't just in the storage you can secure and purge—it's baked into the model, where your traditional privacy controls were never designed to reach.

That shift drives everything. It creates threats with no analog in data at rest—a model that leaks what it memorized, an attacker who can prove someone's data was in the training set, a right to erasure that collides with weights you can't surgically edit. It means privacy has to be designed in across the whole data lifecycle—collect, train, deploy, delete—because the hardest problems are nearly unfixable after the fact, and the single strongest move is the most counterintuitive one: minimize, because the cheapest data to protect is the data you never collected. And it takes a real toolkit—each technique carrying an honest tradeoff, each more effective the earlier it's applied, most powerful layered together, and none yet able to fully solve erasure once data is in the weights. Through all of it runs one truth this book keeps returning to: forgetting is harder than never learning.

Your paramount responsibility as a leader is to fund privacy at design time, make minimization a deliberate risk decision tied to your Chapter 4 appetite, and verify that "we deleted it" is true once models are counted.

Your specialized objective as an implementer is to trace one category of sensitive data end to end through your highest-sensitivity system, and where it flows unprotected into the model, install the cheapest fix first—a de-identification and minimization gate at collection.

Locking these two pieces together shifts privacy from a promise you make at the database to a property you engineer into the model. The leader funds prevention over retrofit and makes minimization a conscious choice; the implementer builds privacy into every stage of the lifecycle, with an honest deletion capability. You stop discovering—during a regulator's inquiry or a customer's deletion request—that your privacy controls stopped at the database door. You protect the data where it actually lives now: inside the model.

Coming next — Everything in the last several chapters—the pipeline defenses, the supply-chain verification, the monitoring, the privacy engineering—has to actually run somewhere, and for most organizations that somewhere is the cloud. The major cloud providers offer powerful AI platforms and services that can implement much of what this book has described—but using them securely is its own discipline, with its own shared-responsibility traps and its own configuration pitfalls. In Chapter 13, we confront the challenge of scaling securely: how to aggressively leverage the AI powerhouses of the major cloud platforms without inheriting a catastrophic new class of exposure. With your foundational principles now firmly established, the critical execution question shifts: How do you run these models at massive enterprise scale when they are hosted on someone else's infrastructure?

CHAPTER 12 IN REVIEW

The core idea: With AI, the privacy problem moves from the database to the model—where traditional controls don't reach and the hardest problems become nearly unfixable after training. Protecting data therefore has to be designed into the AI system from the start, across the whole data lifecycle, because the hardest privacy problems are nearly unfixable once the data is in the weights. (This chapter is about protecting the data; fairness of outputs is Chapter 16.)

The wake-up call: A customer's right-to-erasure request is honored in every database and backup—but the data still lives on inside a model that trained on it months ago and can't simply forget. The deletion is real everywhere except the place it's hardest to perform.

Why AI breaks the privacy playbook (threats with no analog at rest):

- **Training-data extraction** — a model can regurgitate what it memorized, becoming an exfiltration path that looks nothing like a breach.
- **Membership inference** — proving a person's data was in the training set, where membership itself is the sensitive fact.
- **Data baked into the model** — deletion and minimization become genuinely hard; the remedy of last resort (algorithmic disgorgement) can mean destroying the model.

Privacy by design — build it in, not bolt it on: protect data across collect → train → deploy → delete, deciding each stage with the next in mind. The strongest move is data minimization (the cheapest data to protect is the data you never collected), paired with purpose limitation; and design for deletion before you need it.

The privacy-engineering toolkit (each with an honest tradeoff, strongest when layered):

- **Differential privacy** — controlled noise, formal mathematical guarantees, at an accuracy cost; the direct defense against membership inference.
- **Federated learning** — train locally, share only updates; but updates leak, so combine with differential privacy.
- **Confidential computing** — secure enclaves protect data even during processing.
- **Automated PII/PHI discovery & de-identification** — strip sensitive data before it reaches training; minimization made operational.
- **Machine unlearning** — the emerging answer to erasure; genuinely advancing but not solved (verifying true forgetting is hard). Forgetting is harder than never learning.

For the leader (Leadership Lens):

- Fund privacy at design time—retrofitting is the expensive path (and can cost you the model).
- Treat data minimization as risk reduction tied to risk appetite, not a constraint on ambition.
- Verify that "delete my data" is actually true once models are counted.
- Frame privacy by design as a market and regulatory asset, not a tax on innovation.

For the implementer (Execution Lens):

- Minimize and de-identify before data reaches the model (cheapest, highest-leverage).
- Apply differential privacy and federated learning (combined) where data sensitivity justifies the tradeoff; tie intensity to Chapter 6's dials.
- Defend against extraction/inference at deployment, wired into Chapter 9 monitoring.
- Maintain data lineage and build a real erasure capability (machine unlearning with clear eyes; retraining as fallback).

The two actions from this chapter:

- *Strategic Move (leader):* Fund design-time privacy, make minimization a deliberate risk decision, and verify deletion is real.
- *Tactical Move (implementer):* Trace one sensitive-data path end to end; install a de-identification / minimization gate at collection where it's missing.

The throughline to remember: The data ends up where your old controls can't reach. Design privacy in across the lifecycle, layer the techniques, and apply them as early as possible—because the cheapest data to protect is the data you never collected, and forgetting is always harder than never learning.

CHAPTER 13
SCALING SECURELY: LEVERAGING AWS, AZURE, AND GOOGLE AI SERVICES

From Boardroom to Build: A Blueprint for AI Governance, Risk, and Technical Security

(Phase II — The Execution Core)

OPENING

A team needs an AI capability, and the cloud makes it almost magically easy. In an afternoon, they spin up a model endpoint on one of the major cloud platforms—a few clicks, a few lines of configuration, and they have a powerful large language model serving requests through an API. It works. It's fast. They move on to the next thing.

What they didn't do—because the platform didn't force them to, and because it was working without it—was put authentication in front of that endpoint. Or rate limiting. The inference API is just *open*, reachable by anyone who finds the address. And open inference endpoints are not a hypothetical footnote; they're a recurring, documented cloud misconfiguration.[1] The consequences arrive in three flavors, all bad. Anyone can query the model, so it becomes a free resource for strangers—running up a compute bill that can reach thousands of dollars before anyone notices.[1] Anyone can probe it, so it's exposed to the prompt-injection and model-extraction attacks from earlier chapters, now reachable by the entire internet.[1] And the team has no idea any of this is happening, because they were celebrating how easy the deployment was.

Here's the uncomfortable symmetry at the heart of this chapter: *the cloud gave them the power to deploy a sophisticated AI system in an afternoon, and the exact same ease gave them the power to expose it just as fast.* The platform's frictionlessness cuts both ways. It removes the friction that used to make standing up AI hard—and it removes the friction that used to make a catastrophic mistake take effort. A misconfiguration that might once have required provisioning hardware and wiring networks is now a default left unchanged and a checkbox left unticked.

And the part that catches organizations off guard: *the cloud provider was never going to fix this for them.* The provider secured the data center, the hypervisor, the underlying service—an enormous amount of security work the team got for free. But whether that endpoint had authentication in front of it was on the team's side of a line the provider had drawn very deliberately. The breach didn't happen because the cloud was insecure. It happened in the gap between what the provider secures and what the customer must—a gap that most organizations have not updated their mental model to account for now that AI sits inside it.

This is the double-edged nature of running AI in the cloud, and it's why this chapter exists. Nearly every organization runs its AI on cloud infrastructure—by recent measure, at least 81% use managed AI services and around 90% run self-hosted AI software in the cloud.[2] The major platforms offer genuinely powerful, mature security capabilities that can implement much of what this book has described—guardrails, network isolation, identity controls, audit logging—without you having to build any of it. That's real leverage, and refusing it would be foolish. But the same platforms make exposure effortless and draw a shared-responsibility line that AI has quietly redrawn, leaving new and unfamiliar things on *your* side of it. So this chapter covers three things: how the shared-responsibility line moved (and how AI moved it again), the genuine security leverage the cloud hands you for free, and the honest center of cloud AI risk—that the breach is almost never an exotic attack on the provider, and almost always a misconfiguration on your side, now operating at cloud scale.

PART ONE: THE SHARED-RESPONSIBILITY LINE MOVED — AND AI MOVED IT AGAIN

Every major cloud platform operates on a *shared-responsibility model,* and misunderstanding it is the single most common root of cloud security failure. The concept is simple to state and easy to get wrong in practice: the provider is responsible for the security *of* the cloud—the physical data centers, the hardware, the core infrastructure, the managed service itself—and the customer is responsible for security *in* the cloud—how they configure it, who they grant access to, and what data they put in it. The provider secures the building; you're responsible for locking the office they gave you inside it.

For traditional cloud services, most organizations have—often painfully—learned roughly where that line sits. The trouble is that AI moved it, adding new categories of customer-side responsibility that didn't exist before, and that many teams haven't consciously added to their side of the ledger.

What the provider secures (a lot, and it's real). Start by giving the cloud its due, because the leverage in Part Two depends on it. When you use a managed AI service, the provider secures the infrastructure the model runs on, the physical and network security of the data centers, the availability and patching of the underlying service, and—for their own foundation models—a great deal of model-level safety work. This is genuine security you don't have to build, staffed by teams larger than most organizations could ever assemble. Using a managed AI service means inheriting a substantial security foundation for free. That's not marketing; it's the real reason the cloud is the right default for most organizations' AI.

What AI added to your side of the line. But AI deployment puts new things squarely in the customer's column. And these are the ones teams miss because their pre-AI mental model of the line didn't include them:

- *The data you feed it.* The provider secures the service; the sensitivity of the data you send to it, and whether you were permitted to, is yours (everything from Chapter 12 lives here).
- *The access you configure.* Whether that inference endpoint has authentication, whether it's rate-limited, whether it's reachable from the public internet—all yours. The opening's breach lived entirely in this category.
- *The model access you grant.* Which users, services, and *agents* can invoke which models, and what those models are in turn allowed to do, is your configuration to set.
- *The agents you wire to resources.* This is the newest and most consequential addition: when you give an AI agent the ability to act on your cloud resources, the permissions you grant it are entirely your responsibility—and, as Part Three will show, an over-permissioned agent is a new and dangerous class of misconfiguration.

The visibility problem underneath it all. Here's the statistic that exposes how poorly the moved line is understood: even as the overwhelming majority of organizations run AI in the cloud, around 25% still lack visibility into which AI services are even running in their environment: a gap first measured in 2025 and still unclosed.[3] You cannot own your half of a responsibility line for systems you don't know exist. This is the Chapter 2 inventory problem resurfacing at the cloud layer—Shadow AI, now in the form of managed services and self-hosted models spun up across cloud accounts faster than anyone is tracking. The shared-responsibility line didn't just move; for a quarter of organizations, part of it runs through systems they can't see at all.

The reframe. So the foundational mental shift for cloud AI is this: the cloud is not a place where security happens *to* you—it's a partnership with a very precise and very unforgiving division of labor. The provider will hold up its half flawlessly and silently, which is exactly what lulls teams into assuming the whole thing is handled. It isn't. AI added new responsibilities to your half of the line, and the provider will secure its infrastructure perfectly while your unauthenticated endpoint serves the internet. Knowing precisely where the line falls—especially the new AI-era parts of it—is the foundation everything else in this chapter builds on.

PART TWO: THE LEVERAGE — SECURITY CAPABILITIES YOU DIDN'T HAVE TO BUILD

Before the risks, give the cloud its due, because the leverage is the reason to be there. The major platforms have built mature, native AI-security capabilities that would take most organizations years and a specialist team to build themselves—and much of this book's technical program can be implemented by *turning on what the cloud already offers,* rather than constructing it from scratch. The platforms have moved beyond raw infrastructure to offer what one analysis called integrated "AI security fabrics."[4] Here is the leverage, mapped to the chapters where each capability first appeared—because the through-line is that the cloud can implement much of what you've already learned to want.

Managed guardrails (the Chapter 7 runtime defense, pre-built). The inference-layer guardrails from Chapter 7—filtering inputs and outputs, blocking policy violations, screening for sensitive data—are available as native, managed services. The platforms offer guardrail layers that act as interceptor logic between the user and the model, and a genuinely useful property of the better ones is that they're *model-agnostic*: you define a policy once (say, "block all PII") and apply it across different underlying models uniformly.[5] Some platforms put a dedicated screening layer in front of the model specifically to sanitize inputs and scan outputs for secrets before a user sees them.[5] You're not building a guardrail system; you're configuring one.

Network isolation against exfiltration (the Chapter 12 data protection, at the network layer). The data-protection concerns from Chapter 12 get a powerful network-layer ally. Platforms offer ways to keep AI traffic entirely off the public internet—routing it over the provider's private backbone—and, more powerfully, to draw a logical perimeter around your AI resources that prevents data from being copied out to an unauthorized location *even by someone holding valid credentials.*[6] That last capability is a serious defense against the data-exfiltration and extraction threats from Chapters 11 and 12: it means a compromised identity isn't automatically a data-exfiltration path, because the perimeter itself refuses the exit. This is defense-in-depth the cloud hands you, if you configure it.

Identity and least-privilege for agents (the Chapter 7/11 blast-radius limiting, enforced). The least-privilege principle this book has returned to repeatedly—limit what a manipulated model or agent can *do*—is enforced through the cloud's identity and access management. You can write fine-grained policies that constrain exactly what each model, service, and agent is permitted to touch, treating each agent like a service account with a single specific job: if an agent only needs to read from a database, its role can explicitly deny write access, so a misconfiguration or compromise can't escalate.[7] The cloud's IAM is the machinery that turns "limit the blast radius" from a principle into an enforced constraint.

Native audit logging (the Chapter 9 monitoring and Chapter 11 forensics, built in). The monitoring and forensic-capture needs from Chapters 9 and 11 are substantially served by native cloud logging. The platforms can log every API call an AI agent makes, letting you query later for all AI-driven actions, identify unauthorized operations, and maintain compliance audit trails—and you can set alarms on agent actions against sensitive resources or anomalous patterns.[8] This is exactly the behavioral telemetry and forensic record those chapters called for, available as a managed capability rather than a custom build. (It still has to be *turned on, retained, and piped into your SOC*—but the capability is there.)

The synthesis: the cloud can implement this book — if you turn it on. Read those four together and the leverage is striking: managed guardrails, network isolation, least-privilege IAM, and native logging are, respectively, the runtime defense, the data protection, the blast-radius limiting, and the monitoring/forensics that earlier chapters told you to build. The cloud offers them as configurable services. This is the genuine, under-appreciated upside—an organization that knows what it wants (because it read the earlier chapters) can implement a serious fraction of it by configuration rather than construction. But notice the load-bearing phrase in every capability above: *if you configure it, if you turn it on, if you set the policy.* The leverage is real and it is entirely conditional on you using it—which is exactly where Part Three's risk lives.

PART THREE: THE GAP — MISCONFIGURATION IS THE BREACH

Here is the honest center of cloud AI security, and it is almost anticlimactic after the exotic attacks of earlier chapters: the dominant risk is not a brilliant adversary defeating the provider's defenses. It's *you,* misconfiguring your own half of the shared-responsibility line, at cloud scale. Misconfiguration is the documented root cause of the most significant cloud breaches—and the sobering part is that the barrier to fixing it is not capability but prioritization; nearly every common misconfiguration is fixable with native tooling and known commands that teams simply haven't run.[9] The leverage from Part Two is real, but it's inert until configured, and the gap between "available" and "configured" is where the breaches live.

The recurring misconfigurations, now carrying AI data. The classic cloud misconfigurations didn't go away; AI just made their stakes higher by routing sensitive data and powerful capabilities through them. The open inference endpoint from the opening—no authentication, no rate limiting—is the signature AI example.[1] But the old standbys matter more than ever now: publicly-exposed storage buckets that happen to hold *training data* (Chapter 12's sensitive data, now world-readable); over-broad identity permissions; exposed credentials. The three pillars of cloud risk in this era are widely summarized as *identity, AI, and visibility*—and AI sits in the middle precisely because it amplifies the consequences of failures in the other two.[9]

The new, AI-specific misconfiguration: the over-privileged agent. The genuinely new class of misconfiguration—and the most dangerous—is the over-permissioned AI agent. When you wire an AI agent to act on your resources, the permissions you grant it become the blast radius of any compromise, because *a manipulated agent inherits exactly what you* *gave it.* This is where the prompt-injection threat from Chapter 7 and the agentic-incident threat from Chapter 11 land in the cloud: an attacker who manipulates an over-privileged agent doesn't just get bad outputs—they get an authenticated actor with broad permissions operating inside your environment. An agent granted write access "to be safe" that only ever needed read access is a latent breach waiting for the prompt injection that activates it. This is why the least-privilege IAM from Part Two isn't optional hygiene for agents—it's the difference between a contained manipulation and a compromised environment. The misconfiguration here isn't a checkbox; it's an over-generous permission grant that felt convenient at build time.

Why misconfiguration scales worse in the cloud. The cloud's force-multiplier nature, from the opening, applies to mistakes too. A misconfiguration on one server is one exposure; a misconfigured template or default applied across an auto-scaling cloud deployment is the *same mistake replicated everywhere, instantly.* The very elasticity that makes the cloud powerful means an insecure default doesn't stay contained—it propagates. This is why cloud misconfiguration is both the most common cause of breach and the most consequential: it's a single human error, multiplied by the scale the cloud was built to provide.

The honest framing. The lesson of Part Three is deflating in the best way: securing AI in the cloud is, more than anything, the discipline of *not misconfiguring your own half of the line*—and that's mostly achievable with tools and commands the provider already gives you. It's less glamorous than defending against multi-turn jailbreaks, but it's where the actual breaches happen. The organization that obsesses over exotic AI attacks while leaving an inference endpoint open and an agent over-permissioned has aimed its attention exactly wrong. The breach won't be clever. It'll be a default left unchanged.

THE LEADERSHIP LENS

For a leader, cloud AI is a series of decisions about *where to draw your own line*—what to inherit from the provider, what to own, and how to make sure your half is actually held. Four responsibilities.

Know precisely where your half of the line falls — especially the new AI parts. The foundational leadership task is ensuring the organization has an accurate, shared understanding of the shared-responsibility model as AI has redrawn it. The breach in the opening happened because someone assumed the cloud "handled security" in a category that was theirs. A leader's job is to make sure the new AI-era responsibilities—the data fed to models, the access configured, the permissions granted to agents—are explicitly owned, not assumed away. The dangerous phrase to listen for is "the cloud takes care of that," because for the AI-specific parts of the line, increasingly it doesn't.

Treat managed-vs-self-hosted as a security-burden decision, not just a cost or capability one. One of the most consequential leadership choices is how much of the AI stack to run as a managed service versus self-host—and the research frames the trade-off sharply: taking the path of total control with self-hosted open-source models means "inheriting 100% of the security burden."[10] A managed service hands you the native-security leverage and a large inherited security foundation; a self-hosted model hands you maximum control and the entire responsibility. Neither is wrong, but the burden should be weighed consciously rather than discovered later. The organizations running self-hosted AI—by recent measure, the overwhelming majority of cloud environments—have, knowingly or not, taken on that full burden, and self-hosted models are exactly where new visibility blind spots emerge.[2]

Fund visibility first — you cannot secure what you cannot see. Investing in cloud-posture capabilities to discover and enumerate every managed and self-hosted AI service turns an unknowable, Shadow-AI attack surface into a manageable one.

Then exploit native security rather than leaving it on the table out of lock-in fear. Portability has merit, but refusing a provider's mature guardrails, network controls, and IAM means hand-building inferior versions or operating exposed. The pragmatic posture is to use the cloud's native protections where they defend you immediately, while confining lock-in concerns to data and core architecture.

The one question to ask your team this week: *"For our most important cloud AI system, can you show me exactly where the provider's responsi-*

bility ends and ours begins—and can you point to the specific configuration on our side that authenticates the endpoint, limits the agent's permissions, and logs its actions?" If the team can't draw the line crisply, the assumption that "the cloud handles it" is hiding somewhere dangerous. If they can draw the line but can't point to the configurations, you've found the gap where the breach will happen—on your side, in a configuration nobody owned.

THE EXECUTION LENS

For the implementer, securing cloud AI is the disciplined work of owning your half of the line: turning on the native capabilities, catching misconfigurations *before* they deploy, locking down agents, and wiring the cloud's telemetry into the security operations you built in Chapter 9. The good news is that nearly all of it is configuration of tools the provider already gives you.

Turn on the native AI-security capabilities — deliberately, not by default. The Part Two leverage is inert until configured, so make configuring it the baseline:

- Enable the **managed guardrails** in front of every model endpoint, defining policies (block PII, block disallowed content) centrally so they apply uniformly across models.[5]
- Configure **network isolation** — private connectivity so AI traffic never touches the public internet, and a logical perimeter around AI resources that blocks data exfiltration even by credentialed identities.[6]
- Enable **native audit logging** on all AI API calls, set alarms on sensitive-resource access and anomalous patterns, and—critically—*pipe those logs into the Chapter 9 SOC*, because logging the agent's actions only helps if the telemetry reaches the place that watches it.[8]

Secure the inference endpoint — close the opening's gap. The signature AI misconfiguration deserves its own checklist: every inference endpoint gets *authentication* (never public-unauthenticated), *rate* *limiting* (against both abuse and runaway cost), and *network restriction* (reachable only from where it needs to be). This is the most common AI cloud exposure and among the easiest to fix—treat an unauthenticated inference endpoint as a production incident, not a to-do.[1]

Lock down agents with least-privilege IAM — the new critical control. For any AI agent wired to cloud resources, the permissions are the blast radius, so:

- Grant each agent the **minimum permissions for its actual job**, treating it as a service account: read-only if it only reads, with writes and sensitive actions explicitly denied unless required.[7]
- Scope permissions tightly enough that a *manipulated* agent (assume prompt injection will succeed) can't escalate—this is Chapter 7's least-privilege and Chapter 11's blast-radius limiting, enforced through IAM.
- Where agents access resources through emerging integration patterns, use the controls that let you restrict an agent's actions specifically *when taken through the agent path*, and log those actions distinctly for the chain-aware detection from Chapter 11.[8]

Catch misconfiguration before it deploys — security as code. Because misconfiguration is the breach and the cloud replicates it at scale, the highest-leverage engineering move is to catch it *before* it reaches the cloud:

- Define infrastructure as code and **scan the templates against security policies pre-deployment** — a tool that fails the build when someone declares a public storage bucket or an unauthenticated endpoint means the insecure resource is never created.[11]
- Continuously **audit the live environment for drift** — manual changes made outside the pipeline—with always-on posture scanning against benchmarks, so a firewall rule

changed at 3 a.m. to open a port is detected and alerted immediately.[11]

Adopt posture management across the three layers. Use the maturing posture-management tooling to maintain visibility and catch the misconfigurations: **CSPM** for infrastructure misconfigurations, **DSPM** for where sensitive data lives, and **AI-SPM** extending both into the AI layer—discovering managed services and self-hosted models alike, scanning model and dataset configurations, and mapping attack paths from an exposed API to a sensitive training bucket.[12] Crucially, run this *inside your existing DevSecOps workflows,* not as a separate initiative—the same "integrate, don't silo" lesson from Chapter 9.[12]

Cut through the capabilities and the discipline is simple: securing cloud AI is overwhelmingly about configuration discipline on your side of the line—turn on the leverage the provider built, lock down endpoints and agents to least privilege, and catch the inevitable human misconfiguration before it deploys and replicates. You are not, for the most part, building novel defenses here; you are correctly configuring powerful ones the provider already offers, and automating the detection of the configuration mistakes that are statistically certain to occur. The exotic AI attacks from earlier chapters are real—but in the cloud, the breach is far more likely to be the endpoint you left open and the agent you over-permissioned, both fixable with tools already at hand.

The one move to make this week: pick your most important cloud AI endpoint and verify three things, right now: is it authenticated, is it rate-limited, and is its agent (if any) scoped to least privilege? Then run your provider's native IAM analyzer to surface your most over-privileged AI-related roles.[9] If the endpoint is open or the agent is over-permissioned, you've found—in one system, in under an hour—the exact gap where the most common cloud AI breach happens, and closing it uses tools already in your account. One endpoint, three checks, one audit command.

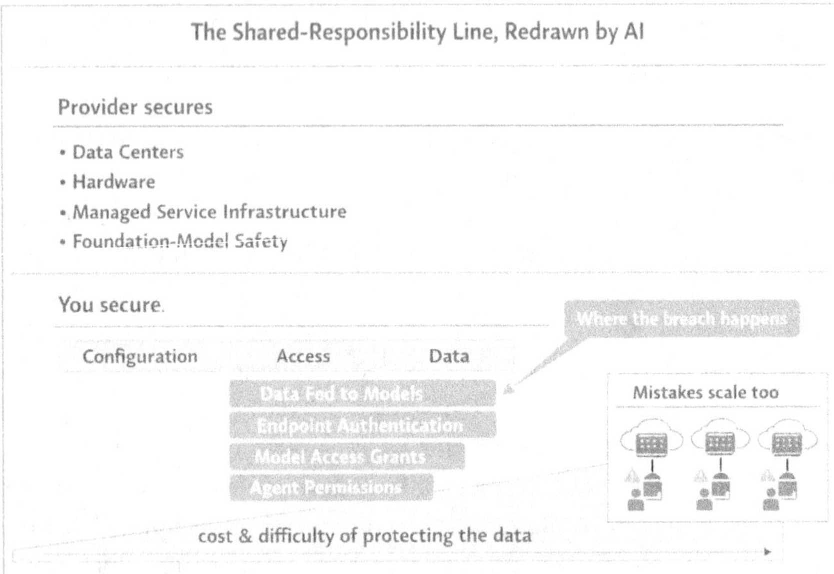

Figure 13.1 — ***The Shared-Responsibility Line, Redrawn by AI*** *AI shifts the shared-responsibility boundary: providers secure the physical and managed layers—data centers, hardware, service infrastructure, and foundation-model safety—while organizations remain responsible for configuration, access, and data. The AI era adds new obligations below the line: data fed to models, endpoint authentication, model-access grants, and agent-permission design. Breaches now occur where these AI-specific controls fail, and misconfigurations scale instantly across auto-scaling deployments.*

BRINGING IT TOGETHER

We opened with a team that deployed a powerful AI model in an afternoon and left its inference endpoint open to the internet—and the recognition that the cloud's frictionless ease cuts both ways: it deploys AI fast and exposes it just as fast. The provider was never going to close the gap the team created. That double edge is the whole chapter.

Understanding it starts with the shared-responsibility line—the provider secures the infrastructure *of* the AI service, you secure how you *configure and use* it—and the recognition that AI redrew that line, adding the data you feed models, the access you configure, and above all the permissions you grant agents to your side of it. The cloud's compensating gift is enormous leverage: the runtime defense, data protection, blast-radius limiting, and monitoring of earlier chapters, all available as configurable services. The cloud can implement much of this book if you turn it on. And the honest center is deflating but liberating: the breach is almost never an exotic attack on the provider and almost always a misconfiguration on your side—an open endpoint, an over-privileged agent—operating at cloud scale, and fixable with tools already in your account. The barrier isn't capability; it's prioritization.

Your overarching strategy as a leader: establish explicitly where your half of the redrawn line falls, treat managed-vs-self-hosted as the security-burden decision it is, fund visibility first, and use the provider's native leverage rather than leaving it on the table out of lock-in fear.

Your tactical mandate as an implementer: verify your most important endpoint is authenticated, rate-limited, and least-privileged, and run the IAM analyzer to surface over-privileged AI roles. Then systematize—turn on native guardrails, network controls, and logging, and scan infrastructure-as-code pre-deployment so the next misconfiguration is caught before it ships.

By operationalizing both the vision and the tactics, you take the cloud's genuine leverage without inheriting its characteristic breach. The leader owns the line and funds the visibility and the burden-aware choices; the implementer configures the powerful defenses the provider built and automates the detection of the misconfigurations that are otherwise statistically certain. You stop treating the cloud as a place where security simply happens to you, and start treating it as what it is—a partnership with a precise division of labor, where your half is mostly the discipline of correctly configuring powerful tools you didn't have to build.

Coming next — This chapter, like the rest of Phase II, has described a lot to do: pipeline defenses, supply-chain verification, monitoring, red-teaming, incident response, privacy engineering, and now cloud configuration. For a large enterprise with a dedicated security team, that's a program. For everyone else—the startup, the lean team, the organization where "the security team" is one person with three other jobs—it can read like an impossible mountain. So Phase II closes with the chapter that makes the rest of it survivable: how to do AI security with limited resources, prioritizing ruthlessly, automating relentlessly, and getting the highest-leverage protection without the headcount of a bank. The principles are universal; the resources are not. Chapter 14 is about security that fits the team you actually have.

CHAPTER 13 IN REVIEW

The core idea: Running AI in the cloud is double-edged. The platforms hand you mature security capabilities you didn't have to build—*and* make a single misconfiguration scale instantly into a major exposure. Securing cloud AI is mostly the discipline of owning your half of a shared-responsibility line that AI quietly redrew.

The wake-up call: A team deploys a powerful model in an afternoon and leaves the inference endpoint open—no auth, no rate limiting—exposing it to abuse, prompt injection, model extraction, and a runaway bill. The cloud made deploying easy and exposing just as easy, and the provider was never going to fix the customer's side of the line.

The shared-responsibility line moved — and AI moved it again:

- The provider secures the infrastructure *of* the service (data centers, hardware, managed service)—a real, free foundation.
- AI added to *your* side: the data you feed models, the endpoint access you configure, the model access you grant, and the permissions you give agents.
- The visibility problem: ~25% of organizations can't see which AI services run in their environment—Chapter 2's Shadow-AI inventory problem at the cloud layer.

The leverage (capabilities you didn't have to build, mapped to earlier chapters):

- **Managed guardrails** — the Chapter 7 runtime defense, model-agnostic, pre-built.

- **Network isolation / private perimeters** — Chapter 12 data protection; blocks exfiltration even by credentialed identities.
- **Least-privilege IAM for agents** — Chapter 7/11 blast-radius limiting, enforced.
- **Native audit logging** — Chapter 9 monitoring and Chapter 11 forensics, built in.
- The catch: all of it is inert until you *turn it on*.

The gap — misconfiguration is the breach:

- The dominant risk isn't an exotic attack; it's your own misconfiguration at cloud scale. The barrier is prioritization, not capability.
- Recurring: open inference endpoints, public buckets holding training data, over-broad permissions.
- New and most dangerous: the **over-privileged AI agent** — a manipulated agent inherits exactly the permissions you granted it.
- Misconfiguration scales worse in the cloud: one insecure default replicates across an auto-scaling deployment instantly.

For the leader (Leadership Lens):

- Know exactly where your half of the line falls, especially the new AI parts; distrust "the cloud handles that."
- Treat managed-vs-self-hosted as a security-burden decision (self-hosting = inheriting 100% of the burden).
- Use the native security leverage fully; don't leave it on the table over lock-in fear.
- Fund visibility first—you can't secure the AI you can't see.

For the implementer (Execution Lens):

- Turn on native guardrails, network isolation, and logging—and pipe logs into the Chapter 9 SOC.

- Secure every inference endpoint: authenticate, rate-limit, network-restrict.
- Lock down agents with least-privilege IAM—the new critical control; assume manipulation and limit blast radius.
- Catch misconfiguration before it ships (scan infrastructure-as-code, detect drift); adopt CSPM / DSPM / AI-SPM inside existing DevSecOps.

The two actions from this chapter:

- *Strategic Move (leader):* Establish where your half of the line falls, make the burden-aware build / buy choice, and fund visibility.
- *Tactical Move (implementer):* Verify your top endpoint is authenticated, rate-limited, and least-privileged; run the IAM analyzer; then systematize with native controls and IaC scanning.

The throughline to remember: The cloud is a force multiplier in both directions—it hands you powerful AI security for free and makes a single misconfiguration scale into a breach. Own your half of the redrawn line: turn on the leverage, lock down endpoints and agents, and catch misconfiguration before it ships. The breach won't be clever; it'll be a default left unchanged.

CHAPTER 14
LEAN SECURITY: ENABLING BUSINESS VELOCITY WITHOUT SACRIFICING PROTECTION

From Boardroom to Build: A Blueprint for AI Governance, Risk, and Technical Security
(Phase II — The Execution Core concludes)

OPENING

Imagine you've just read the seven chapters before this one, and you are not the CISO of a bank. You're the one engineer at a forty-person company who got handed "security" on top of your actual job, or the founder who knows the AI feature you just shipped needs protecting but has no one to assign it to, or the three-person platform team keeping the lights on for a product that suddenly has AI in it.

And the list in front of you is staggering. Secure the training pipeline. Verify the supply chain. Stand up AI observability and a modernized SOC. Run continuous red-teaming. Build an incident response plan with forensic capture. Engineer privacy across the data lifecycle. Catch cloud misconfigurations before they ship. Each chapter was honest that its subject was real and necessary. Stacked together, for a team your size, they read like an instruction to climb a mountain with no equipment and no time.

The natural reaction is despair, and a quiet conclusion that AI security is something only big, well-staffed organizations can actually do—so a small team may as well not really try. That conclusion is wrong, and disproving it is the entire purpose of this chapter. But the reassurance it offers is not the cheap kind. This chapter will not tell you the work isn't real or that there's a shortcut that makes it easy. The work *is* real. Here is the truth that actually helps: **you will never do all of it—and that is not failure. Lean security is the discipline of doing the right fraction of it, on purpose.**

That reframing changes everything. A large enterprise can attempt comprehensive coverage—protect everything, monitor everything, test everything—and a lean team that tries to imitate that posture will fail at all of it, spreading its scarce attention so thin that nothing is actually protected. The lean team's advantage is not resources; it's the *clarity that scarcity forces.* When you obviously can't do everything, you're compelled to answer the question the big team can dodge: *what actually matters most?* A lean team that answers that question well—protecting its highest-stakes systems properly, automating the repeatable work, and using AI to punch above its weight—can achieve security that a sprawling, unfocused enterprise program never does. Constraint, used well, is an edge.

And here is the part you may already half-suspect: this book has been quietly preparing you for this chapter the whole way. Every chapter ended with "the one move to make this week," and nearly every one of those moves was "start with one system—your highest-stakes one." That was never an accident or a beginner's simplification. That was lean security, taught one chapter at a time. The instinct to start with a single, most-important system and do it properly before broadening is the core lean discipline, and you've been practicing it since Chapter 1. This chapter simply names the principle those moves were teaching and turns it into a deliberate operating philosophy—built on three disciplines: prioritize ruthlessly, automate relentlessly, and use AI as a force multiplier where it genuinely helps. The mountain doesn't get smaller. You get deliberate about which parts of it you actually need to climb.

PART ONE: PRIORITIZE RUTHLESSLY — PROTECT THE HIGHEST-STAKES THING FIRST

The first and most important lean discipline is prioritization, because for a resource-constrained team it's the decision that determines whether anything gets protected at all. And the lean failure mode is seductive precisely because it looks responsible: the team tries to give every AI system some security attention, spreads its tiny capacity evenly across everything, and ends up protecting nothing *well*—a thin, uniform layer that stops no determined threat anywhere. Trying to cover everything is how a lean team ends up covering nothing.

The discipline that replaces it is uncomfortable but liberating: *consciously protect the highest-stakes systems properly, and consciously accept more risk on the rest.* You already have the two tools this requires, because earlier chapters built them.

Rank by stakes, using the dials. Chapter 6 gave you the three dials—consequence, data sensitivity, regulatory weight—to read any AI system's stakes. For a lean team, the dials aren't just a calibration tool; they're a *triage* tool. Run every AI system you have through them and you get a ranked list: the systems where a failure is catastrophic, irreversible, regulated, or touches your most sensitive data, versus the ones where a failure is a recoverable inconvenience. That ranking is your work order. The customer-facing AI making consequential decisions on sensitive data gets the real, layered protection from Phase II; the internal tool that summarizes meeting notes gets a light touch and your conscious acceptance of its modest risk. This isn't cutting corners—it's putting your scarce effort where the consequences actually live.

Accept the rest as deliberate risk, not neglect. Here's the distinction that separates lean security from simply *under-securing*: the lean team *decides*, explicitly, which risks it's accepting, and records that decision. This is Chapter 4's risk appetite, now as survival tool. There's a profound difference between "we never got around to securing that system" (neglect, which leaves you blindsided) and "we reviewed that system, judged its stakes low, and consciously accepted its risk for now" (a deliberate risk decision you can defend, revisit, and explain to a board or regulator). The lean team can't eliminate the gap between what it does and what a fully-resourced program would do—but it can convert that gap from an invisible liability into a known, owned, documented set of accepted risks. A lean program isn't one with no gaps; it's one whose gaps are chosen rather than discovered.

Revisit the ranking, because stakes move. The triage isn't a one-time act. The internal summarization tool that was low-stakes last quarter becomes high-stakes the moment someone wires it to customer data or gives it the ability to take actions: a dial spikes, and it should jump your work order. The lean discipline includes periodically re-running the triage so that rising-stakes systems get reclassified *before* they fail, not after. This is the continuous loop from the governance and monitoring chapters, in its most stripped-down form: a small team can't watch everything continuously, but it can periodically re-ask "what matters most now?" and redirect its scarce attention accordingly.

Why this is the foundational lean move. Prioritization comes first because it makes the other two disciplines possible. You can't automate intelligently or deploy a force-multiplier tool usefully until you know *what you're protecting and in what order.* The ranked list of systems-by-stakes is the lean team's single most valuable artifact: it tells you what to protect first and what to defer. The big team can afford to skip this clarity. The lean team's whole strategy depends on it.

PART TWO: AUTOMATE RELENTLESSLY — MAKE THE MACHINE DO THE REPEATABLE WORK

Once you know what to protect first, the second lean discipline is making as much of the protection as possible happen *without a human doing it.* For a team measured in single digits, the binding constraint isn't knowledge—you can learn what to do from this book—it's *attention,* the finite number of things a small team can actively watch and remember to do. Automation is the discipline of spending that scarce attention only on what genuinely requires human judgment, and letting the machine handle everything repeatable. For a lean team, automation isn't an efficiency nicety; it's the only way the math works at all.

Build security into the pipeline so it happens by default, not by memory. The single highest-leverage lean move is to make security *automatic and structural* rather than *manual and remembered*. A control that depends on a person remembering to run it will, on a lean team, eventually not get run—not from negligence but because that person was on fire with three other priorities that day. A control wired into the pipeline runs every time, forever, whether anyone remembers it or not. This is why the cheapest and most durable controls from Phase II are the automated ones: the infrastructure-as-code scanning that fails a build before an insecure resource is ever created (Chapter 13), the guardrails that filter every model interaction without supervision (Chapter 7), the drift detection that watches the trend while everyone sleeps (Chapter 9), the import gate that scans every model automatically (Chapter 8). For each of these, the lean team does the work *once*—wiring it in—and then it protects continuously at zero ongoing attention cost. That trade, one-time setup for permanent automatic coverage, is the best deal available to a small team.

Prefer controls that run continuously over reviews that must be scheduled. A useful lean heuristic for choosing among controls: favor the ones that, once built, run on their own over the ones that require a human to periodically perform them. An automated continuous check beats a quarterly manual review for a lean team not because it's more thorough but because it *actually keeps happening*—the quarterly review is exactly the thing that slips when the team is underwater. Where Phase II offered a choice between a manual practice and an automatable one, the lean team should bias hard toward the automatable, accepting a less perfect control that runs reliably over a better one that runs sporadically or not at all.

Automation is the other half of "start with one system." Beyond the prioritization in Part One, that move carried an automation discipline: building one control properly usually means building it into the pipeline so it runs automatically, and then *replicating* that wired-in control to the next system, and the next. The lean team grows its coverage not by adding manual work it then has to sustain, but by building automatic controls once and propagating them—each new system inheriting the automated protections the previous ones established. Coverage compounds through replication of automation, not through accumulation of manual toil.

The honest limit of automation. Automation handles the repeatable; it does not handle judgment. The lean team still has to make the prioritization calls, the risk-appetite decisions, the "is this acceptable" judgments, and the genuinely novel investigations—and those should be exactly where the team's scarce human attention goes, *because* automation cleared away the toil that would otherwise consume it. The goal isn't to automate the thinking. It's to automate everything that *isn't* thinking, so the small amount of human attention available is spent on the small number of things that actually need a human.

PART THREE: USE AI AS A FORCE MULTIPLIER — WHERE IT GENUINELY HELPS

The third lean discipline is the one that seems most obvious and is most often done badly: using AI itself to help secure your AI. The promise is intoxicating and, handled well, real—AI can let a small team operate as though it had several times its actual resources, automating triage, prioritizing what matters, and investigating at a speed no human team could match.[1] The agentic SOC from Chapter 9, which a large enterprise adopts to reduce alert fatigue, is for a lean team something more fundamental: a way to have *any* coverage at all across hours and systems a tiny team could never watch itself. This is genuine leverage, and a lean team should reach for it.

But beware the two ways it goes wrong. The honest literature on AI for lean security is refreshingly blunt that AI is not plug-and-play magic, and that vendor claims tend to fail in one of two ways.[2] The first is *buzzword baggage*: AI bolted onto legacy workflows with no real impact except, possibly, breaking the workflows you were relying on. The second is *operational burden*: new tools that introduce complexity and noise rather than clarity and simplicity.[2] For a lean team, the second is especially dangerous, because the entire point of adopting AI was to *reduce* the load on scarce human attention—and a tool that adds alerts to triage, dashboards to watch, and integrations to maintain has made the core problem worse while appearing to solve it. The lean team that can least afford wasted effort is the one most often sold tools that waste it.

The lean test: measurable outcomes without added complexity. So the discipline for adopting AI as a force multiplier is a hard-nosed test, not enthusiasm. Before adopting an AI security tool, a lean team should demand a concrete answer to: "does this deliver a measurable outcome—faster detection, fewer false positives, less manual work—without introducing new complexity my team then has to manage?"[2] A tool that genuinely triages alerts so your one analyst sees ten real ones instead of a thousand mostly-false ones has multiplied that analyst. A tool that adds a new console, a new alert stream, and a new integration to babysit has divided them. The test cuts through vendor marketing to the only question that matters for a lean team: did this give me back human attention, or consume more of it?

Keep the human in the loop — and remember to watch the watcher. Two cautions from earlier chapters apply with full force here. First, the mature pattern is human-AI collaboration, not replacement: the AI handles the high-volume tactical work, the human keeps judgment and direction—which for a lean team means the force-multiplier AI extends your reach without removing your control.[1] Second, the recursion from Chapter 9 still holds: the AI you adopt to help secure your environment is itself an AI system that can be manipulated, drift, or fail, and a lean team leaning heavily on it must keep that dependency in view rather than treating the tool as infallible because it's overworked and grateful for the help. The force multiplier is a lever, not a savior—and a lever you're resting weight on deserves a periodic check that it's still holding.

The synthesis of the three disciplines. Put the lean disciplines together and they form a single coherent strategy: *prioritize* so you know what matters most, *automate* so the repeatable protection of those priorities happens without consuming attention, and *multiply* so the human attention you've freed up reaches further than its headcount should allow. Each enables the next—prioritization tells automation what to protect first, automation frees the attention that the force multiplier then extends. A lean team running all three doesn't do everything a big team does. It does the most important things, automatically, with amplified reach—and that focused depth is the whole bet of this chapter.

THE LEADERSHIP LENS

For a leader of a lean organization—a founder, a head of engineering, a one-person security function's manager—this chapter is permission and instruction in equal measure: permission to not do everything, and instruction on how to choose well.

Start by dropping the shame. A lean leader can carry quiet embarrassment about not having a "real" security program, and that shame drives bad decisions—paralysis, panic-buying tools to feel covered, or pretending the risk isn't there. A focused program that protects the highest-stakes systems properly and consciously accepts the rest isn't a lesser version of a big program; it's the correct program for your resources, and often more genuinely secure than a sprawling, unfocused one. Your job isn't to apologize for not being a bank—it's to make the prioritization calls a bank can afford to avoid. Three responsibilities follow from that.

Make the risk-acceptance decisions explicitly — they're yours, and they're the strategy. Part One's "consciously accept the rest" is a leadership act, not a technical one, and it's the heart of lean security. Someone with authority has to look at the lower-stakes systems and decide, on the record, that their risk is accepted for now. That decision is yours (Chapter 5's ownership, Chapter 4's appetite), and making it explicitly is what converts your team's gaps from hidden liabilities into a defensible, deliberate risk posture. A lean leader who refuses to make these calls forces the team into the spread-thin failure mode by default —because without an explicit decision about what *not* to protect, the team tries to protect everything and protects nothing.

Buy the security you can't build. The build-vs-buy calculus tilts decisively toward "buy" for a lean team, and Chapter 13 is the lever: a managed AI service hands you an inherited security foundation and native controls you could never build with your headcount, while self-hosting means inheriting the entire security burden your headcount can't carry. This isn't a close call—the managed path an enterprise weighs against control and lock-in concerns is, for you, often the only way to get serious security at all. Spend your scarce engineering attention configuring powerful managed controls, not hand-building inferior ones.

Fund the force multiplier — but demand the lean test. When you invest in AI security tooling, fund it against the Part Three test, not the vendor's demo: does it give your team back attention, with measurable outcomes and without new complexity? A lean leader's tooling budget is small and hard-won, and the costliest mistake is spending it on buzzword baggage or operational burden that makes an overwhelmed team more overwhelmed. Insist on a real trial against your actual workflow before committing, and be willing to walk away from impressive tools that don't pass. The right tool multiplies your team; the wrong one is a second job.

The one question to ask your team this week: *"If we could only properly secure three of our AI systems, which three would they be—and have we actually, deliberately accepted the risk on everything else, or are we just hoping?"* If the team can name the three instantly, you have a prioritized program. If they can't—if every system feels equally urgent—you've found the problem, and the fix isn't more resources, it's the ranking this chapter is built on.

THE EXECUTION LENS

For the lean implementer, this chapter is the most practical in the book, because it tells you not just what to do but what to do *first, with almost no one.* The playbook is the three disciplines turned into an order of operations.

Build the ranked inventory first — it's your whole strategy in one artifact. Before any control, produce the lean team's most valuable document: every AI system you have, ranked by the Chapter 6 dials. This is the Chapter 2 inventory plus a stakes score, and for a lean team it doubles as the work order, the risk register, and the prioritization map all at once. It tells you which system to protect first, which to defer, and which risks you're accepting—and it fits in a spreadsheet. Don't skip it to "start doing security"; the ranking *is* the lean security strategy, and everything below depends on it.

Protect the top of the list properly, the bottom consciously. Take the highest-stakes system and give it the real Phase II treatment—the pipeline defenses, the guardrails, the monitoring, the least-privilege agent permissions—doing it properly for that one system before broadening. For the bottom of the list, apply light, automated, baseline controls and record the accepted risk. Resist the urge to give every system a medium amount of attention; concentrate, then propagate.

Automate first, and prefer the wired-in control every time. For every protection you build, ask: can this run automatically in the pipeline rather than depending on someone remembering it? Bias hard toward the automatable:

- Wire in the cheap, continuous controls from Phase II — IaC scanning that fails insecure builds (Ch. 13), automated guardrails on endpoints (Ch. 7/13), drift and output-quality monitoring with alerting (Ch. 9), the automated import-scanning gate (Ch. 8).
- Lean on **managed and native cloud controls** over hand-built ones (Ch. 13) — for a lean team, configuring a provider's mature guardrail is hours; building an equivalent is months you don't have.
- Build each automated control *once* and *replicate* it to the next system down the ranked list, so coverage compounds without accumulating manual work.

Adopt force-multiplier AI against the lean test. Where human attention is the bottleneck—alert triage, investigation, prioritization—adopt AI tooling (the agentic-SOC capabilities from Ch. 9, the AI-driven prioritization the lean-SOC tools offer), but only after it passes the test: measurable attention returned, no new complexity, human in the loop.[2] Trial it against your real workflow; keep it if it gives your one analyst back their day, drop it if it adds a console to babysit. And monitor the tool itself as the AI system it is (Ch. 9's recursion).

Hold the three disciplines together and the thesis is unmistakable: lean security isn't a different security program; it's *this* security program, executed in strict order of leverage. You're not learning new controls in this chapter—you're learning the order to apply the ones you already have: rank by stakes, protect the top properly, automate everything repeatable, replicate the automation outward, and multiply your freed attention with AI that passes the test. Every "one move to make this week" from the previous chapters was a single step of this sequence. Strung together and ordered by leverage, they *are* the lean program. The mountain was always meant to be climbed one highest-leverage step at a time.

The one move to make this week: build the ranked inventory—list every AI system, score each on the three dials, and sort. That single spreadsheet tells you, immediately, the one system to protect first and the ones you can consciously defer. It's an afternoon's work, it requires no budget or tools, and it converts the paralyzing Phase II mountain into an ordered queue you can actually start climbing. For a lean team, this one artifact is the difference between a strategy and a spread-thin scramble. One list, ranked, and the top item is your next month.

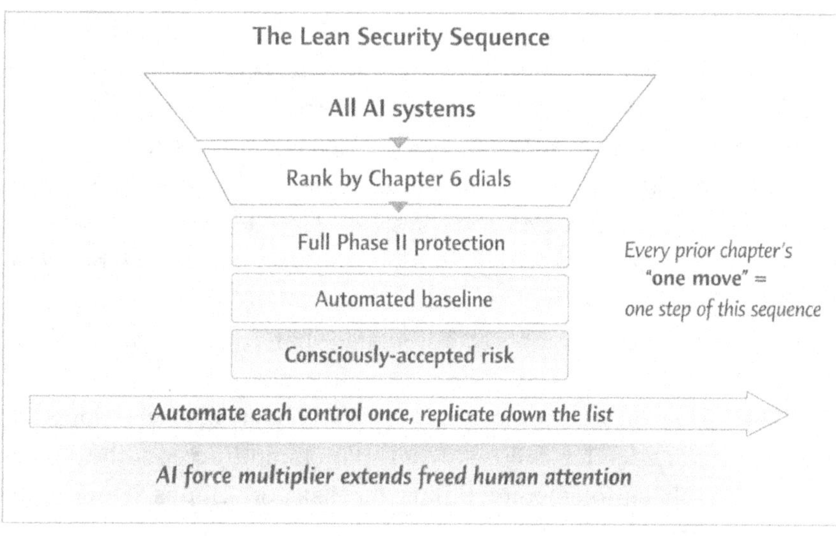

Figure 14.1* — *The Lean Security Sequence *Lean security begins by ranking all AI systems using the Chapter 6 dials, then applying full Phase II protection to the highest-risk tier, automated baselines to the middle, and consciously accepted risk to the lowest. Each control is automated once and replicated down the list, freeing human attention to multiply impact*

through AI assistance. Every prior chapter's "one move" corresponds to one step in this sequence, tying the book's operational loop together.

BRINGING IT TOGETHER

We opened with the lean team staring at the mountain Phase II built—seven chapters of real, necessary work and a team of one or three or five to do it—and the despairing conclusion that AI security is only for the well-staffed. That conclusion is wrong, and the way out isn't a shortcut that makes the work unreal. It's a discipline: you will never do all of it, so you do the right fraction of it, on purpose.

That discipline is three moves that build on each other: prioritize ruthlessly so you know what matters most, automate relentlessly so the protection of those priorities runs without consuming your scarce attention, and use AI as a force multiplier so the attention you've freed reaches further than your headcount should allow. And the deepest truth has been hiding in plain sight the whole book: those per-chapter "one moves" were never warm-ups. They were the lean program, delivered one step at a time.

Your role as a leader is to make the prioritization real: own the risk-acceptance decisions explicitly—which systems get protected properly, which risks you're consciously accepting—and lean hard on managed services to buy the security you can't staff. Treat your lean program not as an embarrassing shortfall but as the correct, focused strategy.

Your immediate task as an implementer is to build the ranked inventory this week—every AI system, scored on the three dials, sorted. It's an afternoon with no budget, and it gives you the one thing the Phase II pile never had: an order of operations, top item first. Then protect that top item properly, automate what you can, and replicate outward.

When these efforts run in parallel, they convert overwhelming into achievable. The leader chooses what matters and accepts the rest on the record; the implementer builds the list and climbs it one automated, replicated step at a time. You stop trying—and failing—to be a big security team in miniature, and start being what a lean team can actually be: focused, automated, and amplified, protecting what matters most genuinely well. For your resources, that's not a lesser program. It's the best one there is.

Coming next — With this chapter, Phase II is complete: you have the full technical program for building and running secure AI, from the pipeline to the cloud, scaled to the team you actually have. But everything you build operates inside a world of rules—laws and regulations that increasingly govern how AI may be built and deployed, and that carry real penalties for getting it wrong. Phase III turns from how you build it to the rules you build it under. We begin in Chapter 15 with the global regulatory landscape: the major AI laws and frameworks, how they fit together (and conflict), and how to navigate compliance without losing the velocity this chapter worked so hard to protect. The engineering is done. Now we map the legal terrain it all runs on.

CHAPTER 14 IN REVIEW

The core idea: A lean team will never do everything Phase II describes —and that's not failure. Lean security is the discipline of doing the right fraction on purpose: prioritize ruthlessly, automate relentlessly, and use AI as a force multiplier where it genuinely helps. Constraint, used well, is an edge—it forces the clarity a big team can dodge.

The wake-up call: A small team facing the stacked-up program of Phase II concludes AI security is only for the well-staffed. The reassurance isn't that the work is unreal—it's that a focused lean program, protecting the right things deliberately, can be more genuinely secure than a sprawling one.

Prioritize ruthlessly:

- The lean failure mode is spreading thin and protecting everything weakly. The discipline is protecting the highest-stakes systems properly and consciously accepting risk on the rest.
- Rank every system by Chapter 6's dials (consequence, data

sensitivity, regulatory weight)—the ranking is your work order.

- Accept the rest as deliberate, documented risk (Chapter 4's appetite), not neglect. A lean program isn't gapless; its gaps are chosen, not discovered.
- Re-run the triage periodically, because stakes move—a dial spikes when a tool gets new data or new powers.

Automate relentlessly:

- The lean constraint is attention, not knowledge. Spend human attention only on judgment; automate everything repeatable.
- Build security into the pipeline so it happens by default, not by memory—a remembered control eventually doesn't get run; a wired-in control runs forever.
- Prefer continuous automated controls over scheduled manual reviews. Coverage compounds through automation, not toil—protect the top item, then propagate the same controls down the list.

Use AI as a force multiplier:

- AI can let a small team operate like a much larger one (triage, prioritization, investigation—Chapter 9's agentic SOC as the lean team's lever).
- Beware buzzword baggage (AI bolted on, breaking workflows) and operational burden (tools adding noise, not clarity).
- The lean test: measurable outcomes (attention returned) without added complexity. Keep humans in the loop; watch the watcher.

For the leader (Leadership Lens):

- Treat lean security as a deliberate strategy, not a deficiency to apologize for.
- Own the risk-acceptance decisions explicitly—they are the strategy.
- Lean hard on managed services—buy the security you can't build (Chapter 13).
- Fund the force multiplier against the lean test, not the vendor demo.

For the implementer (Execution Lens):

- Build the ranked inventory first—it's the whole strategy in one spreadsheet.
- Protect the top of the list properly, the bottom consciously; concentrate, then propagate.
- Automate first; prefer wired-in and managed / native controls; build once, replicate outward.
- Adopt force-multiplier AI only against the lean test; monitor it as the AI system it is.

The two actions from this chapter:

- **Strategic Move (leader):** Make prioritization real, own the risk-acceptance calls, and lean on managed services.
- **Tactical Move (implementer):** Build the ranked inventory this week, then protect the top item properly and automate outward.

The throughline to remember: you can't do all of it, so you do the most important fraction deliberately—rank by stakes, automate the repeatable, and multiply your freed attention with AI that earns its place. The book's per-chapter moves weren't beginner steps; ordered by leverage, they were the lean program all along.

CHAPTER 15
NAVIGATING THE MAZE: GLOBAL AI REGULATION AND COMPLIANCE

From Boardroom to Build: A Blueprint for AI Governance, Risk, and Technical Security

(Phase III — Governance & Future Horizons begins)

OPENING

As this is being written, a company with a high-risk AI system selling into Europe faces a genuinely hard decision, and there is no safe answer.

The EU AI Act—the most comprehensive AI law in the world—has a compliance deadline bearing down on high-risk systems. The obligations are serious: risk management programs, documentation, human oversight, conformity assessments, with penalties for the most serious violations reaching up to €35 million or 7% of worldwide annual turnover, whichever is higher.[1] A responsible company should be racing to meet it. Except that very deadline has been provisionally pushed to late 2027—agreed by EU lawmakers but, as of this writing, not yet formally adopted into law.[2] So the company is caught in a real dilemma the legal press has described plainly: rush ahead with expensive compliance and constrained product launches in case the deadline holds, or stand down and assume the delay will be confirmed—and risk being badly caught out if it isn't.[2]

Sit with that, because it captures something most people get wrong about AI regulation. The hard part isn't that the rules are strict, though some are. The hard part is that *the rules are a moving target, and you have to act before they stop moving.* This company's problem isn't that it doesn't understand the EU AI Act; it understands it perfectly well. The problem is that the law itself is in flux—deadline uncertain, scope being renegotiated—and the company must commit real money and real product decisions *now,* under that uncertainty, knowing it might bet wrong. That is the actual experience of AI compliance in this era, and no amount of carefully reading any single statute solves it.

By the time you read this, that specific deadline will have resolved one way or another—and it almost doesn't matter, because the *situation* it illustrates is the permanent condition. There will always be a looming AI regulation whose final form is uncertain, a deadline that might move, a scope being renegotiated, a new jurisdiction entering the fray. The specific maze in front of you will be different from the one described on this page; the experience of standing in a shifting maze will be identical. This chapter is about how to navigate that—not by memorizing the maze's current layout, which will be obsolete before the ink dries, but by learning to move through *any* configuration of it.

And there's a genuine, almost liberating insight that makes this navigable: *you cannot keep up with AI regulation by tracking individual laws—there are too many, they conflict, and they change monthly—but you don't have to, because beneath the churn the regimes are converging on the same handful of principles.* Build to those shared principles and you are substantially ready for most regimes at once—whichever way any specific deadline happens to fall. So this chapter does three things: it maps the moving maze honestly (and shows why chasing individual laws is a losing game), it identifies the convergent principles that let you build once and comply broadly, and it shows how to make compliance *evidence* rather than theater—by reusing the artifacts your security program already produces. A caveat this chapter wears openly: every specific date, threshold, and penalty here is a snapshot of a fast-moving moment, to be verified against current sources before you rely on it. The structure is durable; the specifics are not, and pretending otherwise would be the least useful thing a book could do.

PART ONE: THE MOVING MAZE — AND WHY CHASING LAWS FAILS

To navigate the maze you first have to see its shape—not to memorize today's layout, but to understand the *kind* of terrain it is. Three features define it, and together they explain why a law-by-law compliance strategy is doomed.

The EU: comprehensive, centralized, and still moving. The EU AI Act is the anchor of the global landscape—the most comprehensive AI law yet, built on a risk-tiered structure that sorts AI systems into categories from prohibited (unacceptable risk), through high-risk (heavy obligations: risk management, documentation, human oversight, conformity assessment), to limited-risk (transparency duties) and minimal-risk (largely unregulated).[3] Its influence reaches far beyond Europe for the same reason GDPR's did: it applies to operators outside the EU whose systems reach the EU market, making it a *de facto* global benchmark that other regulators echo.[1] But even this anchor is not fixed—its deadlines have been renegotiated in real time, as the opening showed. The most comprehensive, most studied AI law in the world is itself a moving target. If *it* won't hold still, nothing will.

The US: fragmenting, and fighting itself. Where the EU is centralized, the United States is the opposite—a fragmenting patchwork with an unresolved power struggle at its center. Individual states have enacted a wave of AI laws covering automated decision-making, training-data transparency, and algorithmic discrimination, each with its own scope and timeline, so that a company operating nationally faces a jurisdiction-by-jurisdiction analysis rather than one federal standard.[4] Layered on top is a genuine federal-versus-state conflict: federal action has moved to *preempt* state AI laws in the name of avoiding burdens on innovation, while a large multi-state coalition of attorneys general signals coordinated enforcement from the other direction.[5] The result for anyone trying to comply is the worst of both worlds: a patchwork that is simultaneously fragmented *and* unsettled, where even the question of *who* gets to set the rules is actively contested.

The rest of the world: more regimes, all at different speeds. Beyond the EU and US, more jurisdictions enter the landscape continually, each with its own approach, timeline, and emphasis—some echoing the EU's risk-tiered model, others charting different paths.[6] For any organization operating across borders, this means the maze has not just many walls but many *map-makers*, each redrawing their section on their own schedule.

Why chasing individual laws fails. Put those three features together—comprehensive-but-moving, fragmented-and-contested, and multiplying—and the conclusion is unavoidable: *a compliance strategy built on tracking individual laws cannot win, because the target moves faster than any compliance project can finish.* By the time you have fully mapped and complied with one jurisdiction's current requirements, another has changed, a deadline has shifted, a new law has passed, a preemption fight has reshuffled the board. An organization that treats compliance as "read each law, build to each law" is signing up for an infinite, always-behind chase—and worse, it's building a brittle compliance posture that shatters the moment any single specific it was built around changes. The law-by-law approach doesn't just fail to keep up; it produces fragile compliance that's obsolete on contact with the next amendment.

This is the trap the rest of the chapter is built to escape. The escape isn't a better tracking system or a bigger legal team to chase the churn faster. It's to stop chasing the specifics altogether and build instead to what *doesn't* change: the principles the regimes are converging on beneath all the motion. That's Part Two.

PART TWO: BUILD TO THE CONVERGENT PRINCIPLES

If chasing individual laws is a losing game, the winning one is this: look beneath the churn for what the regimes have *in common,* and build to that. And when you look, something reassuring emerges—for all their surface differences and conflicts, the major AI regulations are converging on the same handful of underlying expectations. The specifics diverge and change; the principles beneath them are remarkably stable and shared. Build to these five and you are substantially ready for most regimes at once, whichever way any particular deadline or amendment falls.

One — Risk-classify your AI systems. Nearly every serious regime sorts AI by risk and scales obligations accordingly—the EU's explicit tiers (prohibited, high, limited, minimal) are the clearest example, and US state laws increasingly center on "high-risk" or "consequential" decisions as the trigger for heightened duties.[3] [4] The shared principle: *the obligations attach to the stakes.* This is the regulatory echo of Chapter 6's dials—and it means the system-ranking you (a lean team especially) already built isn't just a security tool, it's the foundation of your regulatory posture. Knowing which of your systems are high-stakes is the first thing nearly every regime asks.

Two — Be transparent: disclose that AI is in use. Transparency runs through every regime: people must be informed when AI is being used, especially when its outputs affect their rights, opportunities, or access to services.[7] The forms vary—labeling AI-generated content, disclosing an AI chatbot, watermarking synthetic media, notifying someone an automated decision was made about them—but the principle is constant: *don't hide the AI.* An organization that defaults to disclosing AI use, clearly and proactively, is aligned with the direction of nearly every regime even before the specific labeling rule is finalized.

Three — Document and log: prove accountability exists. Across regimes, documentation, logging, and monitoring are positioned not as optional compliance artifacts but as the "required proof that accountability exists in practice."[7] Regulators increasingly don't just want you to *be* accountable; they want you to *demonstrate* it with records—technical documentation of how a system works, logs of what it did, evidence of the oversight applied. The principle: *if you can't show it, you didn't do it.* This is the single most reusable principle in the chapter, because—as Part Three will develop—the documentation your security program already generates is precisely this proof.

Four — Keep humans in the loop. Human oversight is a near-universal expectation, especially for consequential decisions: a person must be able to understand, oversee, and where appropriate override the AI, rather than letting it make rights-affecting decisions autonomously and unaccountably.[3] [7] This is the regulatory form of the least-privilege and human-checkpoint thinking from the technical chapters—and it means the human-in-the-loop controls you built for high-stakes systems (Chapters 7, 11) are simultaneously satisfying a regulatory principle. Build for human oversight where the stakes are high and you're building what the regimes demand.

Five — Know your role: developer versus deployer. Nearly every regime distinguishes between the entity that *builds* an AI system and the entity that *deploys* it, assigning different obligations to each—mirroring how privacy law separates controllers from processors.[4] [7] This is the regulatory echo of Chapter 8's supply-chain thinking and Chapter 5's ownership question: you must know, for each AI system, whether you are the developer, the deployer, or both, because your obligations differ sharply by role. An organization that can't answer "are we the developer or the deployer of this system?" can't determine its obligations under almost any regime.

Why this is the durable core. Step back and notice what these five principles are: risk-classification, transparency, documentation, human oversight, and role-clarity. None of them is a specific date, threshold, or statute—they are *structural expectations* that recur across regimes precisely because they reflect a shared underlying logic about what responsible AI governance looks like. This is why building to them is durable where building to individual laws is brittle: when a deadline moves or an amendment narrows a definition, your principles-based posture barely flexes, because you built to the thing the amendment was a particular expression *of*. And there's a profound consequence the research states directly: AI regulation now sits squarely *within* privacy and governance programs, because these expectations are familiar ones—the governance frameworks from Chapter 3 already embody them.[7] You are not building a separate compliance apparatus. You are pointing the governance and security program you already built at the regulators who now ask to see it.

PART THREE: MAKE COMPLIANCE EVIDENCE, NOT THEATER

The five principles tell you *what* to build to. This final piece is about how compliance actually gets demanded and delivered—and the good news, genuinely, is that you have already done most of the work.

Compliance is increasingly demanded as proof, by buyers as much as regulators. Two forces now drive AI compliance, and the second surprises people. The first is regulators, who—per principle three—want demonstrated accountability, not asserted accountability. The second, and often the more immediate, is *your customers*: enterprise procurement now routinely asks vendors for AI Act conformity declarations, AI-specific addenda to security certifications, and incident-reporting commitments, exporting their own regulatory burden onto their suppliers through vendor questionnaires.[8] If you sell B2B software, your customers will make their compliance your compliance, and they'll ask for evidence before they sign. This means compliance has a market-access dimension that often bites sooner than enforcement does—procurement closes the door while the regulator is still hypothetical.

The evidence is the artifacts your security program already produces. Here is the chapter's most useful realization, and the payoff of everything before it. The "proof of accountability" that regulators and buyers demand is not a new and separate pile of work—it is, to a remarkable degree, the documentation your security program has been generating all along:

- The **governance documentation** from Chapter 3 (the NIST / ISO frameworks) *is* the demonstrated-accountability proof of principle three.
- The **risk classification** from Chapter 6's dials *is* the risk-tiering of principle one.
- The **red-team evidence** from Chapter 10 *is* the adversarial-testing proof regulators increasingly expect of high-risk and frontier systems.

- The **AI-BOM** from Chapter 8 *is* the provenance and technical documentation the developer/deployer obligations call for.
- The **incident response plan and its notification triggers** from Chapter 11 *are* the incident-reporting commitments buyers ask for in questionnaires.
- The **human-oversight controls** from Chapters 7 and 11 *are* the human-in-the-loop evidence of principle four.

The compliance artifact is the security artifact, presented to a different audience. This is the deepest reason the whole-book approach pays off: an organization that did the security work has, almost as a byproduct, generated the compliance evidence—while an organization that treated security and compliance as separate initiatives is doing the work twice and probably failing at both.

Avoid theater — operate the controls, don't just document them. The honest caution: this only works if the evidence is *real*. The research is pointed that documentation and logging must be proof that accountability exists *in practice,* not checkbox artifacts nobody operates.[7] Compliance theater—policies written to be shown but never followed, controls documented but not running—fails on contact with a serious regulator or a thorough buyer audit, and it's worse than nothing because it manufactures false confidence (the same trap as the hollow red-team from Chapter 10). The principle: generate compliance evidence as the *honest output of controls you actually operate,* not as a documentation exercise performed for show. If the evidence describes a control you genuinely run, it's an asset; if it describes one you don't, it's a liability waiting for an audit.

The synthesis. Compliance, rightly understood, is not a separate discipline bolted onto security—it's the *same work, presented to regulators and buyers as evidence.* Build to the convergent principles using the governance and security program from the rest of this book, operate the controls genuinely, and the documentation those controls produce becomes the proof that satisfies most regimes at once and the answer to the buyer's questionnaire. You navigate the moving maze not by chasing its walls but by building something stable enough to hold its shape no matter how they shift—with the evidence to show it.

THE LEADERSHIP LENS

For a leader, AI regulation is a domain of decision-making under irreducible uncertainty—and the temptation is to handle that uncertainty badly, either by ignoring it or by paralysis. Four responsibilities for handling it well.

Decide under uncertainty deliberately — it's a risk-appetite call. The opening's dilemma (comply now or bet on the delay?) is the defining leadership experience of AI regulation, and it's fundamentally a Chapter 4 risk-appetite decision wearing regulatory clothes. You will rarely have certainty; you'll have a looming deadline that might move, a law whose scope might narrow, a preemption fight that might reshuffle everything. The leadership job is to make the comply-now-or-wait call *deliberately*—weighing the cost of premature compliance against the cost of being caught out, given your actual exposure—rather than defaulting into ignoring it (and getting blindsided) or panicking (and burning resources on a deadline that moves). And the principles-based approach is what makes this bet far safer: if you've built to the convergent principles, you're substantially ready *whichever way the specific resolves*, so the bet matters less. The best way to handle regulatory uncertainty is to build something that's robust to it.

Treat compliance as market access, not just legal risk. The framing that gets compliance funded correctly is recognizing that, increasingly, it's a *commercial* requirement, not only a legal one. Your enterprise customers will demand conformity evidence, AI addenda, and incident commitments through procurement questionnaires—and the deal stalls without them, long before any regulator acts.[8] For a leader, this reframes the compliance investment from "avoiding fines" (a distant, probabilistic cost) to "closing deals" (an immediate, concrete revenue gate). That reframing usually moves compliance from the perpetually-deferred pile to the funded-now pile, which is where, for commercial reasons alone, it increasingly belongs.

Own the developer-versus-deployer determination. A specific, consequential leadership responsibility: ensure the organization knows, for each significant AI system, whether it is the developer, the deployer, or both—because obligations differ sharply by role under nearly every regime, and getting the role wrong means getting the entire obligation set wrong. This is a determination that needs an owner (Chapter 5) and that the business, not just the lawyers, must understand, because it shapes everything from contracts to controls. It's the regulatory question most often left unanswered until an audit forces it.

Build to principles, not headlines — and don't whipsaw the organization. Leaders consume regulatory news, and AI regulation generates a lot of dramatic headlines (a deadline! a delay! a preemption fight!). The discipline is to not let each headline whipsaw the organization into a new crash compliance program or a relieved stand-down. Direct the organization to build to the durable principles, and treat the headline churn as noise around a stable signal. A leader who reorganizes the compliance posture with every news cycle exhausts the team and builds nothing stable; one who holds steady on the convergent principles while monitoring the specifics builds something that survives the churn.

The one question to ask your team this week: *"If the three AI regulations most relevant to us each changed their specifics tomorrow—a deadline moved, a threshold shifted—how much of our compliance work would we have to redo?"* If the answer is "most of it," you've built to the specifics, and you have a brittle, always-behind posture. If the answer is "very little, because we built to risk-classification, transparency, documentation, human oversight, and clear roles," you've built to the principles, and you're robust to exactly the churn that defines this domain.

THE EXECUTION LENS

For the implementer, navigating the regulatory maze means building to the convergent principles and generating the evidence—and the reassuring truth is that most of this is *reusing and presenting work you've already done,* not building anew. The playbook turns the five principles into concrete, durable controls.

Build the five principles as standing controls, not per-law projects. Implement each convergent principle once, as a durable capability, rather than re-implementing per jurisdiction:

- ***Risk-classify*** every AI system using the Chapter 6 dials — this is the regulatory trigger for almost everything, and you likely already have the ranked inventory (Chapter 14). Make the classification an explicit, recorded field.
- ***Transparency*** — build AI-use disclosure in by default: label AI interactions and AI-generated content, and provide notice (and where required, appeal paths) when automated decisions affect people. Defaulting to disclosure is cheaper than per-rule retrofitting.
- ***Documentation and logging*** — ensure every significant system has technical documentation and operational logs sufficient to *prove* what it does and what oversight applies. This is largely the Chapter 9 telemetry and Chapter 3 governance docs, retained and organized for an external audience.
- ***Human oversight*** — implement human-in-the-loop checkpoints on consequential decisions (Chapters 7, 11), and document that they exist and are operated.
- ***Role determination*** — record, per system, whether you're the developer, deployer, or both, and attach the role-appropriate obligations.

Generate the evidence pack from existing artifacts. Assemble a reusable "compliance evidence pack" by *pointing at work you already produced* rather than creating new documents: the governance framework mappings (Ch. 3), the risk classifications (Ch. 6), the red-team reports (Ch. 10), the AI-BOM (Ch. 8), the incident plan and notification triggers (Ch. 11), the human-oversight records. Maintain it as a living collection so that when a regulator's inquiry or a buyer's questionnaire arrives, you're *assembling* from existing evidence, not *scrambling* to create it. The implementer's leverage here is enormous: the security work, organized for presentation, *is* the compliance deliverable.

Overlay jurisdiction-specifics only where they bite. Build to principles first; then add the jurisdiction-specific specifics only where they materially affect you—the particular labeling format the EU requires, the specific notice a given state mandates, the exact threshold that triggers an obligation. The principle-built foundation handles the bulk; the jurisdictional overlay is a thin, maintainable layer on top, not the foundation itself. And keep that overlay *thin and current*, re-verifying the volatile specifics against primary sources on a cadence (the one part of this that genuinely does require ongoing tracking—but only the thin specific layer, not the whole posture).

For lean teams: scope reduction over checkbox policies. A pointed lean tactic the research surfaces: smaller teams should prioritize *reducing scope* over standing up elaborate paper compliance—disabling a high-risk feature you don't need (emotion inference, certain automated decisions), geofencing a capability away from a demanding jurisdiction, or narrowing what a system does so it falls into a lower risk tier.[9] For a lean team, the cheapest compliance is often *not doing the high-risk thing in the first place*—which is the regulatory echo of Chapter 12's data minimization and Chapter 14's ruthless prioritization. Don't build heavy compliance for a risky capability you could simply decline to ship.

Compliance is your security program, organized for an audience: you are not building a compliance system; you are *presenting your security system as compliance evidence.* Every convergent principle maps to controls you've already built across this book, and the implementer's real job is to (a) ensure those controls genuinely run, (b) classify systems by risk so obligations attach correctly, and (c) keep the evidence organized and the thin jurisdictional overlay current. Build to the principles, operate the controls honestly, assemble the evidence from what you already have, and you navigate any configuration of the maze—because you built something stable that the moving walls keep finding you already compliant with.

The one move to make this week: take your highest-stakes AI system and write down two things: its risk classification (using the dials) and whether you are its developer or deployer. Then list which existing artifacts—governance docs, red-team report, AI-BOM, oversight records—you could hand a regulator or enterprise buyer tomorrow as evidence for that system. The gaps in that list are your real compliance work; the items already on it are proof you're further along than you thought. One system, classified, with its evidence inventoried.

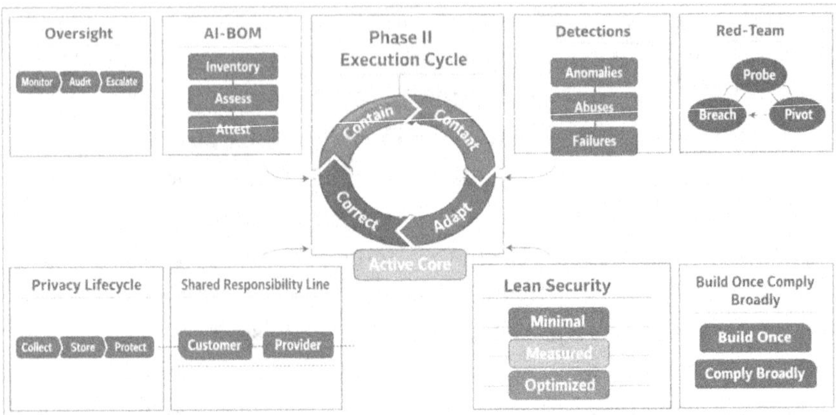

Figure 15.1 — Your Security Work Is Your Compliance Evidence. *The five principles the major AI regimes converge on—risk-classify systems, disclose AI use, document and log, keep humans in the loop, and know your developer/deployer role—each map directly onto an artifact the security program already produces: the Chapter 6 risk dials, the Chapter 7/11 human-oversight controls, the Chapter 3 governance documentation, the Chapter 8 AI-BOM, the Chapter 10 red-team reports. Built once and operated honestly, these become the evidence regulators and buyers ask to see—not a second, parallel body of work.*

BRINGING IT TOGETHER

We opened with a company facing an impossible bet—comply now with a looming EU deadline, or wait on a delay that, as of writing, is agreed but not yet adopted into law—and the recognition that this is the permanent condition of AI compliance: not strict rules, but a *moving target* you must act on before it stops moving. By the time you read this, that specific deadline will have resolved, and it won't matter, because another uncertain one will have taken its place.

The way through is to stop chasing the moving walls. The maze is comprehensive-but-shifting in the EU, fragmented-and-contested in the US, and multiplying across the rest of the world—and a law-by-law compliance strategy loses to all three, producing brittle compliance that's obsolete on contact with the next amendment. So you build instead to what doesn't move: the five principles the regimes are converging on—risk-classify your systems, be transparent about AI use, document and log to prove accountability, keep humans in the loop, and know whether you're developer or deployer. Build to those and you're substantially ready for most of them at once. And the evidence those regimes demand turns out to be the security artifacts you already built, operated honestly and presented to a new audience —which is what the two Moves below put to work.

Your focused guidance as a leader is to direct the organization to build to the convergent principles rather than chasing headlines, make the comply-now-or-wait calls deliberately as the risk-appetite decisions they are, and fund compliance as the market-access requirement it has become—because the deal stalls on a missing conformity declaration long before a regulator calls.

Your practical execution step as an implementer is to take your highest-stakes system, classify its risk and determine your developer/deployer role, then inventory which existing security artifacts you could hand a regulator or buyer as evidence tomorrow. Build the five principles as standing controls, assemble the evidence pack from work you've already done, and keep only a thin jurisdictional overlay current.

Uniting the leader's directive with the implementer's focus turns regulation from a frightening, ever-shifting maze into something navigable. The leader builds to principles and decides under uncertainty deliberately; the implementer turns those principles into standing controls and assembles the evidence from the security program that already exists. You stop trying to memorize a maze whose walls move monthly, and start being the organization that—wherever they move next—is already substantially standing where they ask, with the evidence in hand to prove it.

Coming next — Running through this chapter's principles was a recurring concern: AI systems that make *consequential decisions about people*—credit, employment, essential services—and the demand that those decisions be fair, transparent, and contestable. Regulation increasingly insists on it, but the deeper question isn't only what the law requires; it's what's *right*, and how you build for it technically. In Chapter 16 we turn to the ethical guardrails—bias, fairness, and transparency—the place where AI's impact on real human lives is most direct, and where law, ethics, and engineering meet. Chapter 12 protected the data going in; this chapter is about the fairness of what comes out.

CHAPTER 15 IN REVIEW

The core idea: You cannot keep up with AI regulation law-by-law—there are too many, they conflict, and they change monthly. But beneath the churn the regimes converge on the same handful of principles. Build to those, and you're substantially compliant across most regimes at once, whichever way any specific deadline or amendment falls. *(Every specific date, threshold, and penalty in this domain is a fast-moving snapshot—verify against current sources before relying on it.)*

The wake-up call: A company faces a real bet—comply now with a looming EU AI Act high-risk deadline, or wait on an agreement that, at the time of writing, is not yet formally adopted into law. The hard part of AI compliance isn't strict rules; it's acting under a *moving target* before it stops moving. That uncertainty is the permanent condition, even as specific deadlines resolve.

The moving maze (why chasing laws fails):

- **EU:** the comprehensive, risk-tiered anchor (prohibited / high / limited / minimal) and a de facto global benchmark—but its own deadlines have been renegotiated in real time.
- **US:** a fragmenting state patchwork plus an unresolved federal-vs-state preemption struggle—fragmented *and* unsettled at once.
- **Rest of world:** more regimes continually, each at its own speed.
- **The trap:** law-by-law compliance moves slower than the target and produces brittle posture, obsolete on the next amendment.

The five convergent principles (build to these):

- **Risk-classify** your systems — obligations attach to stakes (the regulatory echo of Chapter 6's dials).
- **Be transparent** — disclose AI use, especially for rights-affecting outputs.
- **Document and log** — proof that accountability exists in practice; "if you can't show it, you didn't do it."
- **Human oversight** — a person can understand, oversee, and override consequential decisions.
- **Know your role** — developer vs. deployer determines your obligations under nearly every regime.

Make compliance evidence, not theater:

- Compliance is demanded by regulators and by enterprise buyers alike, via conformity declarations, AI addenda, and incident SLAs in security questionnaires.
- The evidence is the artifacts you already built: governance docs (Ch. 3), risk classes (Ch. 6), red-team reports (Ch. 10), AI-BOM (Ch. 8), incident plan (Ch. 11), oversight records (Ch. 7/11). The compliance artifact is the security artifact, presented to a new audience.
- Operate the controls honestly — documented-but-unoperated controls are theater that fails on audit.

For the leader (Leadership Lens):

- Decide comply-now-vs-wait deliberately—it's a risk-appetite call, made safer by a principles-based posture.
- Treat compliance as market access, not just legal risk—it gates deals now.
- Own the developer-vs-deployer determination per system.
- Build to principles, not headlines; don't whipsaw the organization with every news cycle.

For the implementer (Execution Lens):

- Build the five principles as standing controls, not per-law projects.
- Assemble a living evidence pack from existing artifacts; assemble, don't scramble.
- Overlay jurisdiction-specifics only where they bite, and keep that thin layer current.
- Lean teams: prefer scope reduction (don't ship the high-risk thing) over checkbox policies.

The two actions from this chapter:

- *Strategic Move (leader):* Build to convergent principles, decide under uncertainty deliberately, fund compliance as market access.
- *Tactical Move (implementer):* Classify your top system's risk and role, and inventory the evidence you could produce tomorrow.

The throughline to remember: Don't chase the moving maze law-by-law—build to the principles the regimes converge on: risk-classification, transparency, documentation, human oversight, and clear roles. Operate the controls honestly, and your security artifacts become your compliance evidence. Build something stable, and wherever the walls move, you're already standing where they ask.

CHAPTER 16
THE ETHICAL GUARDRAILS: BIAS, FAIRNESS, AND TRANSPARENCY

From Boardroom to Build: A Blueprint for AI Governance, Risk, and Technical Security
(Phase III — Governance & Future Horizons)

OPENING

A person applies for a job, or a loan, or has their risk assessed by a court—one of the consequential decisions that shape a life. An AI system processes the application and returns a verdict: rejected, denied, high-risk. The decision is made in milliseconds, applied consistently, and delivered without malice. It is also wrong—not wrong in the sense of a bug, but wrong in the sense that the system has quietly learned to treat people like this applicant worse than people unlike them, for reasons that have nothing to do with their actual qualifications.

Now add the second harm, the one that makes the first so much worse. The applicant wants to know *why*. And no one can fully tell them. The system didn't reason in words; it computed a score from patterns buried in billions of parameters, and even the people who built it cannot point to a clean, human-legible explanation of why this person, specifically, was rejected. The decision was unfair, and it was *unexplainable*: a wrong delivered from inside a black box, with no door the person can knock on to contest it.

This is the dual harm at the heart of AI fairness, and it's worth naming precisely because the two halves compound each other. AI doesn't just make unfair decisions; it makes them invisibly and at scale. A biased human loan officer wrongs the people they personally see; a biased model wrongs everyone it processes, identically, forever, until someone notices—and the opacity is exactly what delays the noticing. The danger isn't only that AI can be unfair. It's that it can be unfair while no one—not even its builders—can readily say why. These cases are not hypothetical: AI hiring tools have faced discrimination litigation, and risk-assessment algorithms used in the justice system have been criticized for producing systematically different predictions across racial groups for the same conduct.[1]

This chapter is about building the guardrails against that dual harm—and it sits deliberately on the far side of a line this book drew earlier. Chapter 12 was about protecting the data going *in*: its confidentiality, its exposure, its presence in the model. This chapter is about the fairness of what comes *out*: whether the model's decisions treat people equitably, and whether those decisions can be understood and contested. Same systems, opposite ends. There, the concern was the data as something to protect; here, it's the *output* as something that affects a human life.

And this is the chapter where three forces the book has treated somewhat separately finally converge on a single problem. The law increasingly mandates fairness: under regimes like the EU AI Act, high-risk systems such as credit scoring carry obligations to identify and assess discrimination—enforceable from August 2026—and employment regulators are pursuing AI-driven discrimination.[1] The *ethics* is the real harm to the real person in the opening—the applicant wronged by a machine. And the *engineering* is the measurable, imperfect toolkit for detecting and reducing that harm. Fairness is where law, ethics, and engineering stop being separate conversations and become one. So this chapter covers why AI is unfair and why you can't simply fix it, the uncomfortable truth that "fair" is a choice rather than a setting, and the practical discipline of measuring, mitigating, monitoring, and explaining—the guardrails that don't make AI perfectly fair (nothing does) but make its unfairness visible, bounded, and accountable.

PART ONE: WHY AI IS UNFAIR — AND WHY YOU CAN'T SIMPLY FIX IT

To build fairness guardrails, you have to start with an uncomfortable truth that rules out the naive goal: *you cannot build a perfectly unbiased AI, because the world the AI learned from is not unbiased.* Models learn from historical data, and that data encodes the real patterns of a society that has discriminated—so a model trained to predict the future from the past will, by default, reproduce and even amplify the inequities baked into that past.[1] This is not a flaw you can patch; it's a property of learning from history. The goal of this chapter, therefore, is not the impossible "unbiased AI" but something achievable and honest: *deliberately measuring, bounding, and accounting for bias,* rather than pretending it can be eliminated. Naming that up front matters, because a team chasing perfect fairness will either despair or, worse, declare victory falsely.

Bias enters AI systems from three distinct sources, and effective guardrails address all three rather than fixating on one.

Data bias: the model learns a biased world. The largest source is the training data itself. If historical hiring data reflects decades of favoring certain groups, a model trained on it learns that pattern as "what success looks like." If the data underrepresents a group, the model performs worse for that group. The data doesn't have to mention a protected attribute directly to encode bias—which leads to the subtlest version of the problem.

Proxy discrimination: the bias hides in innocent-looking features. Even a model that never sees race, gender, or age can discriminate on them, because other features act as *proxies.* A résumé screener that favors "digital native" language can systematically disadvantage older applicants without ever processing age; a model using postal code can encode racial patterns of historical segregation without ever processing race.[1] This is why "we removed the protected attributes" is not a fairness strategy—the bias re-enters through correlated features that look perfectly neutral. Proxy discrimination is the trap that catches teams who believe blinding the model to protected attributes makes it fair.

Algorithmic and human bias: the design choices and the people making them. Bias also enters through how the model is built and tuned—the objective it optimizes, the thresholds chosen—and through the human judgments behind those choices.[1] A team that isn't looking for bias, or that lacks the diversity of perspective to notice whose interests a design choice quietly serves, will build their blind spots into the system. This is why the research consistently pairs technical fairness work with *interdisciplinary, diverse teams*: the people building the system shape whose fairness it protects.[2]

The honest consequence. Put the three sources together and the lesson is clear: because bias enters from the data (which reflects a biased world), from neutral-seeming proxies, and from human design choices, it cannot be switched off—only deliberately surfaced and managed. This reframes the entire task. You are not trying to certify your AI as unbiased; you are building a discipline to *find* the bias that is certainly there, *decide* how much and what kind is tolerable (a value judgment, as Part Two shows), *reduce* it where you can, and *watch* for it continuously. The organizations that get fairness wrong are usually the ones that thought it was a problem you solve once, rather than a property you manage forever.

PART TWO: FAIRNESS IS A CHOICE, NOT A SETTING

Here is the idea that separates a serious treatment of AI fairness from a naive one, and it's the conceptual heart of this chapter: *there is no single, universal definition of "fair." There are several, they are mathematically different, and they often cannot all be satisfied at once—so choosing which one applies to your situation is an irreducibly human, value-laden decision that no tool, metric, or model can make for you.*

Most people approach fairness as if it were a setting—a switch you flip to "on," a box the engineers tick. It is not. When you try to make "fair" precise enough to measure, it fractures into multiple competing definitions, each capturing a real and reasonable intuition about fairness, each measured by a different metric:

- **Demographic parity** asks whether different groups receive positive outcomes at the same *rate*—does the loan-approval rate match across groups?
- **Equal opportunity** asks whether different groups who are *genuinely qualified* have the same chance of a positive outcome—among people who would actually repay, is the approval rate equal across groups?
- **Disparate impact** analysis asks whether any group is disproportionately disadvantaged by the outcomes, regardless of intent.[3]

Each of these is a legitimate notion of fairness. And here is the uncomfortable mathematical fact: *you frequently cannot satisfy all of them simultaneously.* Optimizing for equal outcome rates across groups (demographic parity) can force you to treat genuinely different qualification distributions identically; optimizing for equal treatment of the qualified (equal opportunity) can produce different outcome rates across groups. Improving one fairness metric often *worsens* another. There is no configuration that is fair by every definition at once, because the definitions encode genuinely different—sometimes opposed—values about what fairness *means.*

This is why fairness is a choice. Since you cannot be fair by all definitions, you must *decide which definition of fairness applies to your specific context*—and that decision is not technical. It's a question about values, stakes, and the specific harm you most need to prevent. Is it more unfair, in lending, to approve different *proportions* of each group, or to give qualified applicants from different groups different *chances*? The answer depends on what you believe fairness requires in *that* domain, what the law demands, what the affected communities would say, and what kind of error does the most human damage. An engineer cannot answer that from inside the code; it requires the people who own the decision, the people affected by it, and often the lawyers and ethicists, to make a deliberate, documented value judgment about *which fairness you are choosing and why.*

The consequence for how you build. This reframes the entire fairness effort. The technical work—the metrics, the mitigation—comes *second,* in service of a choice that must be made *first.* A team that skips the choice and lets the engineers pick a metric by default (or pick whichever is easiest to optimize) hasn't avoided the value judgment; it has made it implicitly, badly, and without accountability—letting a convenience decision quietly determine whose fairness the system protects. The mature posture is the opposite: name the fairness definition you're choosing, justify it against your context and the law, document the tradeoff you're accepting against the definitions you're *not* optimizing, and only then turn to the engineering. Fairness done well is a value decision made explicitly and then served by technique—not a technical default dressed up as neutrality.

PART THREE: THE DISCIPLINE — MEASURE, MITIGATE, MONITOR, AND EXPLAIN

With the value choice made, the engineering can serve it. The practical discipline of fairness has four parts, and—consistent with the whole chapter—none of them achieves perfect fairness; together they make unfairness *visible, bounded, contestable, and watched.*

Measure: you can't manage the bias you don't quantify. The foundation is measurement—bias audits that quantify how the system performs across groups, using the fairness metric you chose in Part Two.[4] This means evaluating model performance across demographic groups, checking for representation gaps in the data, and applying the chosen fairness metric (demographic parity, equal opportunity, disparate impact) to produce a concrete number you can track and act on.[4] Crucially, you measure *before* deployment (does this system meet our fairness bar before it touches a person?) *and* after (is it still meeting it?), because—as the monitoring step will stress—bias isn't static. Without measurement, fairness is an assertion; with it, fairness becomes a managed metric like any other.

Mitigate: reduce bias at three stages. When measurement reveals bias beyond your chosen tolerance, mitigation happens at three points in the pipeline, and the research is consistent on all three:[5]

- *Pre-processing* — adjust the data before training: rebalance underrepresented groups, clean skewed data, and remove or neutralize the proxy features that smuggle in protected attributes (Part One's proxy problem).
- *In-processing* — adjust the training itself: fairness-aware algorithms and fairness-constrained learning that penalize biased outcomes in the model's objective, so the model optimizes for accuracy *and* the fairness definition you chose.
- *Post-processing* — adjust the outputs after the decision: calibrate or screen results to ensure fair treatment, including output screens that catch biased content before it reaches a person (the LLM hate-speech-filter pattern).

No single stage is sufficient, and the right combination depends on your system and your chosen fairness definition. The honest note: every mitigation involves the tradeoff from Part Two—reducing one form of unfairness may cost accuracy or worsen another fairness measure, so mitigation is itself a series of value-laden choices, not a mechanical cleanup.

Explain: open the black box enough to contest the decision. This is the transparency leg, and it directly addresses the *second* harm from the opening—the unexplainability. Explainable-AI techniques make a model's decisions interpretable: feature-attribution tools (such as SHAP and LIME) can show which inputs most influenced a given decision, and *model cards* document how a model was built, what data trained it, and what its known limitations and performance-across-groups are.[6] The goal is twofold: internally, so you can detect *why* a model is biased and fix it; and externally, so the person in the opening can be given a reason and a path to contest a decision that affects their life. Explainability is imperfect—these tools approximate rather than fully reveal a model's reasoning—but the difference between "we cannot say why you were rejected" and "here are the principal factors, and here is how to appeal" is the difference between an unaccountable black box and a contestable decision. Transparency is also where this chapter rejoins Chapter 15's principles: disclosure, documentation, and human-legible reasoning are simultaneously an ethical duty and a regulatory expectation.

Monitor: bias drifts, so watching is continuous. Finally, because the world and the data change, a system that was fair at launch can drift into unfairness over time—so fairness, like security, requires *continuous monitoring*, not a one-time certification.[5] This is the Chapter 9 monitoring discipline pointed at fairness: track the fairness metrics in production, watch for drift across groups, and alert when the system crosses the tolerance you set. And pair it with a *bias incident response* path (the Chapter 11 discipline): when monitoring or a user report surfaces a biased outcome, have a defined way to investigate, contain, remediate, and feed the finding back.[5] Provide feedback loops so the people affected can report unfair decisions—they are often your earliest and most accurate bias detector.

The synthesis. Measure, mitigate, explain, monitor—the four together don't deliver the impossible (a perfectly fair AI). They deliver the achievable and the honest: an AI whose fairness is *quantified* against a chosen definition, *improved* where measurement demands, *explainable* enough to be contested, and *watched* so its inevitable drift is caught. That is what ethical guardrails actually are—not a guarantee of fairness, but the disciplined, accountable management of an unfairness you're honest enough to admit you can never fully eliminate.

THE LEADERSHIP LENS

Fairness is the most human of this book's topics, and for that reason the one a leader can least afford to delegate to engineers: its hardest questions are about values, not code. Four responsibilities.

Own the fairness definition — it's a value choice, and it's yours. The central leadership lesson follows directly from Part Two: since "fair" has multiple incompatible definitions and choosing among them is a value judgment, that choice cannot be left to whoever is writing the model. It belongs to leadership, informed by law, ethics, affected communities, and the specific stakes—because it defines what your organization believes fairness means in the decisions it automates. A leader who lets the engineering team pick a fairness metric by default has outsourced a values decision to a convenience decision, and will own the consequences without having made the choice. Name the fairness you're choosing, and own it.

Treat fairness as legal liability and trust, not just ethics. Even a leader unmoved by the ethical argument has two hard-nosed reasons to act: the law increasingly imposes fairness obligations on high-stakes systems and regulators are pursuing AI discrimination, and biased AI destroys the trust of customers, employees, and the public when it surfaces—which it eventually does.[1] Framing fairness as simultaneously the right thing, a legal requirement, and a trust asset is what moves it from "nice to have" to funded priority—because the discriminatory system is not just an ethical failure but a lawsuit, a regulatory finding, and a reputational wound waiting to happen.

Build diverse teams and invite outside perspective — it's a fairness control. Because human blind spots become the system's blind spots (Part One), the composition of the team building the AI is itself a fairness mechanism. A homogeneous team, optimizing in good faith, will still miss harms it has no lived reason to anticipate. The leadership move is to ensure interdisciplinary, demographically diverse input into high-stakes AI—and to invite the perspective of affected communities —not as a diversity gesture but as a practical control that surfaces unfairness a narrow team cannot see.[2] Whose fairness the system protects is shaped by who is in the room when it's built.

Insist on explainability for consequential decisions. A leader should refuse to deploy a fully unexplainable model for decisions that materially affect people's lives. The standard to set: if the system can't offer an affected person a reason and a route to contest, it isn't ready for a consequential role. This is both an ethical line and, increasingly, a regulatory one—and it protects the organization as much as the individual, because a decision you can't explain is a decision you can't defend.

The one question to ask your team this week: *"For our highest-stakes AI decision about people, which definition of fairness did we deliberately choose, who made that choice, and could we explain a single decision to* *the person it affected?"* If the team can't name the chosen fairness definition, the value judgment was made by default, in the code, by no one accountable. If they can't explain a decision, you're operating a black box in a role that demands a glass one. Either gap is the chapter's warning made concrete.

THE EXECUTION LENS

For the implementer, building ethical guardrails means turning the value choice into measured, mitigated, explainable, monitored reality —serving a fairness definition you were *given*, not one you picked by default. The work is a disciplined lifecycle, and much of it reuses machinery from earlier chapters pointed at a new target.

Start with the chosen fairness definition — and refuse to proceed without it. Before writing mitigation code, get the explicit fairness definition from the decision owners (Leadership Lens). If it hasn't been made, *surface that gap rather than papering over it by picking a metric yourself*—choosing the metric in the code is making the value judgment unaccountably, the exact failure Part Two warns against. Your job is to implement the chosen fairness, and to make visible to leadership the tradeoff it implies against the definitions you're not optimizing.

Run the bias self-audit, before and after deployment. Build a repeatable audit that:[4]

- Maps where bias could enter your pipeline (data, proxies, model design—Part One's three sources).
- Profiles the training data for representation gaps and skew.
- Hunts for and removes/neutralizes *proxy features* — the neutral-looking inputs correlated with protected attributes, because dropping the protected attribute alone doesn't work.
- Evaluates model performance across demographic groups using the *chosen* fairness metric, producing a concrete number against a defined tolerance.
- Runs *before* deployment as a gate and *after* as a recurring check.

Mitigate at the three stages, accepting the tradeoffs explicitly. Apply mitigation where measurement demands, combining stages as needed:[5] pre-processing (rebalance and clean data, neutralize proxies), in-processing (fairness-aware / fairness-constrained training that penalizes biased outcomes in the objective), and post-processing (calibrate or screen outputs; output filters for harmful generated content). Document the accuracy-vs-fairness and fairness-vs-fairness tradeoff each mitigation makes—these are the value choices from Part Two, made concrete.

Build explainability in — for diagnosis and for contestability. Implement feature-attribution tooling (SHAP / LIME-style) so you can see which inputs drove a decision, and maintain *model cards* documenting training data, methodology, limitations, and across-group performance.[6] Wire this to two outputs: an internal diagnostic view (why is the model biased, so you can fix it) and an external, human-legible reason plus appeal path for affected people (the answer to the opening's second harm). Treat explainability as approximate—useful for diagnosis and contestability, not a complete window into the model's reasoning.

Monitor continuously and wire bias into the existing loops. Fairness isn't shipped once:[5]

- Track fairness metrics in production and alert on drift across groups—this is the Chapter 9 monitoring discipline, with fairness as the signal.
- Build a *bias incident response* path—investigate, contain, remediate, feed back—as a specialized case of the Chapter 11 plan.
- Provide user feedback loops so affected people can report unfair outcomes; route those reports into the monitoring and incident systems. Affected users are frequently your most accurate bias detector.

Underneath the four-part discipline sits one idea: ethical guardrails aren't a separate ethics module bolted onto the model; they're the *same* security-and-governance machinery—measurement, mitigation, monitoring, incident response, documentation—pointed at fairness as the target, in service of a value choice made above the code. You measure fairness like you measure drift (Ch. 9), respond to bias like you respond to incidents (Ch. 11), document it like you document for compliance (Ch. 15), and gate it like you gate any high-stakes control (Ch. 6's dials decide which systems get this rigor). Build it this way and fairness stops being a vague aspiration and becomes a quantified, monitored, contestable property of the system—imperfect, honestly bounded, but *managed* rather than hoped for.

The one move to make this week: take your highest-stakes AI decision about people and run a single bias measurement—pick the fairness definition (or, if none was chosen, escalate that gap to the decision owners first), and evaluate the system's outcomes across the relevant groups to produce one concrete fairness number. Whether it passes or fails your tolerance, you've converted "we hope it's fair" into "we measured it, here's the number, here's what we'll do." For a decision that shapes human lives, that single measurement is the difference between assuming fairness and managing it. One decision, one chosen definition, one measured number.

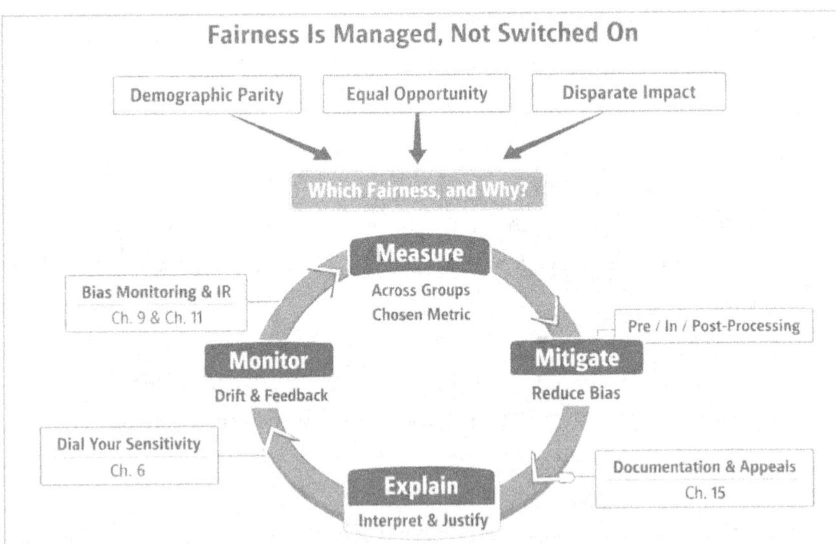

Figure 16.1 — Fairness Is Managed, Not Switched On *Fairness begins as a value choice, not a setting. Three incompatible definitions—demographic parity, equal opportunity, and disparate impact—converge on a human decision: which fairness, and why? From that choice*

flows a continuous discipline: ***Measure*** *(across groups, chosen metric) →* ***Mitigate*** *(pre / in / post-processing) →* ***Explain*** *(feature attribution, model cards, appeal path) →* ***Monitor*** *(drift, bias response, user feedback) → back to Measure. Each stage connects to earlier-chapter machinery—Ch. 9 monitoring, Ch. 11 incident response, Ch. 15 documentation, Ch. 6 dials—forming a living system of accountability. You can't switch fairness on; you choose what it means, then manage it forever.*

BRINGING IT TOGETHER

We opened with a person wronged by a machine—denied a job, a loan, or their liberty by a system that had quietly learned to treat people like them worse, and that could not explain itself when asked why. Two harms in one: unfair, and unexplainable—because opacity is what lets invisible unfairness run at scale until someone finally notices.

Building guardrails against that starts with honesty: you cannot make a perfectly unbiased AI, because it learns from a biased world—through the data, through neutral-looking proxies, and through human design choices—so the goal is not perfection but deliberate management. Then comes the chapter's hardest truth: fairness isn't a setting you switch on. "Fair" has multiple incompatible definitions you cannot satisfy at once, which makes choosing among them a human value judgment no tool can make for you. And only after that choice does the engineering serve it—measure fairness against the definition you chose, mitigate at the data, the training, and the outputs, explain decisions enough to contest them, and monitor continuously because bias drifts. The four together don't promise fairness. They give you the honest most that ethical guardrails can be—far more than the black box in the opening offered.

Your core accountability as a leader is to own the fairness definition as the value choice it is—deciding, with legal, ethical, and affected-community input, what fairness means for your highest-stakes decisions rather than letting the metric default in the code—and to set diversity and explainability as non-negotiables.

Your foundational technical assignment as an implementer is to take your highest-stakes decision about people and produce one concrete fairness measurement against an explicitly chosen definition—escalating first if no definition was chosen. Then build the lifecycle around it: audit for proxies, mitigate across the three stages with documented tradeoffs, implement explainability with an appeal path, and wire fairness monitoring and bias incident response into the loops you already run.

This combination of ethical governance and practical validation makes fairness a managed property rather than a hopeful assumption. The leader makes and owns the value choice and sets the non-negotiables; the implementer serves that choice with measurement, mitigation, explanation, and monitoring drawn from the machinery the book already built. You stop hoping your AI is fair and start being able to say—with a number, a reason, and an appeal path—what fairness you chose, how the system measures against it, and how a wronged person can be heard. That is not perfect fairness. It is accountable fairness, which is the only kind a system learning from an imperfect world can honestly offer.

Coming next — With this chapter, Phase III's substantive work is nearly done, and the book has carried you from the boardroom's first questions about AI to the build-level details of securing it, governing it, complying with its regulation, and making it fair. One chapter remains, and it turns to what comes next. In Chapter 17 we look at where this is all going—the agentic, increasingly autonomous AI that the technical chapters kept gesturing toward—and then pull the entire book together into a single blueprint: the through-line from boardroom to build, and what to actually do on Monday morning. The guardrails are built. The last chapter is about the road ahead, and how to walk it.

CHAPTER 16 IN REVIEW

The core idea: AI can be unfair *and* unexplainable—wronging people invisibly, at scale, while no one can say why. You can't build perfectly unbiased AI (it learns from a biased world), and "fair" isn't a single setting—it's multiple incompatible definitions, so choosing among them is a human value judgment. Ethical guardrails don't make AI perfectly fair; they make its unfairness measurable, bounded, and accountable. *(This chapter is about the fairness of what comes out; Chapter 12 was about protecting the data going in.)*

The wake-up call: A person is denied a job, loan, or liberty by an AI that learned to treat people like them worse—and can't explain why. The dual harm: unfair and unexplainable, each compounding the other, because opacity delays the noticing that would stop the unfairness.

Why AI is unfair — and why you can't simply fix it:

- You can't make perfectly unbiased AI: it learns from historical data that encodes a biased world. The goal is deliberate management, not impossible perfection.
- **Data bias** — the model learns the inequities in its training data.
- **Proxy discrimination** — bias re-enters through neutral-looking features (postal code, "digital native" language); removing protected attributes is *not* a fairness strategy.
- **Algorithmic & human bias** — design choices and the (often non-diverse) people making them build blind spots into the system.

Fairness is a choice, not a setting:

- Multiple legitimate, incompatible definitions: demographic parity (equal outcome rates), equal opportunity (equal chances for the qualified), disparate impact (no group disproportionately disadvantaged).
- You frequently *cannot satisfy all at once*—improving one worsens another.
- So you must *choose* which fairness applies to your context—a value judgment, not a technical one. Skipping the choice means making it implicitly, badly, in the code.

The discipline — measure, mitigate, explain, monitor:

- **Measure** — bias audits across groups using the chosen metric, before *and* after deployment.
- **Mitigate** — at three stages: pre-processing (data), in-processing (fairness-aware training), post-processing (output calibration / screening); every mitigation carries a tradeoff.
- **Explain** — feature attribution (SHAP / LIME) and model cards, for internal diagnosis *and* an external reason + appeal path (the answer to the opening's second harm).
- **Monitor** — continuously, because bias drifts; plus a bias incident-response path and user feedback loops.

For the leader (Leadership Lens):

- Own the fairness definition—it's a value choice, not an engineering default.
- Treat fairness as legal liability and trust, not just ethics.
- Build diverse, interdisciplinary teams as a practical fairness control.
- Refuse to deploy unexplainable models for consequential decisions.

For the implementer (Execution Lens):

- Start from the chosen fairness definition; escalate if none was made—don't pick it in the code.
- Run the bias self-audit (hunt proxies; measure across groups) before and after deployment.
- Mitigate across the three stages with documented tradeoffs.
- Build explainability with an appeal path; monitor fairness and wire bias into the Ch. 9 / Ch. 11 loops.

The two actions from this chapter:

- *Strategic Move (leader):* Own and document the fairness definition for high-stakes decisions; set explainability and diversity as non-negotiables.

- *Tactical Move (implementer):* Produce one concrete fairness measurement for your highest-stakes decision against an explicitly chosen definition.

The throughline to remember: You can't switch fairness on—AI learns from a biased world, and "fair" is several incompatible things at once. So *choose* what fairness means for each high-stakes decision, then manage it forever: measure it, mitigate it, explain it, and monitor it. Accountable fairness—a chosen definition, a measured number, a reason, and an appeal path—is the only honest kind, because no AI trained on a flawed history can offer more.

CHAPTER 17
THE ROAD AHEAD

From Boardroom to Build: A Blueprint for AI Governance, Risk, and Technical Security
(Phase III — Governance & Future Horizons concludes)

OPENING

Think back to where this book began.

It opened in a boardroom, with the most basic questions an organization can ask about artificial intelligence: What is this, really? Should we use it? What could go wrong? Who is responsible if it does? Those were not technical questions. They were questions of judgment, ownership, and risk: the questions a leader asks before a single model is deployed. And from there the book traveled a long way: through the work of naming your AI and governing it, of treating its risks as enterprise risks and assigning someone to own them; and then down into the build itself—securing the pipeline, the supply chain, and the cloud; watching systems in production; attacking them before adversaries do; planning for the incident that gets through anyway; protecting the data and the fairness of the decisions; and doing all of it at whatever scale your team can actually sustain. Finally it widened back out—to the regulations that govern this work and the ethics that should.

That arc has a shape, and the shape is the title of this book: *from boardroom to build.* From the leader's first question to the implementer's last commit, and back again—because, as nearly every chapter showed, the two ends of that journey only work when they're connected. The boardroom decides what matters; the build makes it real; and neither is sufficient alone. A decision no one builds changes nothing; a control no one authorized rarely survives contact with a budget. The whole book has been about closing the distance between those two rooms.

This final chapter does three things, and none of them is teaching a new topic. The topics are done. First, it looks at the horizon, briefly, because the ground this book stands on is already shifting toward something the technical chapters kept gesturing at: agentic, increasingly autonomous AI. Second, and most substantially, it pulls the entire book together into a single blueprint—the through-line from boardroom to build that you can actually hold in your head and act on. And third, it ends where the book has ended every chapter: not with a grand transformation, but with one concrete thing to do this week. The guardrails are built. What remains is to look at the road ahead, and to take the first step down it.

PART ONE — THE HORIZON: THE AGENTIC FUTURE

Every chapter of this book has, quietly, been pointing at the same emerging thing. The monitoring chapter warned about agents whose individual actions are each authorized while only the chain is suspicious. The incident-response chapter described harm at machine speed. The cloud chapter named the over-privileged agent as the new and most dangerous misconfiguration. The red-teaming chapter flagged agentic exploits as the fastest-growing attack category. These were not separate observations. They were early sightings of the same horizon: the shift from AI that *responds* to AI that *acts*—autonomous agents that reason, plan, and take actions in the world, individually and in coordinated multi-agent systems.

That shift is no longer speculative. As this is written, agentic AI is moving into production faster than almost any enterprise technology before it—analysts project that a large and rapidly growing share of enterprise applications will embed task-specific agents within the near term, and surveys already find most technical teams past planning and into active testing or production.[1] And the security community has noticed: in one industry poll, agentic AI and autonomous systems were ranked the *single top attack vector* heading into the year, outranking every other concern.[2] The reason is the recurring danger this book has named from several angles—an autonomous agent operates with broad, cross-system permissions, creates a *non-human identity* that legacy identity systems were never designed to handle, can be manipulated through its inputs into taking harmful actions, and does all of this at machine speed and at a scale where agents may vastly outnumber human users.[1 2]

But here is the most important thing this book can say about the agentic horizon, and it's reassuring rather than alarming: *agentic AI does not require a new book. It intensifies this one.* Look at what the agentic risks actually are, and every one is a concept you have already met:

- The over-privileged agent is **least privilege and blast radius** (Chapters 7, 13), now urgent rather than advisable, because the agent acts on its permissions autonomously.
- The non-human identity explosion is **the inventory and ownership problem** (Chapters 2, 5), now at machine scale.
- Agent manipulation is **prompt injection** (Chapter 7), now with the power to *act* on the manipulation, not just speak it.
- Multi-agent chains are **the chain-aware detection and monitoring problem** (Chapters 9, 11), now the default rather than the exception.
- The governance-lagging-adoption gap is **Shadow AI and the imperative** (Chapter 1), now accelerating.

The pattern is unmistakable: agentic AI takes every principle this book taught and raises the stakes on it. The autonomy that makes agents powerful is exactly what makes the book's disciplines—least privilege, identity, monitoring behavior not just infrastructure, the continuous loop, human oversight, the dials that decide how much rigor a system earns—*more* necessary, not less. The structural truth the research keeps returning to is that adoption is outpacing governance: agents are reaching production without the controls to match.[1] The organization that internalized this book is the one positioned to close that gap, because it already has the principles; the agentic future asks it to apply them with greater rigor and less delay, not to learn them anew.

A word of honesty about the horizon, consistent with the rest of the book: the *specifics* of where AI goes next are genuinely uncertain, and anyone who tells you precisely what the next few years hold is guessing. The particular frameworks, the exact capabilities, the specific threats will all shift. But the *trajectory*—toward more autonomy, more capability, more integration into consequential systems—is not in serious doubt, and that trajectory is enough to act on. You don't need to predict the destination to prepare for the direction. And the preparation is what this entire book has been.

PART TWO — THE BLUEPRINT: FROM BOARDROOM TO BUILD

Here, at the end, is the whole book pulled into a single picture—not a summary of seventeen topics, but the one through-line that connects them, so you can carry the argument rather than the table of contents. The blueprint has three movements, and they map exactly to the journey the book has taken: the boardroom, the build, and the bridge of governance that joins them.

The boardroom: decide what matters and who owns it. The book's first phase was about leadership establishing the foundation, and it reduces to a short, durable sequence. *Recognize the imperative*—AI is already in your organization whether you sanctioned it or not, so the choice is to govern it or be surprised by it (Chapter 1). *Know what you have*—you cannot secure, govern, or comply for AI you can't name, so inventory it (Chapter 2). *Govern it as a structure, not a finish line*—adopt a governance backbone you can implement once and satisfy framework, standard, and law together (Chapter 3). *Treat its risks as enterprise risks*—use the machinery you already have, and decide your risk appetite so you can say yes deliberately rather than no reflexively (Chapter 4). *Give it an owner*—what falls between roles falls to no one, so assign clear ownership with real authority (Chapter 5). And *calibrate to the stakes*—the three dials of consequence, data sensitivity, and regulatory weight tell you how much rigor any given system has earned (Chapter 6). That is the boardroom's work: not to build the controls, but to establish what matters, who is accountable, and how much protection each system deserves. Everything downstream depends on these decisions being made deliberately rather than by default.

The build: secure it in practice. The book's second and largest phase turned those decisions into engineering, and it too has a through-line—a single interconnected loop rather than a list of tasks. You *secure the pipeline* (Chapter 7), recognizing AI as a pipeline not a product, and verify what you can't fully trust. You *secure the supply chain* (Chapter 8), because a model is a dependency your scanners can't read. You *watch it in production* (Chapter 9), because AI fails at the behavior and output layer where traditional monitoring is blind. You *attack it yourself* (Chapter 10), continuously, because the test is never finished. You *plan for the breach that gets through* (Chapter 11), capturing before you contain, and closing the loop by feeding every incident back into your defenses, detections, and tests. You *protect the data* (Chapter 12), building privacy in because it's baked into the model and can't be bolted on. You *scale it securely* (Chapter 13), owning your half of the cloud's shared-responsibility line. And you do all of it *lean* (Chapter 14), prioritizing ruthlessly and automating relentlessly, because you will never do everything—so you do the right fraction on purpose. The deep structure of the build is that these are not eight separate jobs; they are one continuous, self-improving loop, where what you learn in any one feeds all the others.

The bridge: govern what you build, and build what you can govern. The book's third phase is the connective tissue between the boardroom and the build—the accountability that makes the leader's intent real and the implementer's work defensible. You *navigate the regulatory maze* (Chapter 15) not by chasing individual laws but by building to the principles they converge on—and you discover that the evidence regulators and buyers demand is the very security work you already did, presented to a new audience. And you *build the ethical guardrails* (Chapter 16), choosing what fairness means for your consequential decisions and managing it deliberately, because a system learning from an imperfect world can offer accountable fairness, never perfect fairness. This phase is the proof that the boardroom and the build were connected all along: governance is where the leader's "what matters" and the implementer's "how we built it" meet, get documented, and become something you can stand behind.

The through-lines that unify all three. Step back from the three movements and a handful of ideas recur across every one—these are the book's real argument, the threads that make it one blueprint rather than seventeen chapters:

- *The dials.* Consequence, data sensitivity, regulatory weight—introduced for industry context, then reused for control tiering, monitoring intensity, red-team depth, lean triage, regulatory risk-classification, and fairness rigor. One idea, applied everywhere: match the rigor to the stakes.
- *The loop.* Nothing in AI security is done once. Govern, secure, watch, test, respond, learn, and feed it back—because both the systems and the threats keep changing. The test is never finished; the report is a perishable good.
- *Least privilege and blast radius.* Assume manipulation will sometimes succeed, and limit in advance what a compromised model or agent can *do.* This single principle runs from the pipeline to the cloud to the agentic horizon.
- *Your security artifacts are your compliance evidence.* The work doesn't have to be done twice. Build the security program well and the governance, the documentation, and the compliance proof are largely its byproducts.
- *Start with one system.* Every chapter's "one move" was the same move: take your highest-stakes system and do one

thing properly, then replicate. The whole blueprint is climbed one deliberate step at a time.

- *Honest limitation.* Poisoning, prompt injection, machine unlearning, perfect fairness—the book never pretended these were solved. The mature posture is not the elimination of risk but its deliberate, documented, accountable management. Chosen gaps, not discovered ones.

Boardroom and build, one more time. The blueprint speaks to both audiences this book has addressed throughout, and the final word on each is simple. The *leader's* job is to make the decisions that only the boardroom can make—what matters, who owns it, how much risk is acceptable, what fairness means—and then to fund and mandate the work, because intent without authority is just a wish. The *implementer's* job is to turn those decisions into controls that actually run—built into the pipeline, automated, monitored, looped—and to make the gaps visible rather than silent, because execution without honesty is just theater. Each makes the other real. The leader who decides without funding the build has decided nothing; the implementer who builds without the boardroom's mandate has built an orphan. The entire book has been one argument: that AI security works only when the boardroom and the build are connected—when what matters at the top is what gets built at the bottom, and what's learned at the bottom informs the decisions at the top.

PART THREE — THE CALL TO ACTION: MONDAY MORNING

A book like this can leave a reader feeling that the task is enormous—and it is. But the book's most consistent lesson has been that enormity is not faced all at once. It's faced one system, one move, one week at a time.

So here is the entire book reduced to a single instruction you can act on the moment you close it: *pick your highest-stakes AI system—the one that, if it failed or was manipulated, would cause the most harm—and do one concrete thing to make it more secure this week.* Not a strategy. Not a committee. Not a transformation program. One system, one move. Inventory it if you haven't. Classify its stakes with the dials. Put authentication on its endpoint. Limit what its agent can do. Run one bias measurement. Build one automated control into its pipeline. Whichever single move fits where you actually are—make it, this week.

That instruction works for everyone this book has spoken to. If you are a leader, your one move is a decision: name the owner, set the appetite, fund the control, choose the fairness definition—the thing only you can authorize. If you are an implementer, your one move is a control: the wired-in check, the locked-down permission, the measured number that turns a hope into a fact. If you are a team of one wearing both hats, it's whichever of those matters most for your single most important system. The move scales to your role and your resources, because the principle underneath it is universal: *deliberate beats comprehensive.* A small thing done on purpose, on the system that matters most, beats a grand plan that never starts.

And then—because this is a loop and not a line—next week, do it again. The same system, the next move; or the next system, the first move. The blueprint isn't executed in a quarter or a year. It's executed in a sustained habit of deliberate steps, each one making the next possible, each one closing a little more of the distance between the boardroom and the build.

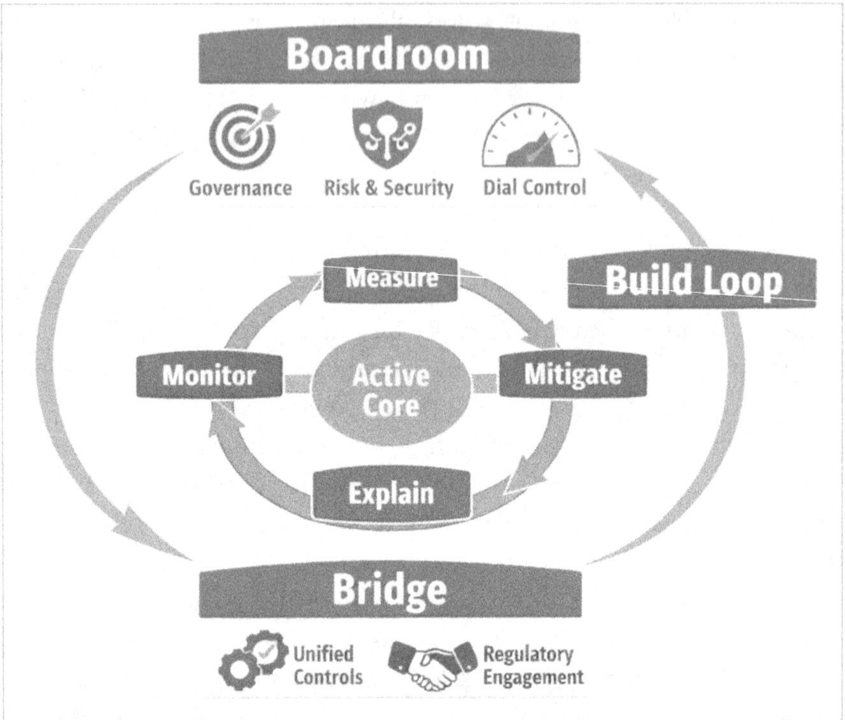

Figure 17.1 — The Connected Blueprint. *AI security is not a ladder you climb once but a loop you run continuously. The* ***Boardroom*** *sets the foundation: recognizing the AI already in the organization, naming it, governing it, owning its risk, and using the three dials to decide how much rigor each system earns. The* ***Build Loop*** *turns those decisions into living controls—securing the pipeline and supply chain, watching systems in production, red-teaming them, responding to what gets through, and protecting data and fairness—each feeding back into the others so the work never finishes. The* ***Bridge*** *closes the circuit: the documentation, evidence, and oversight that turn the build back into something the boardroom can stand behind, satisfying regulators and buyers with the security work already done. Leadership decides what matters; engineering makes it real; governance proves it—and what's learned at the build informs the next decision at the top. From boardroom to build, and back again—the loop that keeps AI secure.*

CLOSING: THE ROAD AHEAD

This book set out to connect two rooms that too often operate as if they were in different buildings: the boardroom where the consequences of AI are owned, and the build where its risks are actually engineered. Everything between them has been one argument made from many angles—and you now hold it.

The ground will keep shifting. The agentic horizon is only the next stretch of a road that does not end—the capabilities will grow, the threats will evolve, the regulations will move, and the specifics in this book will age even as its principles hold. That is not a reason for despair; it's the nature of the work. Security for a technology this powerful and this fast-moving was never going to be a destination you arrive at and rest. It's a road you learn to walk well.

And walking it well does not require predicting the future, or having a bank's resources, or solving problems that are genuinely unsolved. It requires something more durable: the judgment to know what matters most, the discipline to protect it deliberately, the honesty to admit what you can't yet solve, and the will to take the next step even when the road ahead is uncertain. From the boardroom to the build, and back again. That is the whole of it. The road ahead is long, but you are ready to walk it. Start this week, with one system and one move. The rest follows from there.

THE THROUGHLINE OF THE WHOLE BOOK

AI security is the work of connecting the boardroom to the build—deciding what matters and who owns it, then engineering its protection for real, and keeping both connected as the ground shifts. Match your rigor to the stakes, run it as a loop rather than a one-time fix, limit what a compromised system can do, be honest about what you can't solve, and let your security work be its own compliance evidence. You will never do everything—so do the right fraction, on purpose, starting with your highest-stakes system and one deliberate move this week. The road doesn't end; you just learn to walk it well.

GLOSSARY

From Boardroom to Build: A Blueprint for AI Governance, Risk, and Technical Security

Plain-language definitions of the key terms used across this book, written for the reader who needs the concept, not the textbook. Terms are grouped by theme and, within each group, listed alphabetically.

FOUNDATIONS

Agentic AI / AI agent — AI that doesn't just respond but acts: it can reason, plan, and take actions in the world (calling tools, accessing systems), often with broad permissions and minimal human oversight of each step. The emerging frontier and, currently, a top security concern.

Artificial intelligence (AI) / machine learning (ML) — Software that learns patterns from data rather than following only hand-written rules. Machine learning is the most common form of AI in use today.

Context window (context) — The amount of text a model can consider at once — the prompt, the conversation so far, and any documents fed in. Everything the model "sees" when producing an output lives here, which is why it is also where prompt-injection attacks operate.

Foundation model / frontier model — A large, general-purpose model trained on broad data and adapted to many downstream tasks; "frontier model" denotes the largest and most capable of these. The category most AI regulation now targets directly (the EU AI Act's general-purpose AI tier).

Generative AI (GenAI) — AI that produces new content—text, images, code, audio—rather than only classifying or predicting. Large language models are the best-known example.

Inference — The act of using a trained model to produce an output (answering a prompt, scoring an application). The "live" operation of an AI system, as opposed to training it.

Large language model (LLM) — A type of generative AI trained on vast amounts of text to predict and produce language; the engine behind most AI chat and writing tools.

Model — The trained artifact at the center of an AI system: the set of learned parameters (often billions of numbers, called weights) that turns an input into an output.

RAG / retrieval-augmented generation — A technique that lets a model pull in external documents at answer time rather than relying only on what it learned in training. Powerful and now standard—and the channel indirect prompt injection rides in on, since the model trusts what it retrieves.

Shadow AI — AI tools used inside an organization without the knowledge, approval, or oversight of its security or leadership—a major source of unmanaged risk.

Training / fine-tuning — Training is teaching a model from data. Fine-tuning is further training a pretrained model on your own narrower data to specialize it.

Weights / parameters — The internal numbers a model learns during training. The model's "knowledge" lives here, diffused across all of them—which is why specific data, once trained in, is so hard to remove.

HOW AI FAILS AND GETS ATTACKED

Blast radius — How much damage a compromised or manipulated system can do. Limiting the blast radius means restricting in advance what a system can touch, so a breach stays contained.

Data poisoning — Corrupting a model by tampering with its training data, so it learns a hidden flaw or backdoor.

Drift — The gradual degradation of a model's behavior or fairness over time as the world changes around it. Why monitoring must be continuous.

Hallucination — When a model produces fluent, confident output that is simply false—invented facts, citations, or details. Not a malfunction but a property of how these systems generate language, which is why human verification of consequential output is non-negotiable.

Jailbreak — Getting a model to bypass its own safety rules, often through multi-turn conversation rather than a single obvious request.

Membership inference — Determining whether a specific person's data was used to train a model. Dangerous when membership itself is sensitive (e.g., a model trained only on patients with a condition).

Model / training-data extraction — Coaxing a model into revealing data it was trained on—a privacy and confidentiality risk that looks nothing like a traditional breach.

Prompt injection — Manipulating an AI's behavior through crafted input—getting it to ignore its instructions or do something harmful. Indirect prompt injection hides the manipulation in a document or data source the AI reads.

Reasoning compromise — This book's term for an AI incident with no traditional equivalent, where the attack lives in the model's prompts, context, and logic rather than in breached infrastructure. The field describes the phenomenon (attacks on an AI's reasoning process) more than it names it.

DEFENSES AND CONTROLS

AI Bill of Materials (AI-BOM / ML-BOM) — An inventory of everything that went into an AI system (models, datasets, dependencies), used to trace provenance and respond to supply-chain issues. "Forensics, not a firewall."

Guardrails — Controls that filter an AI's inputs and outputs at runtime: blocking disallowed content, screening for sensitive data, enforcing policy. Available as managed cloud services.

Human-in-the-loop — Keeping a person able to understand, oversee, and override an AI's decisions, especially for consequential ones. Both a safety control and a regulatory expectation.

Incident response (IR) — The discipline of preparing for, detecting, containing, and recovering from security failures. For AI, the order inverts: capture forensic evidence before you contain.

Least privilege — Granting any user, system, or AI agent only the minimum access it needs to do its job—a core principle for limiting blast radius.

Provenance — The traceable record of where something came from: which data trained a model, which model version shipped, who changed what. The thing an AI Bill of Materials exists to capture.

Red-teaming — Deliberately attacking your own AI to find its failures before an adversary does—an ongoing practice, not a one-time test.

Shared-responsibility model — The division of security duties between a cloud provider (who secures the infrastructure of the service) and the customer (who secures how they configure and use it). AI added new items to the customer's side.

PRIVACY AND FAIRNESS TECHNIQUES

Algorithmic disgorgement — A regulatory remedy requiring an organization to delete not just improperly obtained data but the models trained on it.

Bias — Systematic unfairness in AI outputs, entering through skewed data, through proxy features that stand in for protected attributes, or through human design choices.

Confidential computing — Using secure hardware enclaves to keep data protected even while it's being processed.

De-identification — Detecting and removing or masking sensitive personal data (names, identifiers, medical codes) before it reaches training.

Differential privacy — Adding carefully calibrated statistical noise so a model learns general patterns while making it provably hard to identify any individual's data. Offers formal guarantees, at some cost to accuracy.

Explainability (XAI) — Techniques (such as SHAP, LIME, and model cards) that make a model's decisions interpretable enough to diagnose and to contest.

Fairness metrics — Different, often mutually incompatible mathematical definitions of "fair"—e.g., demographic parity (equal outcome rates across groups), equal opportunity (equal chances for the genuinely qualified), disparate impact (no group disproportionately disadvantaged—also a specific legal doctrine in US hiring and lending). Choosing among them is a value judgment, not a technical default.

Federated learning — Training a model across many devices or organizations so raw data never leaves its home; only model updates are shared. (Those updates can still leak, so it's often paired with differential privacy.)

Machine unlearning — An emerging set of techniques for making a model selectively "forget" specific data without full retraining—the technique that could one day make algorithmic disgorgement feasible short of rebuilding the model. Advancing, but not yet fully solved.

Model card — A standardized document describing how a model was built, what data trained it, and its known limitations and performance across groups.

Proxy discrimination — When a model discriminates on a protected attribute (race, age) through correlated but innocent-looking features (postal code, word choice) even though the attribute itself was removed.

GOVERNANCE AND FRAMEWORKS

CSPM / DSPM / AI-SPM — Posture-management tooling categories: Cloud Security Posture Management (infrastructure misconfigurations), Data Security Posture Management (where sensitive data lives), and AI Security Posture Management (extending both into the AI layer—discovering models and agents, scanning their configurations).

Developer vs. deployer — The distinction nearly every AI regulation makes between the entity that builds an AI system and the entity that deploys it, assigning different obligations to each. (Mirrors privacy law's controller/processor split.)

EU AI Act — The most comprehensive AI law to date, built on risk tiers (prohibited, high-risk, limited, minimal) with obligations scaled to risk. A de facto global benchmark.

Governance framework — A structured approach to managing AI risk. Major reference points include the NIST AI Risk Management Framework, the ISO 42001 management-system standard, and the EU AI Act.

OWASP LLM Top 10 / MITRE ATLAS / NIST GenAI Profile — Industry reference frameworks cataloguing AI-specific vulnerabilities and adversarial tactics; used to make red-teaming and security work systematic and auditor-ready.

Risk classification / risk tiering — Sorting AI systems by their stakes so obligations and controls attach in proportion. The regulatory echo of this book's "three dials."

A note on terms: this field invents vocabulary faster than any glossary can capture. Where a term here differs from how your team or your regulator uses it, theirs governs—these definitions are for understanding the book, not for settling disputes.

ABOUT THE AUTHOR

CARLOS CABRERA

Carlos Cabrera is a cybersecurity and AI governance professional with nearly three decades of experience—since 1997—helping organizations secure their technology, manage risk, and govern emerging systems responsibly. His work spans the full distance this book describes: from the boardroom, where the consequences of technology are owned, to the build, where its risks are engineered.

Over that career he has worked across the disciplines that converge in artificial intelligence security—engineering and architecture, information security, cloud security, secure software development, enterprise risk, and security leadership—across banking, healthcare, government, and technology organizations, where these questions move from theory to consequence. Along the way he saw firsthand the problem at the heart of this book: that the people who decide to adopt AI and the people who must secure it too often work in isolation from one another. From Boardroom to Build was written to give both audiences a single, shared blueprint.

He holds senior certifications across the field, including the CISSP, CCISO, CRISC, and CISM, along with the CCSP and CSSLP in cloud and application security and the PMP and PMI-ACP in program delivery.

Carlos can be reached at carlosrcabrera@yahoo.com.

NOTES & SOURCES

Sources in this section were verified against primary materials as of June 2026. AI security and regulation move quickly; where a fact is described in the text as a snapshot in time, the citation reflects its status at verification.

Chapter 1 — The AI Imperative: Securing Value in an AI-First World

On the opening account of the Samsung incidents: The Economist Korea. (2023, March 30). Reporting on three Samsung semiconductor data-leak incidents involving ChatGPT (source code, meeting transcript, chip-test sequence). Summarized in English in: Cyber Security Hub. (2023). Samsung employees allegedly leak proprietary information via ChatGPT. https://www.cshub.com/data/news/iotw-samsung-employees-allegedly-leak-proprietary-information-via-chatgpt

1. Fishbowl. (2023, February). 70% of workers using ChatGPT at work are not telling their boss. Fishbowl Insights. https://www.fishbowlapp.com/insights/70-percent-of-workers-using-chatgpt-at-work-are-not-telling-their-boss/—Survey of 11,793 professionals, conducted January 26–30, 2023; of those using AI at work, 68% did not disclose the usage to their manager.
2. On the wave of corporate restrictions: Bloomberg. (2023, May 2). Samsung bans staff's use of AI like ChatGPT after data leak; Reuters. (2023, January). Amazon warns employees not to share code with ChatGPT; Bloomberg. (2023, February). JPMorgan restricts use of ChatGPT; Reuters. (2023, March). Goldman Sachs restricts use of ChatGPT.

Chapter 2 — Know Your Landscape: The Types of AI a Business Actually Uses

1, 5, 6. LayerX Security. (2025). *The LayerX Enterprise AI & SaaS Data Security Report 2025.* https://go.layerxsecurity.com/the-layerx-enterprise-ai-saas-data-security-report-2025—77% of employees paste data into GenAI tools; 82% of that activity occurs via unmanaged personal accounts; GenAI is the #1 corporate-to-personal data-exfiltration channel; employees average 14 pastes per day via non-corporate accounts, of which at least three contain sensitive data.

2. Google. *Gemini Apps Privacy Hub* (consumer), https://support.google.com/gemini/answer/13594961, and *Generative AI in Google Workspace—Privacy and Security* (enterprise). Accessed June 2026. Google's own documentation distinguishes consumer data handling (prompts may be reviewed by humans and used to improve services and models) from enterprise Workspace terms (contractual data isolation; exclusion from model training). [Re-verify before print—live support pages.]

3, 4, 9. Grip Security. (2026). *Top AI Security Risks in 2026.* https://www.grip.security/blog/top-ai-security-risks-in-2026—On the difficulty of discovering embedded AI features across SaaS applications, and on AI risk compounding through access and integration, expanding incident blast radius.

7. National Institute of Standards and Technology. (2023). *Artificial Intelligence Risk*

Management Framework (AI RMF 1.0). https://www.nist.gov/itl/ai-risk-management-framework; OWASP Foundation. (2023). *OWASP API Security Top 10.* On architectural and configuration risk across enterprise app → middleware → API → cloud integration chains.

8. OWASP Foundation. (2025). *OWASP Top 10 for LLM Applications (LLM01: Prompt Injection).* genai.owasp.org; NIST AI RMF 1.0 (2023) on trust boundaries and input governance.
10. OpenAI. *API Data Usage Policies / Enterprise Privacy.* openai.com/enterprise-privacy; Anthropic. *Commercial Terms of Service.* anthropic.com/legal. Accessed June 2026. Provider commitments not to train on API customer data, contingent on the customer's implementation invoking the correct service tier.

Chapter 3 — The Governance Backbone: Adaptive Frameworks for Trustworthy AI

1. EU Artificial Intelligence Act, Regulation (EU) 2024/1689, O.J. (L, 2024/1689) (entered into force August 1, 2024). Original application date for most high-risk (Annex III) obligations: August 2, 2026; for high-risk AI embedded in regulated products (Annex I): August 2, 2027. These dates were subsequently deferred by provisional agreement on the Digital Omnibus on AI (see note 12).
2. National Institute of Standards and Technology. (2023). *Artificial Intelligence Risk Management Framework (AI RMF 1.0).* Voluntary, sector-agnostic; structured around the Govern, Map, Measure, Manage functions.
3. National Institute of Standards and Technology. (2024, July 26). *Artificial Intelligence Risk Management Framework: Generative Artificial Intelligence Profile* (NIST AI-600-1). https://nvlpubs.nist.gov/nistpubs/ai/NIST.AI.600-1.pdf
4. NIST emerging work on agentic AI and on sector-specific AI RMF profiles, including for critical infrastructure (in development at this writing). https://www.nist.gov/artificial-intelligence
5. On international convergence around RMF-style functions: OECD AI Principles; G7 Hiroshima AI Process; Council of Europe Framework Convention on AI; with supporting analysis in Nemko (2026).

6, 7. International Organization for Standardization / International Electrotechnical Commission. (2023). *ISO/IEC 42001:2023—Information technology—Artificial intelligence—Management system.* https://www.iso.org/standard/81230.html—The first certifiable international AI management system standard.

8, 9. A-LIGN. (2026). Market commentary on ISO/IEC 42001 certification as an emerging AI-governance maturity signal for enterprise buyers, and on its shared management-system structure with ISO/IEC 27001 and ISO/IEC 27701.

10, 11, 13. Regulation (EU) 2024/1689, arts. 5–6, 9–17, 99 & Annexes I, III. Risk tiers (prohibited, high, limited, minimal); high-risk obligations (risk management, data governance, technical documentation, record-keeping, transparency, human oversight, quality management); administrative fines up to €35 million or 7% of worldwide annual turnover (prohibited practices), €15 million or 3% (most other obligations), and €7.5 million or 1% (supplying incorrect, incomplete, or misleading information to authorities). Secondary mappings of ISO/IEC 42001 clauses to AI Act obligations: TruvoCyber; Gloceri (2026).

12. On May 7, 2026, the Council of the EU and the European Parliament reached provi-

sional political agreement on the Digital Omnibus on AI, deferring Annex III high-risk obligations from August 2, 2026 to December 2, 2027, and Annex I obligations from August 2, 2027 to August 2, 2028; the agreed text replaced the Commission's originally proposed conditional trigger with these fixed dates. Formal adoption was pending at this writing, so the original dates technically remained in force, with Article 50 transparency obligations largely remaining on the original schedule. The watermarking obligation under Article 50(2) is the exception, deferred to December 2, 2026. Primary source: Council of the EU. (2026, May 7). Artificial Intelligence: Council and Parliament agree to simplify and streamline rules [Press release].

14. On U.S. federal AI policy as of this writing (no comprehensive federal AI law; Executive Order of December 11, 2025; March 2026 White House legislative blueprint; proposed federal legislation; DOJ AI Litigation Task Force; state laws as the operative rules): analyses by Seyfarth; Paul Hastings; Sullivan & Cromwell; Ropes & Gray; Latham & Watkins; Manatt (2025–2026). Fuller treatment in Chapter 15.

Chapter 4 — AI Risk as Enterprise Risk: From Assessment to Alignment

1. PwC Pulse Survey series (2025–2026). A significant share of business leaders now rank AI governance and third-party risk among their top priorities.
2. Committee of Sponsoring Organizations of the Treadway Commission. (2017). *Enterprise Risk Management—Integrating with Strategy and Performance*; International Organization for Standardization. (2018). *ISO 31000:2018—Risk management—Guidelines.* On managing AI risk as an enterprise risk category with a named owner, key risk indicators, and controls drawn from NIST AI RMF, ISO/IEC 42001, and the EU AI Act where in scope.
3. *Moffatt v. Air Canada*, 2024 BCCRT 149 (B.C. Civ. Res. Trib., Feb. 14, 2024). Incorrect information provided by the airline's website chatbot held to constitute negligent misrepresentation attributable to the airline.
4. ISO 31000:2018 and COSO ERM (2017) on aligning risk appetite with organizational objectives and context; Committee of Sponsoring Organizations of the Treadway Commission. (2020). *Risk Appetite—Critical to Success* (Martens, F., & Rittenberg, L.), on risk appetite as an integral part of decision-making rather than a theoretical statement.

Chapter 5 — The New Hierarchy: Who Owns AI Risk?

1. IBM Institute for Business Value. (2026, May). *CEO study: CEOs are reshaping C-suite roles for the AI era.* IBM. (Survey of 2,000 CEOs across 33 countries and 21 industries, conducted February–April 2026; 76% of organizations report a Chief AI Officer in 2026, up from 26% in 2025.) Budget-control figure from: IBM Institute for Business Value, in cooperation with Oxford Economics and the Dubai Future Foundation. (2025, July). *The Chief AI Officer.* IBM. (Survey of 600+ CAIOs across 22 countries and 21 industries, Q1 2025; 61% of CAIOs control their organization's AI budget.)
2. On the CAIO as the coordination point for enterprise-wide AI efforts: IBM Institute for Business Value (2025, July), note 1 above.
3. On the scarcity of qualified AI leadership and fractional arrangements as a middle path for mid-size organizations: McKelvey, J. (2026, May). *Chief AI officer: Role, salary, and when to hire.* https://justinmckelvey.com/blog/chief-ai-officer (practitioner

analysis); Harvard Business Review. (2025, August). *How to make fractional leadership work* [Audio podcast episode].

4. On structured coordination—defined handoffs, joint reviews, and escalation paths—across the security, data, engineering, and legal functions: IBM Institute for Business Value (2025, July), note 1 above.
5. On the number of generative AI models in typical enterprise use—a typical organization runs 11 and plans at least 16 by the end of 2026: IBM Institute for Business Value, The Chief AI Officer (2025, July); see note 1.

Chapter 6 — The Industry Playbook: Reading Your Sector's Stakes

The regulatory readings in this chapter reflect the landscape as of mid-2026.

1, 4. New York State Department of Financial Services. (2026, May 21). Industry Letter: *Heightened Cybersecurity Risks Associated with Frontier AI Models*, issued together with companion guidance, *Measures Regulated Entities Should Consider in a Heightened Cybersecurity Threat Environment.* https://www.dfs.ny.gov/industry-guidance/industry-letters/20260521-heightened-cybersecurity-risks-assoc-with-frontier-ai-models—The letters impose no new requirements; they urge regulated entities to review and update risk assessments and to consider measures beyond the minimums of 23 NYCRR Part 500 in light of frontier AI capabilities.

2. Kiteworks. (2026, January). Analysis of healthcare's contradictory AI regulatory landscape: federal encouragement of AI adoption in care alongside state-level restrictions on AI in mental health, automated patient communication, and automated decision-making.
3. Industrial Cyber. (2025, November). On the Health Sector Coordinating Council Cybersecurity Working Group's AI Cybersecurity Task Group (115 organizations, formed October 2024) and its 2026 guidance program, which by mid-2026 had begun publishing sector playbooks and governance frameworks.
5. Regulation (EU) 2024/1689, art. 6(2) & Annex III, point 5(b) (credit scoring and creditworthiness assessment classified high-risk, excepting fraud detection); high-risk obligations effective August 2, 2026.
6. Corporate Compliance Insights. (2026, January). 2026 operational guide: "non-critical" businesses, including retail, as targets of both attackers and regulators.
7. Kiteworks. (2026, January). On retail AI rising to a higher regulatory tier when it touches consequential decisions; California and Colorado automated-decision rules. Fuller treatment in Chapter 15.

Chapter 7 — Securing Machine Learning and Generative AI Systems

1–5. Souly, A., et al. (2025). Poisoning attacks on LLMs require a near-constant number of poison samples. arXiv:2510.07192. A collaboration between Anthropic's Alignment Science team, the UK AI Security Institute's Safeguards team, and The Alan Turing Institute—the largest pretraining poisoning study to date. Key findings: approximately 250 poisoned documents reliably backdoor models from 600M to 13B parameters, despite the largest models training on more than 20 times more clean data; attack success depends on the absolute count of poisoned documents, not their proportion; the same dynamics were demonstrated during fine-tuning. The study's own caveat: it tested a simple denial-of-service backdoor, and it remains uncertain whether the pattern extends to more dangerous behaviors. See also: Anthropic. (2025, October 9). A small number of samples can poison LLMs of any size; The Alan Turing Institute. (2025, October 9). LLMs may be more vulnerable to data poisoning than we thought.

6, 12. National Institute of Standards and Technology. (2025). Adversarial machine learning: A taxonomy and terminology of attacks and mitigations (NIST AI 100-2e2025); OWASP GenAI Security Project. (2024). OWASP Top 10 for LLM Applications 2025 (LLM04: Data and Model Poisoning). genai.owasp.org

7, 8, 13. OWASP GenAI Security Project. (2026). AI Security Solutions Landscape—on model serialization attacks, safe serialization formats, model scanning, and model signing.

9, 10, 11, 14. OWASP GenAI Security Project. (2024). OWASP Top 10 for LLM Applications 2025 (LLM01: Prompt Injection; LLM02: Sensitive Information Disclosure; LLM05: Improper Output Handling; LLM08: Vector and Embedding Weaknesses). genai.owasp.org; National Institute of Standards and Technology. (2024). Artificial Intelligence Risk Management Framework: Generative Artificial Intelligence Profile (NIST AI 600-1).

Chapter 8 — The AI Supply Chain: Securing Models, Data, and Third-Party Risk

1, 2, 7. JFrog. (2026, May 20). *Software Supply Chain Security State of the Union 2026.* https://jfrog.com/software-supply-chain-state-of-union/—495 malicious AI models identified on Hugging Face; 53% of organizations pull AI models directly from public registries; malicious npm packages surged 451% year over year, reaching 171,592 unique instances in 2025, up from 31,132 in 2024.

3, 6, 18. Cloud Security Alliance AI Safety Initiative. (2026, May). *Poisoned Pipelines: Malicious AI Model and Skill Repositories.* Industry guidance on malicious model files and unsafe pickle deserialization, recommending code-package-level scrutiny for model downloads (provenance, hashing, sandboxed loading, and safe formats). References emerging model-scanning tools such as ModelScan for detecting unsafe operations in serialized AI models.

4, 17. Cloudsmith. (2026, April). *2026 guide to software supply chain security* (models as third-party dependencies traditional scanners can't read; MLSecOps; curation-first; CycloneDX/SLSA); Cloud Security Alliance. (2026, March). Research note on the eight-nation AI/ML supply chain risk and mitigation guidance treating AI-BOMs as baseline.

5. SD Times. (2026, January). *From SBOM to AI BOM* (pretrained models can contain hidden behaviors invisible to component inventory); ties to the poisoning study cited in Chapter 7.

8, 9, 19. SD Times (2026, January); GLACIS. (2025, December). *AI supply chain security guide 2026*; Cloudsmith (2026)—on AI risks absent from conventional inventory, curation-first dependency management, and vendor AI services changing weights, filters, or moderation behavior without notice (GLACIS).

10, 11, 13–16. VentureBeat. (2026, January). *Seven steps to AI supply chain visibility*—AI-BOM/ML-BOM content (models, versions, training and fine-tuning datasets, data sources and licenses, base-model lineage, framework dependencies); CycloneDX 1.6 (ML-BOM support, April 2024) and SPDX 3.0 (AI profiles, April 2024); "treat every model pull as a supply chain decision"; vendor contract requirements; adoption lag (Lineaje survey, June 2025: 48% of security professionals report falling behind on SBOM requirements); "AI-BOMs are forensics, not firewalls."

12. On model signing and cryptographic provenance (GPG/Sigstore; hash comparison against known-good baselines; low adoption on public hubs): GLACIS. (2025, December). *AI Supply Chain Security Guide 2026.* Outlines the need for verifiable model provenance, signing, and integrity checks, and notes that public model hubs show low adoption of cryptographic attestation.

Chapter 9 — Modernizing the SOC: Security Operations for AI

1. CISA, NSA, FBI, and international partners. (2025, May 22). *AI Data Security: Best Practices for Securing Data Used to Train & Operate AI Systems* (Joint Cybersecurity Information Sheet)—names data drift as one of three primary AI data-security risks alongside supply-chain vulnerabilities and maliciously modified data; recommends continuous monitoring and retraining as mitigations.
2. IBM. (2026). *AI agent and LLM observability* (Instana announcement, IBM Think 2026)—continuous discovery of AI components; "success isn't uptime, it's output quality"; scheduled LLM-as-a-judge evaluations to detect drift, hallucination, and degradation.

3, 6. ReliaQuest. (2026, March). *How to build an AI-driven SOC*; D3 Security. (2026, March). *Best AI SOC platforms 2026*—agents triaging, enriching, investigating, and responding under defined confidence thresholds, with humans in the loop.

4. EY. (2026, April). *Agentic SOC: Multi-agent orchestration*—human-AI collaboration rather than analyst replacement; multi-agent SOC structures; LLM prompt-injection vulnerability rates; EU AI Act treatment of security AI.
5. Gartner Security & Risk Management Summit (2026, June, National Harbor, MD)—autonomous AI SOC agents placed at the top of a four-level security-operations maturity model (above manual, semiautomated, and AI-assisted), framed as the direction of travel while warning against "AI washing"; corroborated by Gartner, Hype Cycle for Agentic AI (April 2026) on the early, uneven maturity of agentic capabilities.

Chapter 10 — Red-Teaming AI: Adversarial Testing as an Ongoing Practice

1, 2. NeuralTrust. (2025, August 8). *GPT-5 jailbreak with Echo Chamber and storytelling*; SPLX (SplxAI Inc.). (2025, August). GPT-5 red-team assessment. GPT-5, released August 7, 2025, was jailbroken within 24 hours of release: NeuralTrust combined its Echo Chamber technique (disclosed June 2025) with low-salience narrative storytelling across a few conversational turns, without overtly harmful language in the opening prompts; SPLX found the raw, unguarded model fell for 89% of attacks and was "nearly unusable for enterprise" without a system prompt. The same attack flow was reported effective against prior GPT versions, Gemini, and Grok-4. Contemporaneous coverage: SecurityWeek; Cybernews; Dark Reading (August 2025).

3. Vectra AI. (2026); Mindgard. (2026). On the pattern of major models being jailbroken shortly after release and the rise of agentic attack categories (OWASP Top 10 for Agentic Applications).
4. Vectra AI. (2026). Multi-turn jailbreak success rates (roleplay approaches reported near

90%; multi-turn chains reaching as high as ~97% within five turns, varying by study and target).

5, 9. Gov Capital. (2026). *AI red teaming in 2026: A practical field guide*; Mindgard (2026)—red-teaming an LLM is not penetration testing; output is a list of failure modes; automated plus manual; tools do not replace human red-teamers.

6. Vectra AI. (2026). AI systems behave differently across interactions.

7. Confident AI. (2026). Test the whole application—system prompt, retrieval, tools, guardrails—not just the model behind an API key.

8, 10. OWASP Top 10 for LLM Applications (2025); MITRE ATLAS; NIST AI-600-1 (red-team before and after deployment); NIST AI 100-2 E2025 (adversarial ML taxonomy). Harm categories per Mindgard (2026); Confident AI (2026); Gov Capital (2026).

11, 12. Confident AI (2026); *Automatic LLM red teaming*, arXiv:2508.04451 (2025)—crescendo escalations, conversation hijacking, progressive jailbreak chains, context poisoning via retrieved documents; framework-mapped, severity-scored reporting.

13. Gov Capital. (2026). Six-phase methodology synthesized across Microsoft AIRT, Anthropic, OpenAI, and the OWASP GenAI Red Teaming Guide, treated as gates rather than stages.

14. NVIDIA garak; Microsoft PyRIT; commercial platforms; autonomous red-teaming agents: Gov Capital (2026); Confident AI (2026); *AutoRedTeamer*, arXiv:2503.15754; arXiv:2605.04019 (2026).

15. On regulatory and commercial pressure: Regulation (EU) 2024/1689 requirements for providers of general-purpose AI models with systemic risk to perform adversarial testing; procurement-driven red-team report requests in regulated sectors. Gov Capital (2026); Confident AI (2026). See Chapter 15 for the regulatory timeline.

Chapter 11 — Beyond the Breach: AI-Specific Incident Response

1. ARMO (2026); PurpleSec (2026, April)—machine-speed incidents; a single prompt producing many bad outcomes.

2. NIST SP 800-61, extended with NIST AI-600-1, MITRE ATLAS, OWASP LLM Top 10; GenAI-IRF (MDPI, 2026); GLACIS (2025)—lifecycle backbone.

3. ARMO (2026)—traditional-shaped AI incidents; familiar indicators and containment paths.

4. ARMO (2026)—reasoning compromise; IoCs as prompts and retrieved documents; patient zero as poisoned context source.

5. ARMO (2026); Alice Labs (2026); Kaul, IJCESEN (2026)—containment timing governed by speed of harm and reversibility.

6. PurpleSec (2026, April)—AI forensic artifacts: prompt logs, model state, retrieval context, tool-call history.

7. ARMO (2026)—"kill the pod, image the disk" destroys volatile model state; capture that survives containment.

8. ARMO (2026); Alice Labs (2026); Kaul, IJCESEN (2026)—evidence decay; least-disruptive-intervention rule; "remediation is not restoration."

9. GLACIS (2025, December)—graduated containment levers: rollback, traffic reduction, feature flags, circuit breakers, kill switch.

10. ARMO (2026); PurpleSec (2026, April)—agentic chains where each link is individually authorized; chain-aware detection.

11. PurpleSec (2026, February); GLACIS (2025)—AI incident archetypes with distinct containment, eradication, recovery paths.
12. NIST SP 800-61 + NIST AI-600-1, MITRE ATLAS, OWASP LLM Top 10—framework mapping for archetype playbooks.
13. GenAI-IRF (MDPI, 2026, January 19)—peer-reviewed framework supplying the operational "how" the standards omit.
14. Regulation (EU) 2016/679 (GDPR), art. 33; Regulation (EU) 2024/1689 serious-incident reporting. See Chapter 15.
15. PurpleSec (2026, April)—tabletop exercises by archetype; MTTD/MTTC metrics; blameless root-cause culture.

Chapter 12 — Privacy by Design: Protecting the Data Fuel

1. IAPP. (2025, July). Privacy engineering for AI machine learning: Addressing algorithmic disgorgement risks during product development. On algorithmic disgorgement—the US FTC remedy (used since 2019) of deleting not just improperly-obtained data but the models trained on it—and machine unlearning as a mitigation raised in privacy consultations. Separately, on the EU right to erasure: Regulation (EU) 2016/679, art. 17.
2. Alation. (2025, August). *Privacy-preserving machine learning: Minimizing PII & PHI.* Differential privacy; federated learning; homomorphic encryption; confidential computing; automated PII/PHI discovery and de-identification. Representative tooling: TensorFlow Privacy; PySyft; FATE; Flower.
3. Flower Framework documentation. *Differential privacy* (accessed 2026). Federated learning's residual leakage via model updates; membership-inference, property-inference, and model-inversion attacks; clipped, noised aggregation as mitigation.
4. IAPP. (2025, July). Machine unlearning: selective removal of specific data's contribution to a trained model while preserving utility.
5. IEEE Communications Society. (2025, December). Special-issue call for papers: *Federated machine learning and unlearning for privacy-preserving networked intelligence*—establishing the convergence as an active research frontier.
6. *FedRecovery: Differentially private machine unlearning.* (2026). IEEE Xplore; *Efficient federated unlearning with adaptive differential privacy preservation,* arXiv:2411.11044; *f-FUM: Federated unlearning,* arXiv:2602.06187—machine unlearning remains genuinely hard; approximate unlearning trades completeness for efficiency; stored historical updates can introduce reconstruction risks.

Chapter 13 — Scaling Securely: Leveraging AWS, Azure, and Google AI Services

Provider capabilities below are cited as illustrations of general principles, not as a feature comparison; product specifics change.

1, 9. Cloudanix. (2026, April). *Top 15 cloud misconfigurations in 2026 and how to fix them*—open or unauthenticated inference endpoints as a recurring documented misconfiguration; native IAM analyzers (AWS IAM Access Analyzer, Azure PIM review, GCP IAM Recommender).

2, 3. Wiz Research. (2026). *State of AI in the Cloud 2026* and *AI Security Readiness* reports. https://www.wiz.io/reports/state-of-ai-in-the-cloud-2026—At least 81% of observed cloud environments use managed AI services and at least 90% run self-hosted AI software, while 25% of organizations lack visibility into which AI services run in their environment.

4, 12. Giri, B. (2026, January). *AI for security, security for AI—a cloud-native perspective in 2026*. Medium; Wiz AI-SPM documentation (2026)—AI-SPM extending CSPM and DSPM into the AI layer; "AI security fabrics."

5, 6, 11. Revolgy. (2025, December). *Cloud security in 2026 (part 3): Securing generative AI on AWS and Google*—managed model-agnostic guardrails as interceptor logic; private-backbone network isolation and logical data perimeters blocking exfiltration even by credentialed identities; infrastructure-as-code pre-deployment policy scanning and drift detection.

7, 8, 10. ToxSec. (2025, November). *Cloud AI security: A pro's field guide for 2026 challenges.* Medium; AWS Security Blog. (2026, April). *Secure AI agent access patterns to AWS resources using Model Context Protocol*—least-privilege identity for agents; native audit logging of agent API calls; distinct logging of agent-path actions; self-hosting as inheriting 100% of the security burden.

Chapter 14 — Lean Security: Enabling Business Velocity Without Sacrificing Protection

1. Bitdefender / The Hacker News. (2026, February–March). *AI in cybersecurity: Is it worth the effort for lean security teams?*; BizTech Magazine. (2026). *How can AI agents support lean security teams?*; Radiant Security. (2026). *Best SOC platforms for lean security teams* —AI as a force multiplier for lean teams; human-AI collaboration rather than replacement.
2. Bitdefender / The Hacker News (2026)—the two failure modes ("buzzword baggage" and operational burden); the lean test of measurable outcomes without added complexity; AI is "not plug-and-play magic for defenders."
3. Supporting context: Safe Security. (2026, January). *The modern risk prioritization framework for 2026* (multi-dimensional risk scoring, including velocity); Graylog lean-SOC announcements (2026, March).

Chapter 15 — Navigating the Maze: Global AI Regulation and Compliance

1. Regulation (EU) 2024/1689—comprehensive, extraterritorial scope reaching operators outside the EU whose systems reach the EU market; administrative fines up to €35 million or 7% of worldwide annual turnover for prohibited practices, €15 million or 3% for most other obligations, and €7.5 million or 1% for supplying incorrect or misleading information to authorities (art. 99). Supporting analyses: Tredence (2026, April); Holland & Knight (2026, April).
2. Digital Omnibus on AI: provisional political agreement of the Council and Parliament, May 7, 2026, confirmed by Member State representatives May 13, 2026, deferring Annex III high-risk obligations to December 2, 2027 and Annex I obligations to August 2, 2028; formal adoption and Official Journal publication were expected before the original August 2, 2026 deadline, after which the deferral becomes settled law. Transparency-related timing is mixed—watermarking obligations under Article 50(2) are deferred to December 2, 2026 (a shorter delay than the six-month deferral originally proposed), while the remaining Article 50 transparency duties continue to

apply from the original August 2, 2026 date; verify the specific obligation before relying on it.

3. Regulation (EU) 2024/1689 four-tier structure and high-risk categories per Annexes I and III (biometric identification, critical infrastructure, education, employment, essential services including credit scoring and insurance, law enforcement, migration, justice). Tredence (2026); Holland & Knight (2026).
4. U.S. state patchwork as of this writing: Colorado AI Act (SB 24-205; enforcement stayed by federal court April 27, 2026, then repealed and replaced by SB 26-189 on May 14, 2026, which narrows it to an ADMT disclosure framework effective January 1, 2027—itself an illustration of the volatility this chapter describes); California ADMT regulations under the CCPA (pre-use notices and opt-outs phasing in ~January 2027); California AB 2013 (generative AI training-data disclosure); Texas Responsible Artificial Intelligence Governance Act; with additional activity in New York, Utah, Nevada, Maine, and Illinois. Analyses: Cooley (2026, April); Kiteworks (2026, January); OneTrust (2026, March); Beyond Tomorrow (2026).
5. U.S. federal-state dynamics: Executive Order of December 11, 2025; 2026 White House national policy framework urging federal preemption; multistate attorney-general coordination; increased AG enforcement against AI deployers. techresearchonline (2026, January); Kiteworks (2026, January); Cooley (2026, April).
6. OneTrust. (2026, March). *Where AI regulation is heading in 2026: A global outlook*—other jurisdictions entering at varied speeds, several echoing the EU's risk-tiered model.
7. OneTrust (2026, March)—convergent principles across regimes: transparency for rights-affecting outcomes; documentation, logging, and monitoring as proof that accountability exists in practice; the developer/deployer distinction mirroring privacy's controller/processor.
8. Beyond Tomorrow. (2026). Compliance demanded through procurement: conformity declarations, SOC 2 AI addenda, and incident SLAs in vendor questionnaires; B2B customers exporting regulatory burden to suppliers.
9. Beyond Tomorrow. (2026). Scope reduction (disabling emotion inference, geofencing features, narrowing to a lower risk tier) as the lean team's highest-leverage compliance tactic.

Chapter 16 — The Ethical Guardrails: Bias, Fairness, and Transparency

1. On fairness harms and the law/ethics/engineering convergence: Clarifai. (2026, January). *Top AI risks 2026*; Crescendo. *AI bias examples* (proxy discrimination; risk-assessment algorithms in criminal justice); *Mobley v. Workday, Inc.*, No. 3:23-cv-00770-RFL (N.D. Cal., filed Feb. 21, 2023)—alleging age, race, and disability discrimination in AI applicant screening; preliminary collective certification of the ADEA claim granted May 16, 2025; collective later expanded to applicants screened via Workday's HiredScore features (July 2025); on March 6, 2026 the court rejected Workday's argument that the ADEA does not protect job applicants (while dismissing certain California state-law and individual disability claims with leave to amend, which plaintiffs re-pleaded March 30, 2026). The ADEA claim is the only one certified on a collective basis; Title VII race, ADA disability, and certain California claims remain individually litigated. Litigation ongoing as of this writing (June 06). Regulation (EU)

2024/1689 high-risk obligations for credit scoring, including discrimination identification and assessment: arXiv:2408.02558.

2. IBM. (2026, February). *What is algorithmic bias?*; EY. (2026, April). *Addressing AI bias: A human-centric approach*—diverse, interdisciplinary teams as a practical fairness control.
3. On multiple, mathematically incompatible fairness definitions (demographic parity, equal opportunity, disparate-impact analysis): the fairness impossibility literature, with practitioner treatments in TCS, *Algorithmic bias and mitigation strategies*; SmartDev. (2025, April). *AI bias and fairness*; Codewave. (2026, March). *8 best practices.*
4. On bias measurement and audits (cross-group performance evaluation, representation-gap analysis, pre- and post-deployment testing; causal fairness auditing): Codewave (2026); SmartDev (2025); arXiv:2408.02558.
5. On three-stage mitigation (pre-processing, in-processing, post-processing), continuous monitoring, bias incident response, and feedback loops: SAP, *What is AI bias?*; TCS; Codewave (2026).
6. On explainability and transparency (XAI; SHAP; LIME; model cards; contestability): TCS; Crescendo; IBM (2026, February).

Chapter 17 — The Road Ahead

1. On agentic adoption outpacing governance: Gartner projection that approximately 40% of enterprise applications will embed task-specific AI agents by the end of 2026, up from under 5% in 2025; Deloitte finding that close to three-quarters of companies plan to deploy agentic AI within two years, with only 21% reporting a mature agent-governance model; survey findings that most technical teams are past planning into active testing or production, with only a small fraction of agents going live with full security approval. Deloitte AI Institute. (2026, January). State of AI in the enterprise: The untapped edge; Recorded Future. (2026, April). Emerging enterprise security risks of AI; Gravitee. (2026, February). State of AI agent security 2026; Strata. (2026, April). Agentic AI risks: A 2026 guide; Salesmate. (2026). The future of AI agents.
2. Kiteworks. (2026, February). *Agentic AI: Biggest enterprise security threat for 2026*, reporting a Dark Reading readership poll in which approximately 48% of cybersecurity professionals identified agentic AI and autonomous systems as the top attack vector heading into 2026.
3. Supporting context: Cloud Security Alliance. (2026, January). *Top 10 predictions for agentic AI in 2026* (MAESTRO, OWASP AIVSS, CSA AICM, NIST AI RMF alignment); Palo Alto Networks. (2025, November–December). *2026 predictions for autonomous AI* (vendor projections, cited as illustrative).